The War Against the Past

The War Against the Past

Why the West Must Fight for Its History

Frank Furedi

polity

First published in 2024 by Polity Press

Polity Press
65 Bridge Street
Cambridge CB2 1UR, UK

Polity Press
101 Station Landing
Suite 300
Medford, MA 02155, USA

ISBN-13: 978-1-5095-61254

A catalogue record for this book is available from the British Library.

Library of Congress Control Number: 2024930231

Typeset in 11.5 on 14 Adobe Garamond
by Fakenham Prepress Solutions, Fakenham, Norfolk NR21 8NL

For further information on Polity, visit our website:
politybooks.com

Contents

Preface

This book was born in October 2020, on a street thousands of miles from where I live. It was almost 9 p.m. in Portland, Oregon, when the city's police department tweeted that a mass gathering had formed on the corner of Southwest Park Avenue and Southwest Madison Street. 'Some are trying to pull down a statue with a chain,' they warned. Within the hour, Abraham Lincoln had been pulled from his plinth, assassinated for the second time. Images were swiftly shared online and found their way to my computer in England.

The rioters who were responsible for this act of mindless vandalism reminded me of a lynch mob, albeit one with a difference. Their target was an inanimate statue of someone who had died more than a century ago. It was as if they had invaded the past to exact revenge on the present.

And yet it seemed to me that this outburst was merely the culmination of a new form of iconoclasm – one that is far more ominous than the tearing down of important symbols of the past. As I explain in this book, the entire historical legacy of Western civilization has been turned into a battlefield. The defiling of Lincoln was just one flashpoint.

The chapters that follow argue that the stakes in this conflict could not be higher. For when the past is contaminated, it becomes near impossible to endow people's life with meaning in the present. The aim of this book is to explain why the War Against the Past must be defeated.

Acknowledgements

Over the past year and more, I have been the beneficiary of intelligent and probing criticism from friends and comrades involved with the charity Ideas Matter, and the organizers of the Battle of Ideas conference. My colleagues at MCC Brussels have provided a stimulating environment for the conduct of my research and I have gained important insights in engaging with their views. A noble Norman Lewis read and critiqued the draft chapters, while my son Jacob and wife Ann offered invaluable advice about how to improve their arguments.

This book is dedicated to the formidable fighter Claire Fox, known to many as Baroness Fox of Buckley.

Introduction

There was no formal declaration of war. No gunshots rang out. It didn't even make the local news. But, sure enough, at some point at the turn of the 21st century, a war against the past was launched.

Who were the culprits? They are hard to pin down. The partisans supporting the assault on the legacy of European civilization are not members of a party. They have not issued any war aims and have never formulated an explicit strategic vision. They are also a heterogeneous bunch, a coalition of disparate interests and movements.

In an earlier era, the 1990s, when the first wave of mobilization was taking shape, the English historian J.C.D. Clark warned against representing the promotion of this conflict as the 'outcome of a grand conspiracy'. He wrote that it was 'the result of a thousand separate, distantly related acts, the promptings of widely absorbed assumptions'. Nevertheless, argued Clark, despite its diverse and uncoordinated prompting, it amounted to a 'distinct enterprise of historical disinheritance'.[1]

As I shall argue in the chapters to follow, hostility towards the past evolved slowly, and then all at once, its intensification occurring haphazardly without any serious long-term thought. The use of the term 'war' to account for the systematic pursuit of historical disinheritance is not simply metaphorical. In effect, this war leads to the diminishing of the authority of the past, to the discrediting of its legacy, and to the killing of the soul of communities whose way of life remains underpinned by European culture.

This book's principal argument is that the main driver of the Culture Wars is an undeclared War Against the Past. At times, supporters of these Culture Wars against Western civilization behave as if this perilous territory continues to represent a menace to the contemporary world. Their constant targeting of the legacy of the past – its physical symbols, values, and achievements – resembles a frenetic moral crusade seeking to make people feel ashamed about their origins and who they are. Culture warriors have, in effect, opened up a second front to gain mastery over how the past is viewed.

The goal of cancelling the legacy of Western civilization is pursued through reorganizing society's historical memory and disputing and delegitimizing its ideals and achievement. Activists seek to erase the temporal distinction between the present and the past to achieve this objective. There has never been a time in living memory when so much energy has been devoted to readjusting the past and questioning and criticizing historical figures and institutions. At times, it seems as if the boundary between the present and the past has disappeared as activists casually cross over it and seek to fix contemporary problems through readjusting what has already occurred.

The crusade against the past has proven remarkably successful in alienating society from its history. Public and private institutions ceaselessly paint their communities' past in the darkest colours. There is no longer any need to prompt institutions of education and culture to apologize for just about everything that occurred in the past. Even the spectacular achievements of human civilization, from Greek philosophy to the intellectual revolution of the Enlightenment to the scientific inventions of modernity, are now regularly indicted for their supposed association with exploitation and oppression. The representation of the past through a narrative that highlights its malevolent, oppressive, exploitative, and abusive dimension is not confined to a small number of headline-seeking historians. The frequency with which history is told as a tale of human degradation indicates that in popular culture the past now possesses the status of the 'Bad Old Days'.

Anyone visiting a gallery or a museum will soon be confronted with troubling reminders regarding the malevolent influence of the past. There is a veritable army of grievance archaeologists whose role is to indict the objects on display with some kind of offence. Any painting or object created in the 18th or 19th century has a good chance of being directly or indirectly linked to colonialism or the slave trade. Glasgow's Burrell Collection features the most bizarre reminders of the misdeeds of history. A note attached to a bronze bust of a young Roman man, 100 BC–AD 100, states: 'Roman artists copied Greek sculptors, who used mathematical formulas to work out what they thought were people's perfect proportions. This has been wrongly used to promote racist ideas about the ideal proportions of faces.' The absurd attribution of racist motives to the sculpting of facial proportions in ancient times speaks to a veritable cultural addiction to shaming the achievements of the past. In its own terms, a condescending comment about a bronze bust of a young Roman man does not signify very much. But when similar reminders of historical injustices are attached to numerous other objects on display in a museum, viewers are left with a very clear and negative story of the past.

As we note in later chapters, even some of the most inspiring contributions to human history have been targeted by mean-spirited activists determined to empty the past of any redeeming features. Practitioners of accusatory history are committed to poisoning the reputation of the Enlightenment by claiming that it was 'from the outset a racist endeavour'.[2] The targeting of the past has proved to be remarkably successful. Historical dramas and films invariably represent the legacy of Western civilization, particularly its Anglo-American component, in an unfavourable light. The past is anachronistically rewritten in accordance with the playbook of contemporary identity politics.

Public and private institutions have uncritically embraced the cause of decolonization and revel in discovering their own 'shameful' past. The embrace of decolonization now works as a performance of virtue and has become an obligatory ritual for any institution that wishes to demonstrate that it is of the time. All that the crusade against the past lacks is the addition of the word 'holy'. Consider the statement 'Supporting Decolonisation in Museums' issued by the UK's Museums Association. It notes that 'at a time' when 'history is under more scrutiny than ever, it is vital that that museums engage' in 'discussions and reappraise their own historical role in empire'. It adds that 'we will continue to work with museums to support them on this journey'.[3]

One of the aims of this book is to explain why 'history is under more scrutiny than ever'. There is no doubt that, at least outwardly, this is the case, However, on closer inspection, it becomes evident that 'scrutiny' is the wrong term to describe the current project of rewriting the past. *The Oxford English Dictionary* defines scrutiny as investigation and critical inquiry.[4] There is, however, little genuine investigation and certainly nothing critical about the obsessive attempt to seek revenge on the past.

The English social historian E.P. Thompson's phrase the 'immense condescension of posterity' is far better than 'scrutiny' as a way to describe the current project of delegitimizing the past.[5]

In the chapters that follow, I refer to the current obsession with scrutinizing the past as the practice of grievance archaeology. Outwardly, grievance archaeology is committed to uncovering historical injustices and misdeeds that require the atonement of institutions and actors in the here and now. Culture warriors justify their project on the grounds that the past injustices they unearth are consequential for the lives of numerous identity groups today. Grievance archaeology, however, is not simply about excavating hitherto unknown facts or events. It is principally about repackaging the past in accordance with the values and objectives of present-day identity politics. Through reading history backwards, the behaviour and actions of individuals and groups who inhabited the world hundreds and even thousands of years ago are cast in the role of an offender of present-day sensibilities. In this way, key historical figures are effectively cancelled from the canon of the greats.

Consider the case of Immanuel Kant, one of the most influential philosophers of the modern era. If the grievance archaeologists associated with the decolonization movement are to be believed, Kant is just another common-or-garden racist. Moreover, almost every major philosopher of the 17th- and 18th-century Enlightenment has been cast into this role. According to the cultural warriors' judgement, Locke, Hume, Hegel, and Kant are all deemed guilty. No doubt, these individuals shared many of the prejudices of 18th-century society. But they also developed the universalistic outlook that led them to give meaning to the ideal of human equality. Kant, for one, was unequivocally opposed to colonialism and the behaviour of the conquering European powers, warning that they 'oppress the natives, excite widespread wars among the various states, spread famine, rebellion, perfidy, and the whole litany of evils which afflict mankind'.[6] But for the grievance archaeologists, it does not matter that Kant's ethics offers a precious resource for upholding the moral dignity and worth of all humans. What matters is that his language, attitude, and behaviour violate the recently cobbled-together norms codified in the virtue-seeking language guides of 21st-century Anglo-American institutions.

Still, the War Against the Past is not simply a conflict involving words. It also involves the physical act of removing symbols of the past. *The Guardian* refers to this development as 'The Statue Wars', yet it is not only statues that are pulled down, disfigured, or removed. As discussed in chapter 4, troublesome books are hidden from the public in libraries and, in some cases, destroyed. Even the burning of books has made an unwelcome return.[7] Precious and historically significant objects are rendered 'troublesome' and presented to the public with a note of disparagement. The world-famous British Museum is so worried about the impact of its 'troublesome' collection that it has decided to give 'emotional support' to its staff and help them add trigger warnings to its archive.[8]

Children and young people are the main target audience for the representation of the past as a story of shame. From a very young age, they are exposed to a form of education that aims to morally distance them from their cultural legacy and deprive them of a sense of pride in their past. In the UK, primary schoolchildren as young as five are offered US-style lessons about 'white privilege'.[9] Teachers are instructed to avoid teaching 'white saviour narratives' during lessons on slavery by de-emphasizing the role of white abolitionists such as William Wilberforce.

Such successes are not due to the crusade's supporters' intellectual coherence and effective organization. Of course, movements such as Black Lives Matter contributed to this feverish ahistoricism. But their success was, to a considerable extent, underwritten by a pre-existing cultural climate favourable to their objective. One of the most striking and fascinating features of the War Against the Past is the relative lack of resistance to it. In the UK over the last couple of decades, successive regimes – the majority of them *Conservative* – have refused to respond to the assault on Britain's heritage. This reluctance to fight for our history constitutes a veritable act of cultural betrayal.

An important reason why the War Against the Past has successfully influenced the current zeitgeist is the defensive stance assumed by those charged with upholding and transmitting the legacy of Western civilization. In retrospect, it is evident that sections of the cultural and political establishment have, for some time, become estranged from their society's tradition and historical legacy. By the late 20th century, numerous observers drew attention to the uneasy relationship Western culture had developed with its historical legacy. As I explained over 30 years ago, in *Mythical Past, Elusive Future: History and Society in an*

Anxious Age, Western societies' cultural and political establishments had already become all too aware that they had lost touch with their past. The realization that there was no longer a commonly accepted version of the past was widely echoed by leading commentators in the 1970s. Society's estrangement from the past was a symptom of an all-pervasive moral drift afflicting society in that decade.[10] This sentiment was captured by the transatlantic thinker Stanley Hoffman in 1979, who, in his discussion on the 'demise of the past', warned that 'through speed and the savagery of history, we have not simply lost touch with the world that is behind us; it also appears that this world said many things that turned out to be false and thus has nothing more to say to the average European'.[11] Numerous observers echoed Hoffman's conviction that the leaders of Western society had become estranged from their own cultural traditions.

When Hoffman mused 'is there a Europe, was there a past, and will there be a future?',[12] he voiced a concern deeply felt by leading thinkers across the political mainstream. An awareness that Europe had lost touch with its past and was therefore disoriented about its place in the world led to what proved to be half-hearted attempts to reaffirm its cultural traditions. As it turned out, this was the last time that the Western European mainstream political establishment – Christian Democrats, Conservatives, and Liberals – seriously tried to 'go back to basics' and revive and act by the tradition bequeathed by history. From its inception, British Prime Minister John Major's 'Back to Basics' campaign of 1993 was an object of ridicule. The swiftness of its embarrassing demise indicated that there were no 'basics' to return to.

Small groups of conservative intellectuals sought to fight a rear-guard action against their society's alienation from its historical past. The American conservative sociologist Robert Nisbet's *History of the Idea of Progress* (1980) highlighted what he saw as the tragic consequence of a society that had become physically and morally detached from its past. He presented a bleak historical vision in Manichean terms: 'In no period of Western history, not even the Dark Ages, has alienation from, lack of confidence in, and hostility toward fundamental institutions been as deep and widespread as in this final part of the twentieth century in the West,' he warned.[13] On the other side of the Atlantic, the soon-to-be prime minister of the UK, Margaret Thatcher, also sounded the alarm.

> We are witnessing a deliberate attack on those who wish to promote merit and excellence, a deliberate attack on our heritage and our past, and there are those who gnaw away at our national self-respect, rewriting British history as centuries of unrelieved doom, oppression and failure – as days of hopelessness, not days of hope.[14]

Nisbet's and Thatcher's diagnosis of the threat facing the historical traditions of their societies was well observed. Yet the threat they faced was far less serious and omnipresent than today. Were they alive now, both would genuinely be shocked by the depth of the animosity directed at the past.

By the time the Culture Wars erupted in the 1980s, the intellectual and cultural defenders of the past were fast becoming an endangered species within society's key institutions. Oddly, during the Reagan and Thatcher era of the 1980s, the moral devaluation of Western culture and its past gained great momentum. Oddly, because at least outwardly, the Reagan–Thatcher years were associated with the triumph of conservatism. However, the ideological triumph of Reagonomics and the formidable support that it enjoyed were not matched in the sphere of culture. Indeed, in the cultural domain, traditional conservative ideals regarding tradition, the family, sexuality, morality, and the past were on the defensive. It was precisely during this decade that cultural norms calling into question the traditional values of the West gained rapid ascendancy. What American conservatives had previously characterized as 'adversary culture' was fast acquiring hegemonic influence. The verdict of the American sociologist Alan Wolfe on these key developments in this era is pertinent to this day. He noted that 'the right won the economic war, the left won the cultural war, and the center won the political war'.[15] Wolfe's assessment was echoed by Gertrude Himmelfarb, a leading American conservative thinker, who concluded that 'having been spared the class revolution that Marx predicted, we have succumbed to the cultural revolution'.[16]

The opposition to the newly emergent crusade against the past crumbled with remarkable ease. At the time, the import of this development was obscured by the appearance of triumphalism surrounding the Reagan–Thatcher Revolution. What was overlooked in the 1980s and the decades to follow was that mainstream conservatism had more or less given up on the past. Society's estrangement from its past led to a situation where its traditions meant little for the conduct of everyday life. The growth of this sense of estrangement was steady but very gradual. It was underpinned by a loss of confidence and a sense of exhaustion. Hoffman captured well this slow unravelling of confidence in the past when he wrote;

> The disappearance of the past is partly a disappointment with that past – with what history and human action have wrought – thus it is very different from that deliberate historical break that revolutionaries intent on building a new order and creating a new man provoked in 1792, or in 1917, or in 1949 in China. It means exhaustion, not energy; drainage, not arson. In turn, the lack of a sense of the future has further depressed, devalued, and discoloured the past; when one does not know where one is going, when there seems to be nowhere to go and nothing new and better to accomplish, what is the point of retracing one's steps? It takes a combination of faith in, ideas about, and will to build one's future to keep an interest in the past from becoming mere scholarship or leisure.[17]

Hoffman's emphasis on the motif of exhaustion and disappointment as key factors in the de-authorization of the past helps explain the undramatic quiet retreat of supporters of traditionalism from the battleground of ideas. At the turn of the 1980s, there was no dramatic historical break with the past, just a sense of defeatism brought on by a loss of confidence in the legacy of European civilization.

What is the War Against the Past?

Outwardly, the Culture Wars present themselves as mainly about conflicts over moral values touching on sex, abortion, gender and cultural identity, sovereignty, and race. Disputes about freedom of speech, language use, and the different dimensions of human communication often target what they dismiss as outdated norms and ideals. Always lurking behind these conflicts are competing attitudes towards the past. As the chapters that follow suggest, the territory of the past is the most important site on which the Culture Wars are fought. The underlying impulse driving these wars is the aspiration to replace the norms and attitudes rooted in the past with ones that validate the outlook of the various present-day groups and individuals associated with identity politics. Though the promoters of the different versions of identity politics are not always conscious of their objectives, their energies always work towards the same purpose: the de-authorization of the civilizational accomplishments associated with the West.

The noisy protesters demanding the pulling down of statues or the decolonization of education are by no means the only parties targeting the past. Modernizing technocrats, profit-seeking corporates, and flashy, modish cultural entrepreneurs in Hollywood, New York, London, and Paris often communicate an attitude of disrespect towards the legacy of the past. Business publications such as *The Harvard Business Review* frequently warn about the risk of outdated company practices. They often declare that 'there's no need to dwell on the past; what matters is the future'. The flourishing of change management in business and educational fads in school represents a compulsive desire to leave the past behind. Overall, the cumulative outcome of these disparate influences is to encourage a perspective that regards the past as morally inferior to the ways of the present.

The stamping of moral inferiority on the past is habitually, almost thoughtlessly, practised by Western elites. Their practice is motivated by an aspiration for securing legitimation. Since the dominant narratives used to interpret political and socio-economic developments lost much of their authority, the political and cultural establishments have been confronted with the problem of legitimacy. One response to this problem has been an attempt to attain authority by favourably contrasting the present-day sensibilities of an 'aware' elite to a dark, morally inferior past. At a time when a mood of political exhaustion has led to the decline of future-oriented projects, elite culture frequently finds refuge in advertising its superiority over the supposedly unenlightened traditional practices of previous generations.

This complacent, presentist approach relies on continually reminding the world of its superior ways. It constantly compares itself to historical protagonists and finds them wanting. The term 'moral anachronism' best captures the ritual of humbling characters from the past. By treating individuals and events in the past as having to account for themselves in relation to the standards of the present, moral anachronism effectively erodes the temporal distinction between the present and the past, assessing historical figures as if they are our peers. And so the likes of Aristotle, Chaucer, Shakespeare, Hume, and Kant are frequently hauled before the contemporary court of public opinion and charged with various recently formulated cultural crimes. Ostensibly, these rituals aim to 'raise awareness' about past injustices. But at times, it appears that the ritualistic thrashing of the reputation of historically significant figures is also designed to re-educate the dead. In this way, the present is projected backwards so that our ancestors are forced to account for themselves in accordance with the spirit of our time.

Regardless of their philosophical or political differences, until recently, most serious thinkers believed that important lessons could be learned from history. Those disposed towards a conservative outlook went so far as to claim that the traditions of the past could convey transcendental truths relevant to people at all times. Others drew different lessons and regarded history as an inspiration for showing the possibility of progressive change. Today's presentist zeitgeist encourages a very different approach. It dispossesses the past of its claim to truth. At best, the past is indicted as irrelevant; at worst, it is charged with causing harm to the generations that have followed.

By the turn of the 21st century, the outlook of Western elites had become thoroughly imbued with the essence of presentism. They concluded that they inhabited a world where the rate of change was so rapid that just about everything from the past had turned obsolete and was irrelevant to their lives.[18] Moreover, they had become disenchanted with the value of their historical inheritance. In particular, they regarded many of the values transmitted by previous generations as no longer appropriate for the conduct of life. Upholding the traditions of the past was not a cause they were prepared to defend. Within institutions of culture and education, the past was often represented as an alien, if not hostile, territory. Consequently, decades before the explosion of support for the decolonization of society, the prevailing cultural norms were frequently antithetical to those of the past. Once these attitudes were in place, society's estrangement from its history became susceptible to politicization. At this point, the crusade against the past gained momentum and erupted into what I characterize as a War Against the Past.

The Culture Wars have always exuded hostility towards the past. Their frequent rhetorical reference to outdated language, behaviour, and attitudes convey a tone of disparagement towards history. When TV channels warn about 'outdated attitudes and language', their message regarding established ways is clear.[19] They frame the past in the language of harm to deprive its influence of positive content. The ritual of issuing a warning about the outdated already conveys an implicit call to treat it with suspicion.

Numerous interpretations of the Culture Wars represent their agents as external to the mainstream of Western societies. Often, modern 'radicals' are assigned responsibility for attempting to dethrone the authority of the West's normative outlook. No doubt, the activists associated with these movements have played an important role in this conflict. Yet their remarkable success was made possible by the complicity of sections of the Western political and cultural establishment. Since this establishment had lost enthusiasm for its historical legacy, it did little to oppose the cultural warriors assembling at its gates. On the contrary, in many institutions, those formally charged with their defence left the gates wide open. Like those Romans who stopped believing in their way of life and lost the will to fight, the elites of Western society did little to uphold and protect its historical legacy.

Unlike the Romans, however, the elites of Western societies did not merely stop at giving up their traditional values and way of life, they also sought to actively negate it. That is why they are often in the vanguard of an army determined to attack the cultural legacy of their society. In his characterization of this development, the commentator Paul Kingsnorth claimed that we are passing through a *culture of inversion* phase.[20] He noted that,

> The West's ongoing decline has caused its elites to lose faith in their cultural inheritance, and this loss of faith has now reached pathological proportions. As a result, the leading lights in Western society – the cultural elites, and sometimes the political and economic elites too – are dedicated not to upholding the cultural forms they inherited, but to turning them on their heads, or erasing them entirely.

In their subconscious, this loss of faith is expressed through a sensibility that strives to dispossess society of its cultural inheritance and history.

The key themes in the War Against the Past

The dominant impulse driving the assault on the past is the aspiration to detach society from its influence. In the Western world, cultural continuity was long maintained through the absorption of custom into law and the continuous modification and development of tradition. Despite the frequent outbreak of conflicts over values throughout history, the different protagonists understood the necessity for retaining this continuity. This was the case even after the decline of religion and the emergence of secularism and the spirit of science. During the 18th and 19th centuries, neither side sought to abolish the continuity of culture but offered different interpretations of how to relate to the legacy of human civilization.

There were, naturally, historical moments – such as the First World War – when cultural continuity was threatened and severely undermined by serious disruptions. 'Old authority and traditional values no longer had credibility,' wrote Modris Eksteins in his *Rites of Spring: The Great War and the Birth of the Modern.* Yet 'no new authority and no new values had emerged in their stead'.[21]

Until the late 1960s, the distancing of society from its past was gradual – occasionally punctuated by calls to bring back tradition or religion. As noted previously, such calls were confined to small groups of conservative thinkers by the 1970s. From the late 1970s onwards, we see not simply the continuous weakening of cultural continuity but much more explicit attacks against it. At this point, the Culture Wars started to kick in, and it was only a matter of time before their adversarial sensibility became crystallized into what would become a veritable crusade against the past. Their target was not certain aspects of the West, but the entirety of its cultural legacy.

To this end, their supporters strive to attain widespread support for a Year Zero ideology. In previous times, the evocation of a Year Zero was heralded by radical and revolutionary movements who sought to represent the world they were building as fundamentally different to the evil days of the past. This sentiment was most systematically expressed in recent decades during the Khmer Rouge takeover of Cambodia in the mid-1970s (which it renamed Kampuchea). Advocates of establishing Year Zero claimed that the evil traditions of the past had to be destroyed, old ideas had to be purged, and society needed to start again from scratch.

The mutation of hostility towards the past in Western societies into a veritable ideology offers a moderate version of this Year Zero outlook. Today, its main emphasis is on enforcing a moral quarantine between the present and the past and seeking to wreak vengeance on the latter's legacy. Through highlighting the present's moral superiority over the past, it attempts to wrest authority to influence contemporary affairs.

At first sight, there appears to be an irresolvable contradiction between the outlook of Year Zero ideology and the outlook of presentism. Year Zero ideology is fervently devoted to the policing of temporal boundaries. It wishes to throw a quarantine around the past and declare it to be a no-go zone. This is an ideology which appears wholeheartedly committed to the eradication of the past. In contrast to the dictates of Year Zero ideology, presentism promotes a very different agenda of rejecting the boundary that separates its world from the past. It promotes a worldview that invites people to cross this important temporal boundary to fix the problems of the past. One manifestation of this trend is the emergence of a form of cultural politics which seems more interested in solving past problems than in engaging with those rooted in the present era. The ever-expanding activism of grievance archaeology serves as testimony to the growing interest in seeking retribution for misdeeds going as far back as ancient times.

The politicization of identity has radicalized presentism. Identity politics has encouraged presentism to become increasingly obsessive about its orientation towards the past. Those with politicized identities regard the past as a fertile terrain for historical validation. They achieve this objective by denouncing the past for failing to acknowledge that they have always been around but hidden from view. The Burrell Collection, mentioned previously, offers an exemplary presentation of politicized presentism in action. Next to the porcelain figure of Guanyin made during the Qing Dynasty in China, a note states, 'Trans people have always existed and are rooted in history.' It asserts that the figure of Guanyin 'reflects this, showing that gender and identity are not always fixed'. Almost effortlessly, this note jumps back into the age of the Qing Dynasty (1662–1722) and unilaterally declares that Guanyin, the Chinese

Goddess of mercy, is trans! Without any regard or sensitivity to historical context, it projects the current concern with trans identity and gender into an era where it could not have possessed any cultural relevance.

The curators at the Burrell Collection wish to insert the 21st-century politics of inclusion into the lifeworld of the Qing Dynasty. The absurdity of this exercise in moral anachronism is overlooked by presumably intelligent museologists ideologically committed to validating recently invented identities through sighting them in 17th- and 18th-century China. The politicization of presentism is used to both validate and invalidate present-day concerns. In the following chapters, this apparent contradiction between using the past to validate and invalidate and between Year Zero ideology and presentism is referred to as *the paradox of the past.* The paradox of the past draws attention to the shifting and, at times, uneasy relationship between these two outwardly contradictory themes in the crusade against the past.

In practice, the coexistence of hatred towards the past and an obsessive impulse to change it are reconciled through a revengeful and accusatory approach towards it. The paradoxical relationship between demanding a break with the past and exacting revenge on it is mediated through the politicization of presentism. Once the boundary between the present and past is rendered porous, political conflicts become detached from the restraints of temporality. In this way, the past can be represented as a dark place where human degradation, abuse, victimization, and genocide were the normal features of daily life. One purpose of this sanctimonious spiteful history is to create a moral distance between the present and the legacy of the past. The other is to convert the injustices of the past into a moral currency that can be used as a resource for claiming attention, respect, and authority in the here and now.

It is tempting to interpret the crusade against the past as merely the latest chapter in the centuries-long conflict between different interpretations of history. To be sure, the War Against the Past has unleashed an intensely polarized debate about the facts of history and their interpretation. Arguments about the history of Anglo-American societies are often conveyed in a tone of venom and hate. 'Whitewashing US history with "patriotic education",' declared *The Guardian.*[22] *The Independent* attacked what it described as Trump's insidious attempt to rewrite history.[23] 'We must clear away the twisted web of lies in our schools and classrooms and teach our children the magnificent truth about our country,' replied Trump.[24]

Heated exchanges about historical facts are an acceptable feature of democratic public life. It is entirely legitimate to adopt a questioning approach towards studying history. In my *Colonial Wars and the Politics of Third World Nationalism* (1994), I dealt at length with the imperial powers' attempt to gain control of decolonization to render it harmless, calling into question the representation of the anti-colonial movements by the apologists of colonial domination. As someone who has published several historical books offering a radical critique of imperialism, colonialism, and racism, I remain sympathetic to continuing the debate of these global issues.[25]

However, the present-day representation of decolonization has little to do with a commitment to set straight the historical record. As the American philosopher Olúfẹ́mi Táíwò observed, the current version of decolonization constitutes the 'absolutization of colonialism'.[26] Decolonization today is no longer about gaining freedom and independence from the influence of colonial power. It is a movement that has voluntarily adopted the role of the historical victim and whose identity is entirely dependent on living in the past. Advocates of the contemporary reinterpretation of decolonization cannot let go of the past since so much of their identity depends on its perpetuation.

The crusade against the past today differs greatly from previous attempts to rewrite history. During the 20th century, the project of rewriting or reinterpreting history was mainly motivated by the determination of the Left and the Right to elaborate a version of the past that could provide legitimation for their political projects. The historians of the Right were drawn towards the objective of revitalizing and defending the past's apparently irrelevant tradition and legacy. In particular, they were interested in the rehabilitation of national histories. Historians on the Left, meanwhile, were devoted to developing a sense of the past that recognized the role of working people and oppressed and marginalized minorities. Theirs was an 'underdog history' that sought to supplement the narrative of different identity groups with greater coherence and meaning. Until recently, these histories were far more devoted to validating and glorifying their constituent's past than detaching society from it.

The War Against the Past only superficially resembles the classical project of rewriting history. Though it can be mistakenly perceived as a conflict between contrasting views of history, it is much more than that: it is about dispossessing the past of any redeeming features.

Why does all this matter?

Society's relation to its past and how it views and understands it has profound implications for everyday life. 'When hegemonic ideas capture our understandings of the past, they capture the present too, and what we can make out of it,' observed the sociologist David Inglis.[27] Should the negative and destructive narrative of the past consolidate its growing authority, it will succeed in undermining people's confidence in themselves, their communities, and their capacity to confront the challenges posed in the future. Once the past is cast in an entirely negative light, there is little possibility of cultivating a sense of hope for the future. In such circumstances, the past ceases to provide any guidance. The continuous serving up of the horrors of the past has the effect of lowering human ambition.

A pathologized history calls into question the capacity of humanity to change for the better and improve its circumstances. A preoccupation with reinterpreting the past as a story of human abuse, atrocity, genocide, ethnic cleansing, slavery, and Holocausts coexists with the tendency of society to regard itself as the object rather than the subject of historical change. A morose fascination with human evil threatens to overwhelm our capacity to imagine an individual's potential for altruism, heroism, or simply doing good.

In its place, humankind is condemned to a world whose history is endlessly recycled as a cautionary tale against the aspiration to exercise human subjectivity. In its most extreme form, humanity's historical role becomes a self-loathing story of ecocide, with humans as the destroyers of all things good. This teleology of evil transmits the message that there is very little that people can do to influence their future: we have created a Hell that cannot be escaped.

Yet, if we are to avoid the genuine mistakes of the past and correct its injustices, society needs to believe in its ability to do good so as to cultivate a politics of hope. This is the paradox of the War Against the

Past: those who are waging it are, inadvertently, denying themselves the capacity to win. For if your past is evil, if your centuries-old story is defined by bitterness and bad faith, how can you possibly hope to redeem yourself?

But what is the past that has now become the target of so much concern and conflict? In the chapter to follow, we will explore the meaning of this term and outline how ideas about the past have evolved and changed over the centuries. Its focus is on the emergence of a sensibility that differentiated between the present and the past. Once this distinction became entrenched in the cultural imagination, then the relationship between the present and the past could become a subject of discussion and debate. Throughout most of history, the past possessed authority and was often perceived as an important resource that could be used to guide society's journey towards its future. The gradual erosion of the authority of the past created the precondition for the crystallization of negative narratives towards it. This chapter outlines the different stages of modern society's estrangement from the past and explains how the loss of its authority has led to a dramatic revision of its cultural status.

The aim of chapter 2 is to outline the slow emergence of the War Against the Past by looking at the historical phases that led up to it. The goal of this chapter is to explain what is distinct about contemporary society's attitude and relation to its past. Chapter 3 is devoted to a discussion of the Ideology of Year Zero. The powerful influence of this ideology legitimates the demand for breaking with the past and starting the world anew. Year Zero ideology justifies this rupture on the grounds that the influence of the past is toxic and that therefore society needs to liberate itself from its influence. It draws a moral contrast between two temporal states, one that demonizes the past. This ideology encourages society to feel a sense of shame about its past and fosters a cultural climate hospitable to estranging people from their origins.

Year Zero's demotion of the past is sustained by a zeitgeist that is obsessively focused on the present. This development has led to ascendancy of the outlook of presentism, which is the subject of chapter 4. Having left the past behind, contemporary Western society has opted to inhabit an endless present. Presentism has encouraged a loss of historical sensibility, and, as a result, everything that precedes it is looked upon as merely an earlier version of itself. Presentism promotes an anachronistic orientation towards the different stages of history to the point that it treats individuals who lived thousands of years ago as if they are our contemporaries. One of the most important consequences of the ascendancy of presentism is the erosion of temporal boundaries. This chapter argues that the influence of presentism has led to the contemporary Culture Wars being fought out on the terrain of the past.

Chapter 5 moves the discussion forwards by investigating the way in which the politicization of identity interacts with the War Against the Past. It suggests that the very rise of identity politics is a by-product of society's detachment from its past. In turn, the politicization of identity has run in parallel with the invention of a negative narrative of never-ending oppression in the past. Since the injustices of the past serve as a resource for establishing the moral authority of identity groups, grievance archaeologists are incentivized to constantly provide material for a gloomy version of history.

Chapter 6 explains how the War Against the Past directs so much of its energy towards gaining control over everyday vocabulary. Through the promotion of linguistic engineering, it seeks to displace traditional vocabulary on the grounds that its words are outdated and offend minorities and identity groups. New words are constantly invented, and through the policing of language, people face pressure to alter their vocabulary. The project of dispossessing people of their language is one of the most insidious manifestations of the War Against the Past. From the standpoint of culture warriors, the taking of control over language serves as a prelude to controlling the way we think.

Chapter 7 draws attention to an extremely disturbing development, which is the disruption of the kind of generational transaction necessary for the socialization of young people. The War Against the Past directs its energies towards the objective of disconnecting the young from the experience and achievement of their ancestors. It seeks to undermine the intergenerational transmission of the values and ideals that are rooted in the past. Consequently, young people's understanding of who they are and where they come from is compromised. This chapter argues that young people's loss of connection with the legacy of the past has created the condition for the flourishing of a crisis of identity. The difficulty that the young have in resolving this crisis has ensured that identity has become a permanent issue in society.

Finally, the book's Conclusion puts forward the case for a nuanced and responsible orientation to the past. It suggests that the defence of the past and learning from its legacy is the precondition for possessing a capacity to face the future.

1

What Is the Past?

Before exploring how the past became a battleground, it is necessary to review the evolution of society's *sense of the past*. Our present attitude towards the past is paradoxical. Strident calls to break with history coexist with an obsessive desire to settle the score with it. As I shall argue in this and the following chapters, the outcome of this contradictory approach to the past is to erode the boundary that separates it from present times.

Consider how events that occurred centuries ago are often treated by sections of the media as *current* events. *The Guardian*, for instance, copying a previous endeavour by *The New York Times*, has commissioned academics to write a report about its founding in 1821 and the newspaper's owners' relation to the slave trade.[1] Elsewhere, institutions such as the Church of England appear to feel more comfortable about accounting for their behaviour two centuries ago than with confronting the challenges of our time. In setting aside a fund to investigate the C of E's links with slavery, Archbishop Justin Welby claimed that he was motivated by 'the presence of the risen Christ alive in the church'.[2]

Since, as the American historian David Lowenthal reminds us, 'the past is everywhere', we tend to take its meaning for granted. 'Noticed or ignored, cherished or spurned, the past is omnipresent,' he wrote in his *The Past Is a Foreign Country* (1985) – its title a reference to the widely cited observation of L.P. Hartley in his novel *The Go-Between* (1953): 'The past is a foreign country ... they do things differently there.'[3] In its most literal sense, the past refers to what has preceded our moment. According to the common-sense definition offered by Wikipedia, the past refers to 'the set of all events that occurred before a given point in time' and 'the past denotes a period of time that has already happened, in contrast to *the present* and *the future*'.[4] According to *The Oxford English Dictionary*, the past 'is the time that has gone by'; it 'existed or occurred prior to the current time'.[5]

In reality, the past does not simply refer to events that occurred before the current moment. It is also a distinct temporal realm that is perceived in the contemporary world as different from the present and the future. Nor does the past simply refer to the domain of temporality. Our consciousness of the past is principally a cultural accomplishment. It is strongly shaped by people's perception of their predicament in the present. Although societies possess a collective memory or sense of the past, different groups and individuals may experience them dissimilarly. The past can incite a wide range of emotions.

> Watch, for example, any of those ancestry programmes in which experts 'dig up' documents and records of some celebrity's forebears. You may see some individuals react with pride and pleasure to the discovery that one of their ancestors was a notable historical character; for others the past brings tears to their eyes, when they realise that one of their relatives had a hard life and experienced the most trying of social conditions. The past, like the present, can elicit the full range of human emotions.[6]

Individuals may only sometimes be aware of their consciousness of the past but the relationship that they have to it is constitutive of who they are. Whether or not individuals are interested in studying their history and finding out about the life of their ancestors, they are inescapably the products of a community that preceded their existence. As the historian Eric Hobsbawm argued, 'For where we stand in regard to the past, what the relationships are between past, present and future are not only matters of vital interest to all: they are quite indispensable.' He added, 'We cannot help situating ourselves in the continuum of our own life, of the family and group to which we belong.'[7]

Society's perception of bygone days is best captured by the term *the sense of the past*. The literary critic Lionel Trilling has persuasively argued that possessing a sense of the past is an 'actual faculty of the mind, a "sixth sense"', through which we become conscious of history and our place in it.[8] From this perspective, the working of this faculty is informed by how people position themselves in relation to the past. There are a range of possible reactions, from nostalgia towards the past to the impulse to leave it behind. However, in all modern societies, all human beings are conscious of history's existence. As Hobsbawm noted:

> To be a member of any human community is to situate oneself with regard to one's (its) past, if only by rejecting it. The past is therefore a permanent dimension of the human consciousness, an inevitable component of the institutions, values and other patterns of human society. The problem for historians is to analyse the nature of this 'sense of the past' in society and to trace its changes and transformations.[9]

The 'sense of the past' constitutes a problem to be investigated because it is constantly subject to shifts in the cultural mood prevailing in society. Society's sensibility towards the past has a history, and how we view it very much depends on our circumstances in the present.

As I shall note later, the past and its meaning for society today is very different from how it was seen and experienced by previous generations. Even during my adult life, there has been a dramatic shift in attitudes towards the past. Back in 1992, when I published my study *Mythical Past, Elusive Future: History and Society in an Anxious Age*, I was struck by the all-pervasive sense of nostalgia that encouraged Western societies to reimagine their history. The focus of *Mythical Past* was on the loss of confidence and the anxiety about the future prevailing in Western societies, which 'stimulated a scramble to appropriate the past'.[10] At the time, other historians and scholars also drew attention to what appeared to be a desperate attempt to sustain a sense of continuity with the past. Nostalgia towards bygone days led to the emergence of what came to be known as the Heritage Industry. The titles of Robert Hewison's *The Heritage Industry: Britain in a Climate of Decline* (1987) and Patrick Wright's *On Living in an Old Country: The National Past in Contemporary Britain* (1985) drew attention to a society that felt more comfortable living in the past than in the present. Wright associated what seemed as the compulsive celebration of heritage during the 1980s as an 'expression of loss of confidence in the future'.[11] According to Nick Merriman, 'The rise of the pejoratively-termed "heritage industry" has been seen as a symptom of the failure of modern society to face the future after the decline of industry. Instead, society is looking back to a more glorious past, but this past, as portrayed in displays led by marketing policies, is a romanticised fiction.'[12]

The project of cultivating the sense of the past during the latter part of the 20th century was, to a considerable extent, a response to the fear of being too detached from it. Lowenthal's *The Past Is a Foreign Country* offered a compelling account of the steady erosion of the sense of continuity, which led to a breach with the past. This development was most astutely captured by the historian J.H. Plumb in his seminal study *The Death of The Past* (1969). Though Plumb was sympathetic to the loss of authority of the past, he was sensitive to the fact that something important was lost. He observed that 'whenever we look, in all areas of social and personal life, the hold of the past is weakening'.[13]

Plumb drew attention to the widespread derision towards what he posited as the 'hollow values' that emanated from the past. According to him, the consequence of this putative death of the past was that attitudes to it became primarily nostalgic: 'The new methods, new processes, new forms of living of scientific and industrial society have no sanction in the past, and no roots in it. The past becomes, therefore, a matter of curiosity, nostalgia, a sentimentality.'[14] In a memorable and scathing remark, Plumb stated that 'the most remarkable aspect of Western ideology is its leech-like addiction to its past'.[15]

Far from serving as the principal cultural frame for perceiving the past, nostalgia and uncritical sentimentality towards it have given way to a mood of uncritical criticism. Today's society is conscious of its loss of historical continuity, but its principal impulse is to reject it. There is – as the title of our book indicates – a veritable War Against the Past, and nostalgia towards it has given way to rejection and detachment. For many, the past is not so much a foreign country as an enemy territory.

The popularity of period dramas such as *Downton Abbey* and *The Crown* can lead to the conclusion that sentimentality towards the past still retains a powerful influence over society. While its presence is manifestly evident, however, it has far from a dominant influence on the contemporary zeitgeist. The paradox of our times is that hostility towards the historical legacy of Western culture exists in an uneasy relationship with a sense of nostalgia. To be more precise, the paradox of the past is best understood as the coexistence of a dominant culture of estrangement and detachment with a search for roots and identity at the level of the individual. The coexistence of these two contradictory elements has unleashed an unprecedented impulse towards eroding the boundary between the present and the past.

Estrangement from the past often runs in parallel with blaming it for the problems of the present. While the fatalistic tendency to blame our current predicament on the past has a long history, it is only in recent times that it has led to the crystallization of the trend of attempting to fix the problems created in the historical past. This development is continually visible in the world of museums, whose mission was once devoted to conserving a subject's legacy. Today, many curators have adopted the habit of attaching signs to old artefacts and works of art that inform visitors of the cultural crimes and sins associated with them. It is as if these curators are putting the past in its place and ensuring that visitors are protected from its baneful influence. In this case, what is paradoxical about the relation of the targeting of outdated views to history is that it rejects the past as irrelevant and best left behind, while at the same it is often obsessively treated as if it is very much alive.

The tendency to treat the past as a clear and present danger is often justified on the grounds that it is a reality that contaminates people's lives in the present moment. Take the blurb advertising a book titled *Rhodes Must Fall.* It states:

> When students at Oxford University called for a statue of Cecil Rhodes to be removed, following similar calls by students in Cape Town, the significance of these protests was felt across continents. This was not simply about tearing down an outward symbol of British imperialism – a monument glorifying a colonial conqueror – but about confronting the toxic inheritance of the past.[16]

Representing the past as a 'toxic inheritance' is significant because it conveys the conviction that it continues to impact human existence negatively. Like all poisonous substances that threaten human life, people need to be protected from its harmful effects. As I previously discussed in my study *Therapy Culture: Cultivating Vulnerability in an Anxious Age* (2004), in the contemporary era, where many problems of existence are interpreted through the prism of mental health, the threat of the past is often assumed to be a psychological one. Arguing in this vein, a petition to remove the statue of Thomas Jefferson from the campus of the University of Missouri asserted that its presence 'perpetuates a sexist-racist atmosphere that continues to reside on campus'. The petitioners wrote that the statue 'alone will not eliminate the racial problem we face in America today, but it will cure the emotional and psychological strain of history'.[17]

The presumption that the past lives on as a dangerous contaminant is frequently asserted by advocates of the different decolonization campaigns. Promoters of Rhodes Must Fall at Oxford University argued that the statue not only reminded them of Rhodes's legacy of racism, colonialism, and oppression but also served to re-traumatize them. As Annie Teriba, one campaign member, explained, 'There's a violence to having to walk past the statue every day on the way to your lectures, there's a violence to having to sit with paintings of former slaveholders whilst writing your exams – that's really problematic.'[18] The language used by some of the Oxford students indicates that a toxic past represents a direct threat to their well-being. This representation of the past was further elaborated by Omar Khan, a director of the advocacy group the Runnymede Trust, who stated that for some students, the sight of Rhodes caused a 'deep wound' that was not 'merely in people's heads nor in any way irrational'.[19] Khan's metaphor of a deep wound that afflicts Oxford students communicates a view of the past that represents it as the source of permanent cultural trauma. The leader of this campaign at the University of Cape Town in South Africa, Kealeboga Ramaru, similarly, insisted that Rhodes's statue was 'a source of pain and trauma to a lot of black students'.[20]

The removal of the statue of the Confederate General Robert E. Lee in Charlottesville, Virginia, was represented by some of its advocates as if it was akin to an intervention promoting their mental health and well-being. Jalane Schmidt, a University of Virginia religious studies professor, stated that the presence of the statue was 'like if there's a rabid dog in the neighbourhood that's been hurting people, and it needs to be euthanized'.[21]

The Pitt Rivers Museum in Oxford illustrates the tendency of Western cultural institutions to represent the past as toxic and a source of shame. There is very little that is nostalgic about the practice of its curators. In 2020, it decided to remove its popular exhibit of shrunken human heads from public view.[22] The Museum's director, Laura Van Broekhoven, decided that this exhibition reinforced 'racist and stereotypical thinking'.[23] For over 80 years, visitors have been fascinated by the display of shrunken heads, decorated skulls, scalps, and Egyptian mummies. It requires a dogmatic belief in the pathological influence of the past to imagine that the exhibition of shrunken heads is likely to incite racist thinking. On the contrary, the visitors exposed to this exhibit are likely to feel stimulated to take an interest in other cultures.

That Van Broekhoven prefers to regard her institution as a Hall of Shame serves as testimony to the radical reconceptualization of the meaning of the past. The project of liberating the Pitt Rivers Museum from its supposed sordid past is framed as integral to the decolonization of cultural institutions sweeping the Western world. However, although the campaign to decolonize museums focuses on de-racializing their collections, its objective goes way beyond the issues of colonialism and race: it is to call into question the history and cultural past of the communities they serve.

In this vein, during the summer of 2019, the Victoria and Albert Museum in London posted signs outside an exhibition on the history of British humour, stating, 'This display confronts uncomfortable truths about the past.' According to the narrative promoted by 21st-century cultural institutions, the past is always immersed in 'uncomfortable truths'. The V&A exhibition did not display any exotic colonial objects; it was merely devoted to a display of British humour. But just in case visitors decided to treat this exhibition light-heartedly, a sign warned them about the risk of being put off by 'some offensive historical materials and language'.[24] For these cultural killjoys, not even the humour voiced by people of yesteryear can be immune from being the target of their sanctimonious sermons and condemnation.

It is important to note that throughout modern history, museums and related cultural institutions have served as powerful instruments of social memory. They have often embraced the role of glorifying the past and promoting celebratory myths about community and nation. Today they appear to pursue a very different mission of throwing a negative light on the past. In our era, museums are much more likely to promote counter-cultural myths about the legacy of the past. It is a past that is fundamentally flawed, and just about all its achievements are said to be corrupted and contaminated by a malevolent culture devoted to oppression and exploitation. Excavating uncomfortable truths about the past has turned into a growth industry. It is an industry that relentlessly works towards rupturing society's emotional connection and organic link with its past.

There have been numerous historical examples of attempts to break with the past. In different ways, the French and Russian Revolutions promoted radical measures to free their societies from the legacy of their history. However, not even these radical revolutionaries went so far as today's culture warriors in their rejection of what preceded them. It is important to underline that whatever hostility it demonstrated towards aspects of the past, even the Western radical and revolutionary tradition continually appealed to its legacy.

Although Karl Marx warned, in his *The Eighteenth Brumaire of Louis Bonaparte*, that the 'social revolution of the nineteenth century cannot take its poetry from the past but only from the future', he was aware of the tremendous influence that the past exercised over the outlook of radical movements. Writing about how 'the tradition of all dead generations weighs like a nightmare on the brain of the living',[25] he observed that, at a time when radicals and revolutionaries are engaged in creating something that has never yet existed, they anxiously conjure up the spirits of the past to their service and borrow from them names, battle cries, and costumes. As examples of this trend, Marx wrote that 'Luther donned the mask of the Apostle Paul, the Revolution of 1789 to 1814 draped itself alternatively as the Roman republic and the Roman empire'; and the leaders of the French Revolution – Danton, Robespierre, Saint-Just, Napoleon – 'performed the task of their time in Roman costume and with Roman phrases'. The power exercised by the legacy of ancient Rome even influenced modern revolutions 'which we commonly regard as radical breaks with tradition'. The French Revolutionary Republic sought to communicate its ideals by appropriating the symbols of the ancient Romans.

Generations of European revolutionaries were educated in the classics and regarded its legacy as foundational to their outlook. The leading Italian communist theoretician Antonio Gramsci argued that 'one doesn't learn Latin and Greek in order to speak them, to become a waiter, or an interpreter, or whatever. One learns them in order to know the civilisations of Greece and Rome, whose existence is posited as a foundation of world culture.'[26] No doubt Gramsci's sense of the past was in many ways radically different to those with conservative inclinations, but what bound together both sides was their attachment to those achievements of the past that constituted the foundations of world culture.

Hobsbawm, a Marxist historian, echoed this sentiment when he wrote that:

> The sense of the past as a collective continuity of experience remains surprisingly important, even to those most dedicated to innovation and the belief that novelty equals improvement: as witness the universal inclusion of 'history' in the syllabus of every modern educational system, or the search for ancestors (Spartacus, More, Winstanley) by modern revolutionaries whose theory, if they are Marxists, assumes their irrelevance.[27]

When Hobsbawm made this observation in the early 1970s, the importance that even modern revolutionaries attached to the sense of the past as a 'continuity of collective experience' could be taken for granted. No doubt, many of them possessed bitterness and anger towards historical injustices and the violent and oppressive actions of rapacious rulers. Nevertheless, their awareness of these 'uncomfortable truths' ran in parallel with the inspiration drawn from the accomplishment of exemplary ancestors in earlier times.

Today, when even the continuity of collective experience is under question, it is evident that we are confronted with a radical revision of the meaning of the past. The past is rarely called upon to serve as a source of authority. On the contrary, it has been recast as a source of contemporary pathology.

The past in history

The current tendency to de-authorize the influence of the past and negate and defeat its legacy stands in sharp contrast to how it was conceptualized across the ages. Throughout most of history, the past served as a focus of cultural reverence. It was frequently perceived as a corrective to the ills suffered by communities in the present. Indeed, the past more often than not served as a model to which people were expected to conform. Calls to recapture or return to the ways of the past are common themes in the history of humanity.

Ideas about the past are inextricably bound up with perceptions concerning its relationship to the present and the future. Not all societies make a sharp temporal distinction between the present and the past, and many believe that what we call the future is the past foretold. Greek tragedies are saturated with a powerful sense of fatalism where events set in motion in the past work inexorably towards a predictable end. In Sophocles' *Oedipus*, the main protagonist 'lives in the illusion of his future life without having access to his past, in which his present life is rooted'. The tragedy surrounding Oedipus' life 'can be explained by the fact that he hoped to avoid his future without knowing his past'. According to a review of this tragedy, 'The Greeks believed that since the past had already happened, we can see it "in front of us", while we can't see the future, so it is "behind our back".'[28] In certain respects, for the protagonists of this drama, the past was more real than what today we call the present, and, in all likelihood, they regarded knowledge about it as the key to grasping their predicament.

Many societies possessed a cyclical view of time where the past was perceived as a stage in a cycle that would eventually, in all essentials, reoccur. This cyclical view of history was prevalent among the Chinese and Hindu societies, the ancient Greeks, and the Aztecs. In historical periods where little appeared to change, there was not much to distinguish the past from the present and therefore it made sense to perceive change through the prism of natural cycles.

The meaning of the past for Greeks in the ancient era was very different than for modern society. There is even a dispute about the point at which human communities began to possess a consciousness of history based on a distinction between the present and the past. A consciousness of history required that the past be seen not only as an era that preceded the present but also as qualitatively different. In his fascinating study *The Birth of the Past* (2011), the historian Zachary Schiffman explained that the distinction between the present and the past 'rests on something other than a priority in time; it reflects an abiding awareness that different historical entities exist in different historical contexts'. The awareness of this difference led to the development of the notion of the past. Schiffman claimed that the concept of the past is not universally given but the 'intellectual creation of a particular historical moment'.[29] Once the sense of the past is perceived as the subject of intellectual creation, it follows that it becomes a legitimate topic for contrasting interpretation and controversy. Such interpretations are often specific to a particular moment in time, and therefore the meaning that communities attach to the past becomes subject to historical variations.

According to most scholarly accounts, the sense of the past in the West emerged during the Renaissance between the 14th and 17th centuries. Schiffman claimed that the idea of the past originated during this period and only acquired the status of common sense in the 18th century.[30] The historian Richard Southern contended that the 'cultivation of a sense of the past is a fairly recent development', and that 'in its most articulate form it is a product of the breakdown of the relatively stable intellectual system which had been created in the Middle Ages and remained substantially operative till the mid-nineteenth century'.[31]

The historian Roy Porter wrote that 'a crowning achievement of Renaissance humanism was to generate "a sense of the past"'. Renaissance humanism differentiated between its immediate past – the medieval era – which it cast in a negative light, and the distant past – antiquity – which it extolled. 'The very act of playing off the luminaries of Antiquity against the barbarians of the "Dark Ages" forced scholars to see difference, time, transformation and periodization.'[32] The historian Richard Marius, too, drew attention to the pioneering role of Renaissance historians, who 'began to perceive the difference between their own times and the past they described'. According to Marius, this discovery was barely grasped in the Middle Ages, when the 'past faded into vague folk memory where men and women of antiquity were no different from the people one saw in the throng of a feudal procession'.[33]

One of the outcomes of the emergence of historical consciousness during the Renaissance was that the past became an object of critical investigation. Previously, the most significant prior precedent for adopting a critical orientation towards the past occurred in early imperial Rome, where philosophers like Cicero warned of the danger of unthinkingly accepting and imitating the legacy of pre-existing Greek culture. The Romans never tired of pointing out 'the weaknesses of the Athenian political system in comparison to their own'.[34] Whatever praise the Romans voiced towards the accomplishments of Greek culture, they were in no doubt about the superiority of their political arrangements. The lessons that Romans drew from the experience of Athens were not simply motivated by the impulse to avoid the upheavals that blighted this city-state. The construction of a distinct Roman tradition and way of life required that the influence of the older Greek culture should be kept in check. In their extensive discussion about the Greeks, the 'Romans were intensely anxious about what it meant to be Roman and not Greek'.[35]

What was remarkable about Rome's uneasy relationship with the influence of the Greeks was that, despite cultural tensions, it nevertheless opted to integrate the Homeric past into its tradition.[36] Whilst distancing itself from the 'corrupt' and 'degenerate' customs of latter-day Greek city-states, Rome appropriated the heroic Homeric era into its founding myth. In this way, it could claim the inheritance of the best of the Greek past while also boasting a superior political wisdom to that possessed by the Hellenic world. The Romans adopted the myth of descent from Aeneas, and 'through the *Aeneid*'s foundation legend the Roman populace bound itself to Greek history'.[37] In this way, Rome came to be represented as the inheritor of the legacy of Greek culture. In Virgil's *Aeneid*, the founding of Rome is depicted as the culmination of a prophecy, and through this act, 'the spirit of the best of the Greek ancestors lives on through its resurrection on Italian soil'.[38]

The self-conscious construction of a narrative of Rome's past set an important precedent for the development of Western political thought. The Romans systematically developed a political culture that situated the concept of authority and of legitimacy on the foundation of the past. They expressly attempted to consolidate a powerful sense of tradition and continuity. They believed that through drawing and maintaining an organic continuity between successive generations, a robust sense of the past would contribute to the development of solidarity and stability. This appeal to the authority of the past and its customs and traditions was a self-consciously pursued enterprise. The affirmation of continuity, with its connotations of a thriving and living tradition, played an important role in constructing a unique Roman sensibility towards the past. The Romans continually wrote about their history and were self-consciously devoted to their ancestors, traditions, and customs.[39]

The political life of Rome was dominated by custom and tradition, and day-to-day decisions were often shaped by the tacit knowledge that its political and cultural elite possessed about it. The absence of a systematic presentation of its theory of government did not mean that it lacked political skills. Roman political life possessed an impressive capacity for institutional adaptation and innovation. The Roman constitution, or, to put it more accurately, constitutional arrangement, expressed a powerful sense of continuity with the past as well as an open orientation towards further development in the future. It offered a synthesis of tradition with a willingness to adapt to new experiences. The values of origins, preservation, and continuity were points of references for the working of the constitution. The Roman philosopher Cicero claimed that the association of these values with the constitution accounted for its superiority to others. He noted that the transmission of ancient values from one generation to the next helped explain the distinct form of the government of Rome. Through the process of continuous generational transactions, the constitution succeeded in evolving through assimilating new experiences. Cicero stated that this constitution was 'superior to others' because it 'had been established not by one man's life but over several ages and generations'. For the Roman elites, the virtue of this arrangement was that it was not simply based on 'one man's ability' but on 'that of many' over a long period of time. He noted that since 'no collection of able people at a single point of time could have sufficient foresight to take into account of everything; there had to be practical experience over a long period of history'.[40]

Rome's so-called ancient constitution should be conceptualized not as a legal document or a code but as a set of informal guidelines based on custom and precedent and transmitted from one generation to the next. Its lack of formality possessed the virtue of adaptability that allowed it to evolve in line with the shift from Rome as a city-state to becoming a vast empire. The emphasis which Cicero and others placed on a foundation as a sacred moment in the constitution of the community was motivated by the understanding that a consensus on common origins and a way of life was essential if the city was to cope with the internal tensions and external pressures that confronted it. From 250 BC onwards, a series of major foreign wars and imperial expansion irrevocably transformed the Roman world in a way that began to expose the 'weakness of a governmental system that relied upon respect for authority and adherence to tradition'.[41] In such circumstances, tradition needed to be nurtured and cultivated.

As one overview of this period noted, 'Constant expansion required a basic consensus at home.'[42] That is why, arguably, the Romans were not simply traditionalists but also self-consciously traditionalists. Cicero's emphasis on the state's 'foundation and preservation' represented an attempt to endow custom and tradition with life.[43] Through this construction of a dialectic of foundation and preservation, the story of Rome's origins served as a source of validation for subsequent events. The preservation of tradition was represented as an obligatory duty of all. In this way, every generation was bound to the previous one and, through this process of interaction, to the foundation of the city.

For Cicero, the foundation for belief, including religious belief, was tradition. However, religion was not so much focused on gods as on *the affirmation of the past*. In the Roman case, religion 'literally meant *religare*: to be tied back, obligated, to the enormous, almost superhuman and hence always legendary effort to lay the foundations, to build the cornerstone, to found for eternity'.[44] The act of venerating the past had a distinct religious quality. The founding of Rome was presented as the culmination of historical events that could never be re-created. It was an authoritative event that contained within itself the potential to authorize. In her reflections on this process, the political philosopher Hannah Arendt posits the act of foundation as the source of authority. The act of foundation represents a unique experience which Roman tradition developed to authorize belief and behaviour.[45] From this perspective, authority meant 'fundamentally the wisdom of the ancestors, the *mos maiorum*, in the form of the necessity of religious belief for the solidarity, loyalty, cooperation, and dynamism of the citizenry'.[46]

Rome was by no means the only society that venerated its past and took its founding myth and traditions seriously. Yet it went further than most societies in antiquity in its cultivation of the past and, indeed, the politicization of tradition. Numerous accounts of ancient times write of Rome's strong sense of traditionalism and of its suspicion of innovation. What's interesting about Rome, however, was not its rigid conservatism but its understanding that tradition had to be cultivated and imaginatively reconstructed. The historian Harriet Flower wrote how the 'sense of a shared set of values was cultivated for a surprisingly long time' despite the upheavals experienced by the Republic.[47]

For the Romans, the distinction they drew between their society and that of Athens was motivated by pragmatic concerns. Their reflection lacked the depth of Renaissance humanists, whose elaboration of historical thinking led to an important conceptual clarification of the meaning of the past. Lowenthal pointed out that it was 'only in the fourteenth century, with Petrarch', that the 'rival merits of old and new become a major concern, first in Italy, then in France and England'.[48] During this era, different epochs in history were assessed, contrasted, and criticized. These reflections on the past stimulated lively debates about the merits of antiquity and modern times. It is important to note that the Renaissance was the first era where leading thinkers self-consciously regarded themselves as modern and as possessing achievements that were superior to their forebears in the recent Dark Ages.

The spell that the authority of the past cast over the people of the Western world ensured that new ideas about the superiority of modern thought did not enter the mainstream of society. It would take several centuries before the Renaissance's discovery of the past and its qualitative difference with modernity would enter the popular consciousness of Western society. Lowenthal has argued that until the 19th century the historical past was generally thought of much like the present. He added that:

> To be sure, history recorded major changes of life and landscape, gains and losses, but human nature supposedly remained constant, events actuated by unchanging passions and prejudices. Even when ennobled by nostalgia or deprecated by partisans of progress, the past seemed not a foreign country but part of their own. And chroniclers portrayed bygone times with an immediacy and intimacy that reflected the supposed likeness.[49]

One reason why the past continued to have such a hold on the public imagination was that it continued to be perceived as the source of knowledge and of authority. 'Men ever praise the olden times and find fault in the present,' wrote the Renaissance political thinker Machiavelli in his observation on the *Discourses in the First Ten Books of Titus Livius*.[50] Machiavelli, the father of modern political philosophy, nevertheless regarded the past as a source of both inspiration and of authority. For its part, despite its animosity towards medieval society, Renaissance humanism venerated the ancient and the traditional.

Historia magistra vitae

Throughout much of history, the past was regarded from the perspective of what Cicero described as *historia magistra vitae*, the idea that studying the past offers a lesson for the future. This Latin expression conveyed the idea of history as 'life's teacher'. This sensibility continues to influence human thought to this day. After all, we cannot help but learn from our experience, and therefore, consciously or intuitively, we often turn to the past for guidance.

Historically, the past has almost always served as the pattern for the present.[51] Even when people began to perceive a difference between their circumstances and those of their ancestors, the old ways continued to exercise an influence on their daily lives. Respect for the customs of ancestors extended to the attribution of wisdom to the old. Elders served as models for the younger generations to follow, and it was not until the 19th century that generational conflict leading to a rejection of the ways of the old gained momentum. The precondition for the persistence of the traditional ways of the old was a relatively slow rate of change. A growing consciousness of change in the 18th century, coinciding with the intellectual and scientific revolutions that ran in parallel with the Enlightenment, created a cultural landscape that became more and more inhospitable to the flourishing of the authority of the past.

The German historian Reinhart Koselleck persuasively argues that the Ciceronian *topos* called *historia magistra vitae* started fading in the late 18th century, owing to the new aspects of irreversibility and acceleration that history had gained.[52] History could thus no longer provide lessons for a deeply uncertain world after the French Revolution. A rapid acceleration of social change created a condition where many drew the conclusion that the past could offer little guidance and could no longer provide them with a model for making sense of the present. During the 19th century, the past ceased to be seen by many as offering a pattern for the present and innovation was recognized, according to Hobsbawm, as both 'inescapable and socially desirable'.[53]

The literary and popular culture of the time was increasingly drawn away from the celebration of the past and sometimes sought to distance its audience from previous norms and values. There emerged a cult of the young that directly counterposed itself to the archaic ways of the elder generation. Literature often touched on the conflict between the cultural attitudes of different generations. Ivan Turgenev's powerful novel *Fathers and Sons* (1862) is paradigmatic in this respect. It offered a powerful dramatization of a growing generational divide. Despite resistance from traditionalist quarters, the idealization of the young swiftly gained momentum and became ascendant by the turn of the 20th century.

The 19th-century reaction to the past was most pronounced in the United States, where its idealization often ran counter to society's proclivity to celebrate novelty. This was, after all, the New World, and Americans were often ambivalent about cherishing the legacy of the past. The past was a territory that many left behind when they set sail from the ports of the Old World. They had little sentimental attachment to the society they willingly rejected and were often excited about the prospect of starting their life anew. 'I like the dreams of the future better than the history of the past,' noted Thomas Jefferson, a Founding Father of the United States.[54]As Lowenthal explained, 'The sheer novelty of America made history irrelevant.' He cited Benjamin Gratz Brown, a future governor of Missouri, stating, 'With the Past we have literally nothing to do. Its lessons are lost and its tongue is silent.' He added: 'Precedents have lost their virtue and all their authority is gone.'[55]

'A nation is much to be pitied that is weighed down by the past,' its 'industry and enterprise are constantly impeded by . . . its recollections', asserts a character in one of James Fenimore Cooper's new frontier novels.[56] This sentiment is forcefully affirmed by the American essayist Ralph Waldo Emerson in his argument against revering the past. He warned that 'whatever is old is corrupt, and the past turns to snakes. The reverence for the deeds of our ancestors is a treacherous sentiment.'[57] Emerson's disdain towards the deeds of ancestors resonated with American society's idealization of youth. Freed from the supposed burden of the legacy of the past, the youth of America were invested with the task of creating the world anew. By the turn of the 20th century, the cult of novelty had succeeded in thoroughly undermining the cultural authority of the past in the United States.

The flip side of the celebration of the youth was the devaluation of the old and of ageing. In particular, this attitude influenced the outlook of many thinkers and commentators associated with the American progressive movement at the turn of the 20th century. A leading radical progressive intellectual, Ralph Bourne, wrote a veritable manifesto, *Youth and Life* (1913), which celebrated the young as the saviours of civilization. Adults were dismissed by him as obstacles to progress:

> There is no scorn so fierce as that of youth for the inertia of older men. Adults are little more than grown-up children. This is what makes their arrogance so insulting. . . . Youth has no right to be humble. The ideals it forms will be the highest it will ever have, the insight the clearest, the ideas the most stimulating. The best that it can hope to do is to conserve those resources, and keep its flame of imagination and daring bright.[58]

At the turn of the 20th century, Bourne and many leading American liberals invested their hopes in the youth because it appeared to them that unlike their elders, they were not weighed down by the traditions of the past. Bourne portrayed the young as the saviours of civilization. He called on intelligent youth to be 'the incarnation of reason pitted against the rigidity of tradition'.[59] In the eyes of Bourne, there was little that one could value in adulthood. He explained that it is the young 'who have all the really valuable experience'.[60] For him, the experience of the elderly counted for little since it was based on a bygone age that was made irrelevant by the impact of rapid change. Not only were the older generations irrelevant, but their behaviour and attitude also inhibited young people from realizing their destiny. In an accusatory tone, Bourne complained that 'an unpleasantly large proportion of our energy is now drained off in fighting the fetishes which you of the elder generation have passed along to us'.[61]

Sentiments like that of Bourne were voiced in Europe. The Italian Futurist movement fetishized novelty and youth and communicated an unrestrained sense of contempt for the old. *The Futurist Manifesto*, published in 1909, warned young people that:

> To admire an old picture is to pour our sensibility into a funeral urn instead of casting it forward with violent spurts of creation and action. Do you want to waste the best part of your strength in a useless admiration of the past, from which you will emerge exhausted, diminished, trampled on?[62]

The *Manifesto* depicted ageing as a form of social death that possessed no redeeming features. It observed:

> The oldest among us are not yet thirty years old: we have therefore at least ten years to accomplish our task. When we are forty let younger and stronger men than we throw us in the waste paper basket like useless manuscripts![63]

The sentiments articulated by the Futurists were more extreme than most commentaries devoted to the glorification of youth. Nevertheless, it is important to note that this movement exercised an important influence on the aesthetic sensibility of several generations of young Europeans, particularly in the domain of art, design, and architecture.

At the time, the unrestrained contempt of the Futurists for the 'useless admiration of the past' did not yet exercise a hegemonic impact over European society. However, in a more muted form, large sections of society had become distanced from their traditions. The ways of the old had lost much of their appeal and the authority of the past was now put into question. These modernist sentiments gained force during the 20th century, and gradually there were fewer and fewer appeals to the authority of the past. Even the knowledge that was gained through experience of the past was often dismissed as redundant, supposedly because it had been overtaken by events. *Historia magistra vitae* was no longer fit for purpose.

From the perspective of the post-*Historia magistra vitae* era, rapid change negates the wisdom of the past and the elders have little of value to transmit to the young. This outlook gained widespread force during the rise of the Counter-Culture in the 1960s. The American social psychologist Kenneth Keniston voiced this sentiment when he starkly stated that

> the relations between the generations are weakened as the rate of innovation increases. The wisdom and skills of fathers can no longer be transmitted to sons with any assurance that they will be appropriate for them; truth must as often be created by children as learned from parents.[64]

The claim that the intergenerational transmission of wisdom and skills has become undermined because of the supposed irrelevance of the past implicitly calls into question the conventions and norms through which society gives meaning to human experience.

Since adulthood is meant to provide the model to guide the formation of identity, the weakening of its status and appeal has important implications for the process of transition from adolescence. This issue was alluded to by the psychologist Eric Erikson when he raised concerns about the problem of giving meaning to authority. He was critical of the failure of adult society to provide the leadership that adolescents required to resolve their crisis of identity. What was at stake was not simply a question of adults not providing inspiring leadership but also their inability to uphold the ideals to which the young should aspire. Erikson warned that 'we must not overlook what appears to be a certain abrogation of responsibility on the part of the older generation in providing those forceful ideals which must antecede identity formation in the next generation – if only so that youth can rebel against a well-defined set of older values'.[65] Ideals that antecede identity formation are the ones that link young generations to society's past.

Erikson's concern with the failure of adult society to provide the forceful ideals that are necessary for identity formation is to the point. However, the absence of such forceful ideals is not due to a character defect of the older generations. By the time Erikson penned his thoughts on this issue, not only was the normative foundation of adulthood fatally undermined, but also adult society was struggling to articulate the ideals and philosophical outlook needed to share with the younger generation. Over the decades, the norms and values that guided generations in the past were systematically called into question by experts, who continually claimed that rapid change had made them irrelevant. This loss of continuity with the values of the past had important implications for the cultivation of adolescent identity. As Keniston urged us to recall, 'One of the chief tasks of identity formation is the creation of a sense of self that will link the past, the present and the future.'[66] Having invested so much emotion and energy in renouncing the influence of the past and its traditions, psychologists and related professionals unwittingly made a significant contribution to the erosion of the sense of continuity required for the formation of stable identities.

It is difficult to develop a sturdy sense of collective identity without a shared memory and a common attachment to conventions or customs that are rooted in the past. Collective identities are intergenerational accomplishments that are cultivated through the absorption of a common cultural inheritance. Through transmitting the values of the past, socialization is integral to an intergenerational transaction whereby moral norms are communicated by authoritative adults to the young.

Although adulthood and childhood are often discussed as separate and stand-alone concepts, they exist and thrive as part of an intergenerational community where their relationship is mediated by a common web of meaning. Because they are heirs to a common past, adults can transfer to the young the cultural resources that they will need to make their way in this world. Through this generational continuity – which is not just biological but also cultural – the organic relationship between a community's present and past is reproduced and reinforced.

The detachment of the present from the past meant that adulthood lacked a narrative with which it could confidently assist the project of identity formation. As I argued in *100 Years of Identity Crisis: Culture War Over Socialisation* (2021), the disruption of the intergenerational transmission of values complicates the socialization of the young, which in turn leads to the proliferation of the phenomenon known as the crisis of identity. The relationship between the erosion of the authority of the past and the crisis of identity is one of the main themes discussed in the chapters to follow.

Reflections on the loss of the authority of the past

The weakening of the sense of the past had profound implications for how people made sense of their place in the world. Society's sense of the past is inextricably bound up with how its members perceive the world. Society's consciousness of its origins and traditions provides the cultural foundations for community life. Despite numerous declarations of the death of the past, it cannot but continue to inform people's lives. The past is not a phenomenon that can remain entirely detached from individuals' lives or the community they inhabit. From the moment that children become humanized and socialized, they become aware of the fact that what preceded them has an important bearing on who they are. The past is an integral element of human consciousness, and society's reaction to it is communicated through the way it ascribes meaning to experience. When, today, the past often appears to have ceased to be a repository of meaningful values with which to influence and socialize the younger generation, society is confronted with serious problems.

Since the late 18th century, in one form or another, concern about the potential consequences of the loss of the past has haunted the imagination of philosophers and thinkers across the political divide. The attempt to retain the authoritative status of the past was most systematically pursued by conservative intellectuals who were most sensitive to the psychic and cultural distance dividing their present from the past. In many respects, it can be argued that classical conservatism emerged in the 19th century to retain the relevance and force of the ideal of *historia magistra vitae*. Edmund Burke, the intellectual father of modern conservatism, stressed custom and tradition and the influence of prejudice and prescription as the foundation for validating authority. In an often-cited speech to the House of Commons in May 1782, he outlined his traditionalist orientation:

> Our constitution is a prescriptive constitution whose sole authority is that it has existed time out of mind. . . . Prescription is the most solid of titles, not only to property, but, which is to secure that property, to government. . . . It is accompanied with another ground of authority in the constitution of the human mind – presumption. It is a presumption in favour of any settled scheme of government against any untried project, that a nation has long existed and flourished under it.

Burke insisted that the 'wisdom' of prejudice built up over centuries was a far more reliable guide than an individual's 'own private stock of reason'.[67]

Burke sought to depict the principle of authority and liberty as complementary. People's loyalties to their traditional institutions expressed a balance between liberty and constraint. In his 'Reflections on the Revolution in France' (1790), he stated that the authority of established institutions encouraged loyal assent, and its 'power' was rendered 'gentle' by 'pleasing illusions' and the support of 'ancient opinions and rules of life'.[68] Burke, of course, recognized that rendering power 'gentle' required a sensibility inconsistent with the modern mind, which is why he used the phrase 'pleasing illusions'. His frank acknowledgement that illusions were necessary is testimony to his struggle to sustain the mystery of tradition.

The defence of the past was of central concern to 19th-century conservative thinkers such as the Swiss-German historian Jacob Burckhardt. He was concerned with what he perceived as an overreaction to the legacy of the preceding centuries. Burckhardt feared the 'sudden attack against everything inherited from the Middle Ages' and the 'hatred' for the historical legacy of the pre-Enlightenment era.[69] From his standpoint, hostility towards past traditions encouraged an anti-historical orientation that coincided with a naïve optimism about human perfectibility and the inevitability of progress.

Classical liberal thinkers were also preoccupied with ensuring that society retained a balanced sense of the past. In 1831, the liberal English political theorist J.S. Mill published a series of articles titled *The Spirit of Age*. In part, these essays sought how to address the issues posed by the de-authorization of the past. In the first of his articles, he explained that 'the times are pregnant with change; and that the nineteenth century will be known to posterity as the era of one of the greatest revolutions of which history has preserved the remembrance, in the human mind, and in the whole constitution of human society'.[70] Mill characterized his era as an 'age of transition' where 'mankind have outgrown old institutions and old doctrines, and have not yet acquired new ones'. The old maxims, argued Mill, have become irrelevant and people have ceased to defer to their influence. 'Who can hope to sway the minds of the public by the old maxims of law, or commerce, or foreign policy, or ecclesiastical policy?,' he asked. But although the authority of the past had become exhausted, there continued to be no new alternatives:

> Now, it is self-evident that no fixed opinions have yet generally established themselves in the place of those which we have abandoned; that no new doctrines, philosophical or social, as yet command, or appear likely soon to command, an assent at all comparable in unanimity to that which the ancient doctrines could boast of while they continued in vogue.[71]

For Mill, 'this intellectual anarchy' was symptomatic of a grave threat facing society, which is that its elites have become disorganized – the 'divisions among the instructed nullify their authority' – and as a result, the 'multitude are without a guide'.[72] Time and again, Mill reiterated his concern that without the authorization of the past, the foundation of intellectual authority is rendered fragile.

Despite his radical vision, Mill could not quite let go of the past. He counselled his readers against becoming obsessed with novel forms of authority and, at times, appears to find it difficult to avoid celebrating the wisdom of the past. He wrote that the 'great authority for political doctrines' in past governments 'was the wisdom of ancestors: their old laws, their old maxims, the opinions of their ancient statesmen'. He reminded his sceptical modernist 19th-century audience that 'this may sound strange to those who have imbibed the silly persuasion, that fickleness and love of innovation are the characteristics of popular government', but that it is a 'matter of authentic history'.

Pointing to the French Revolution as the point at which Europe 'entered into the state of transition', Mill warned about the tendency to 'disregard the authority of ancestors, which characterise an age of transition'.[73] That Mill, who was no traditionalist, could reflect so wistfully on the authority of the past indicates the seriousness with which he regarded the absence of a recognized form of moral authority. Nine years after writing this article, he asserted the need for a source of unquestioned authority in his essay on Coleridge. He wrote that in 'all political societies which have had a durable existence, there has been some fixed point; something which men agreed in holding sacred'. But when these 'fundamental principles' are habitually questioned, the 'state is virtually in a position of civil war'.[74] He criticized the *philosophes* of the 18th century for 'ignoring the conditions necessary for the stability of society' and put forward a plea to reformers 'to be sensitive to whatever values may reside in old institutions and beliefs, and not to destroy everything which is regarded as bad without at the same time being able to replace it with something else'.[75]

Burke's and Mill's preoccupation with the unravelling of the past as a central component of the normative foundation of society anticipated concerns that would be raised and raised again in the centuries to follow. The growing tendency to detach society from its traditions and pre-existing norms has created the condition where values become a source of conflict instead of serving as an instrument for the achievement of unity. In the absence of a web of meaning based on common norms, the fear of disunity that haunted successive generations of conservative and liberal thinkers has become a reality.

Today, in everyday life, people tend to be encouraged to disassociate themselves from the past. According to the editor of *Archaeology Ireland*:

> More often than not, the proverbial past is seen as a problem – a container for all that was/is wrong with the world. We have all heard the phrase 'living in the past' being used in that unmistakably accusatory tone, often applied to someone who is extolling the merits of an older method of doing something or other. Unfortunately, the use of this phrase not only implies a total condemnation of former times and the people who lived through them but also displays a lack of interest in understanding the substance of what we are and what surrounds us.[76]

The crystallization of an accusatory tone directed at the past has been a long time coming. However, as we shall see, what's unique about 21st-century society's account of the past is not its hostility to it but its uniquely paradoxical presentist orientation towards it.

The paradox of our past is that it is said to be less and less relevant to our existence while, at the same time, it is seen to have a uniquely negative influence on contemporary society. Blaming the past and attacking historical figures that were until recently widely acclaimed signifies a shift in focus from facing up to the challenges of today to settling scores with the past. In all but name, a war has been declared against the past. In his discussion of the past, Lowenthal noted that 'what is once done can never be undone'.[77] That is not how the culture warriors who have declared against the past view matters today. They believe that they can reverse the past and settle scores with it to ensure that its legacy can become a source of shame.

It is important to note that the precondition for the War Against the Past was the gradual erosion of its authority. The weakening of the sense of the past has led important sections of society to lose interest in its historical legacy. A feeble sense of historical consciousness coexisting with the palpable mood of presentism created a cultural environment where the principal reaction to the declaration of a War Against the Past is appeasement and defeatism.

2

The War's Long Gestation

It is only in recent times that the rejection of the authority of the past has led to a declaration of hostility towards it. To understand the unique features of the current conflict, it is necessary to explore the different stages of its evolution.

The rise of modernity coincided with the emergence of ambivalent attitudes towards the authority of the past. From this point onwards, the distinction between old and new began to acquire moral connotations. The historian John Lukacs has noted that the term 'modern' acquired the connotation of newness at this point. As he explained:

> The word 'modern' first appeared in English about four hundred years ago, circa 1580. At first its sense was close to the original Latin *modernus*: 'today's', 'present'. (Shakespeare occasionally used it, meaning 'now common'.) Gradually the weight of its sense shifted a bit forward, including the meaning of 'new' – that is, something divergent from 'old'.[1]

The contrast between old and new was paralleled by the emergence of a form of historical consciousness that regarded the modern as a distinct stage in the evolution of humanity. Gradually, the modern and the new came to be associated with intrinsically positive qualities by the intellectual and cultural influencers of the time. This sentiment dominated the Western world's outlook during the centuries to follow. *Make It New* was the title of a 1934 collection of essays by the American expatriate poet Ezra Pound. For Pound, modernism and making it new were intertwined. In a seminal essay published in 1959, the American art critic Harold Rosenberg characterized this outlook as 'the tradition of the new'.[2] This was a reference to the cultural validation of novelty, based on the belief that it possessed an intrinsic value. At times, this belief was supported by the conviction that science and technology had the answer for everything and, therefore, what was new is likely to be better than what was old.

By the 19th century, it was evident that the tendency towards celebrating the new was often coupled with disdain for the past. In a series of lectures delivered between 1868 and 1885, the historian Jacob Burckhardt raised concerns about this development. 'To me, as a teacher of history, a very peculiar phenomenon has become manifest', he noted, 'namely the sudden devaluation of all "mere" events of the past.'[3] He drew attention to what he regarded as a disturbing matter: since the French Revolution, 'men took upon themselves the right to indict the past as a whole'. He added that 'the arrogant belief in the moral superiority of the present, however, has only fully developed of late years; it makes no exceptions, even in favor of classical antiquity'.[4]

Burckhardt's observation regarding the practice of indicting the 'past as a whole' drew attention to a radically new occurrence in European culture. At this point, the rendering of the past as morally inferior to the present was still in its early phase, a point of view held by a minority. Nevertheless, in the decades to follow, an aggressive modernist disdain for the authority of the past gained ascendancy within European society. What I characterize as the War Against the Past originates in the emergence of a moral contrast between the new and the old and the present and the past. The modernist sensibility that assumed itself to be superior to everything that preceded it provided the disposition towards cultivating a climate hospitable to the delegitimization of the authority of the past.

Initially, the diminished significance that society attached to the authority of the past did not necessarily lead to a hostile and negative outlook. In the 19th century, the spirit of modernism was far more drawn towards celebrating the new than denigrating the old. The characteristic response of modernists and progressives towards the past was one of indifferent contempt. The idealization of progress and the growing authority of the new influenced the spirit of the times. From the standpoint of the modernist imagination in the 19th century, change was synonymous with progress, and progressivism systematically expressed this sensibility. Except for reactionary and conservative movements, by the turn of the 20th century, progressivist ideals gained influence among parties across the political divide.

Contemporary discussions on progressivism tend to overlook the appeal of this ideology to virtually every section of the political class. To be sure, there were left- and right-wing versions of progressivism, but regardless of their ideological goals, both sides had become estranged from the past and came to regard its legacy as irrelevant to their project. Progressives were devoted to reforming and changing the world. They were confident that 'man could make and remake his own world'.[5] They also believed that the experience of the past had little value to adherents of progress, who were attempting to introduce radically new measures to reform society.

Those who, socially and politically, usually disagreed on the main issues of the time nevertheless shared a common sensibility towards the past. Influenced by political and cultural modernism, they dismissed the legacy of the past as of little worth and, therefore, did not attach any significance to preserving cultural continuity, seeking, on the contrary, to challenge those who still endorsed it. Their implicit and sometimes explicit objective was to detach modern society from the traditions of the past. This goal was most systematically pursued by modernizing groups of social engineers who believed that the continuing influence of the past represented an obstacle to the realization of progress.

Though a variety of radical and revolutionary movements had as their goal the liberation of society from the legacy of exploitation and oppression of the past, the most coherent and zealous opponents of tradition were the adherents of American progressivism. However, virtually every modernist movement – New Liberals in Britain, Social Democrats in Sweden, European socialists and eugenicists, communists and fascists – endorsed and embraced aspects of this outlook. In their wildest dreams, they often advanced a utopian vision of a new world fundamentally re-engineered by scientific principles.

The main site of progressivist activism was in the sphere of education and socialization. Political movements, therapeutic professionals, pedagogues, and modernizing capitalists regarded the re-engineering of socialization as the main site for social/cultural/economic reform and renewal. Insulating children and young people from the influence of the past was one of their principal goals. Across the conventional ideological divide, movements sought to diminish the influence of the past and replace traditional values with new 'up-to-date' modern ones.

All shades of political opinion became drawn towards training and educating children to embrace a physical and moral outlook that was not distorted by the superstitions and irrational customs of the past. During the first three decades of the 20th century, political movements often invested their hopes in the figure of a New Man, who, untainted by past distortions, would serve to transform or revitalize society. Movements from Left and Right promoted their version of what this New Man would look like and achieve.

Leon Trotsky, one of the leaders of the Russian Revolution, projected a utopian vision of a new 'superman'. In his *Literature and Revolution* (1924), he wrote:

> Man will make it his purpose to master his own feelings, to raise his instincts to the heights of consciousness, to make them transparent, to extend the wires of his will into hidden recesses, and thereby to raise himself to a new plane, to create a higher social biologic type, or, if you please, a superman.[6]

Far right and fascist movements were also attracted to the myth of the New Man. The fascists idealized their New Man as virile, physically hard, forceful, and committed to the taking of initiative. Adolf Hitler described the New Man as 'slim and slender, quick like a greyhound, tough like leather, and hard like Krupp steel'.[7]

This idealization of the New Man did not perish in the interwar era. It re-emerged in the 1980s to refer to a male who embraced anti-sexist attitudes and rejected outdated masculine values and traditional male roles.[8] In contemporary times, gender-neutral and anti-sexist socialization promises to produce young people who are not tainted by the heteronormative attitudes of the past. Today, these sentiments are constantly conveyed by those who promote the cause of 'raising awareness' of those still in the thrall of outdated attitudes.

The intensification of the consciousness of change

The erosion of the authority of the past was influenced by the widespread belief that the modern world was in constant motion. It was claimed that because of the unprecedented rate of change, the legacy and achievements of previous generations had lost much of their relevance. During the 19th and early 20th centuries, as the development of science and technology led to the industrialization of Western societies and social transformation, there was a prevalent expectation of rapid and constant change. In many instances, expanding the psychological gulf between the present and past led to a feeling of disconnection from the achievements of previous generations. Whatever their political views or inclinations, people who fell under the influence of the zeitgeist of rapid change began to feel detached from their community's history.

The intensification of the consciousness of rapid change led many commentators, especially social scientists and educators, to magnify and objectify the psychic distance between the present and the past. Consequently, from the late 19th century onwards, change was often represented in a dramatic and mechanistic manner that exaggerated breaks, ruptures, and the decoupling of the present from the past. In retrospect, this response to change is entirely understandable. This was an era when the sheer scale of social transformation made it difficult for many – including social scientists – to draw on the resources of the past to make sense of a new world. Philip Abrams, author of a study of 'The Sense of the Past and the Origins of Sociology', noted:

> The generation that gave birth to sociology was probably the first generation of human beings ever to have experienced within the span of their own lifetime socially induced social change of a totally transformative nature – change which could not be identified, explained and accommodated as a limited historical variation within the encompassing order of the past.[9]

The influence of this cultural conjuncture on the subsequent evolution of the social sciences is evident to this day. One manifestation of this trend is the 'academic and intellectual dissociation of history and sociology'.[10] Numerous social scientists and educators assume that ideas drawn from the experience of the past are of little relevance to their work. They conclude that if the experience of the past can no longer illuminate the present, there is little point in studying it.

The estrangement of social scientists and educators from the past by the turn of the 20th century was not simply a direct reaction to the scale of social transformation but also an outcome of the estrangement of modernity from the authority of the past. The American historian Dorothy Ross has argued persuasively that during this period, social scientists were fast losing interest in the past.[11] Consequently, social science works often displayed a sense of historical illiteracy. Unfortunately, this orientation persists in the present era. As David Inglis argued in his reflection on 'The Death of History in British Sociology', mainstream 'British sociology currently exhibits very weak forms of historical consciousness'. He added that 'over the last two decades or so, it has had a very poor record of building sophisticated awareness of long-term historical processes systematically into its analytic practices'.[12] This observation, made in 2010, retains its relevance to the present day. Social science's weak sense of historical consciousness is paralleled by an intense consciousness of rapid change.

The consciousness of rapid change not only inflated the contrast between the present and the past but also doomed the latter to irrelevance. For if indeed change was so all-encompassing and rapid, then the experience of the past would lose much of its relevance. This claim about the irrelevance of the experience of the past was forcefully advanced by the English writer and social commentator H.G. Wells. Widely regarded as a prophetic critic of society, Wells dismissed the experience of the past as irrelevant to the conditions of the early 20th century. In his novel *The New Machiavelli* (1911), Wells's progressive liberal protagonist observed that the world had changed so much that 'suddenly, almost inadvertently, people found themselves doing things that would have amazed their ancestors'.[13] Wells's depiction of the consciousness of ceaseless change captured the attitude of reformers, commentators, and politicians with social-engineering ambitions at the time.

It is entirely understandable that under the pressure of rapid change, educators, philosophers, and intellectuals across all the disciplines would wish to review and reflect on society's relationship to its past. However, an awareness of changing conditions need not necessarily lead to the writing off of previous experience. The response of rendering the experience of the past irrelevant was strongly influenced by the pre-existing moral contrast drawn between the old and the new and the past and the present.

Since the early 20th century, the writing off of the experience of the past has been a constant theme within pedagogy. Despite the formal commitment of schools and educators to acquaint children with the cultural legacy of the past, the modern curriculum has become less and less devoted to it. The discipline of pedagogy is influenced by an outlook that attaches little significance to the experience of history. Looking back over the approach adopted by educators since the turn of the 20th century, it becomes evident that schools have devoted less and less energy to transmitting the values and experiences of the past to their pupils. In effect, generations of young people have been deprived of their historical inheritance. Since their elders have also been instructed to embrace a presentist mode of learning, it is not surprising that Western culture has become disconnected from its historical legacy over the decades.

Progressivist-minded educators were at the forefront of the downsizing of the authority of the past. They constantly asserted that in a rapidly changing world, it was pointless to socialize children to embrace values that would soon become outdated. They claimed that since children had to be adaptable and flexible, they should not be weighed down by the burden of old dogmas. The conviction that people inhabited a world that was qualitatively different to that of their parents served as the premise for the claim that the knowledge and insights acquired over previous centuries had lost their relevance. These views have endured to this day and continue to influence the work of experts charged with ceaseless curriculum modernization.

The First World War and the rupture of cultural continuity

The loss of a sense of the past was not simply an outcome of society's perception of hyper-change. The sensibility of an ever-widening psychic distance between the present and the past was reinforced and intensified by dramatic historical experiences – the most important being the First World War.[14] Members of the European cultural and political elites concluded that this catastrophic war had created an insurmountable rupture in time.

The Great War fundamentally undermined the cultural continuity of the West.[15] For many Europeans, their relationship with their past had become fatally undermined. Millions of people – especially the elderly – lamented losing the old order. It became apparent to even those with a strong conservative impulse, however, that there was no obvious road back to the past. Attempts to preserve the old ways of being were marginalized and overwhelmed by a zeitgeist that sought to create the world anew. The authority of the past appeared to be a lost cause. The cultural influence of novelty captured the temper of the times. Many intellectuals and artists experienced the end of the war as a point of no return to the past and felt that history ceased to have anything positive to say to society. The sensibility of epochal rupture and disdain for the past dominated the modernist intellectual and artistic imagination. A more radical version of this sentiment was communicated by interwar radicalism, which fervently believed that a break with the past was both possible and necessary.

One of the most momentous and durable legacies of the Great War was that it disrupted and disorganized the prevailing web of meaning through which Western societies made sense of their world. 'Europe was exhausted, not just physically, but also morally', and there was a 'crisis of confidence'[16] among the early 20th-century elites as suddenly the key values and ideals they were socialized into appeared meaningless.

In historical moments, when people are confused about their beliefs, they also become disoriented about who they are and where they stand in relation to others. The psychiatrist Patrick Bracken writes about the 'dread brought on by a struggle with meaning'. 'When the meaningfulness of our lives is called into question,' he says, 'people become painfully aware that they lack the moral and intellectual resources to give direction to their lives.'[17]

The historical phases in the evolution of society's estrangement from the past

The loss of the authority of the past and society's estrangement from it first gained momentum in the United States before enveloping the whole Anglo-American world and other Western societies. It unfolded in four distinct stages.

Phase one: The past as no longer relevant

Initially, the impulse to reject the past was closely linked to the optimistic modernist outlook, claiming that it had lost much relevance.

Until the 19th century, the authority of the past remained relatively intact. However, during the course of this century, many liberals and progressives adopted an uncritical, one-dimensional orientation towards the future. As Dorothy Ross explained in her important study *The Origins of American Social Science* (1991), this orientation had the regrettable consequence of weakening 'historical understanding'. She noted that leading liberals and utilitarians like the English philosopher Jeremy Bentham

> believed a modern society had nothing to learn from the past and should go directly to the universal principles of human nature. … For those engaged in understanding the historical course of progress, the whole past could be telescoped into a single stage which progress was leaving behind.[18]

A similar sentiment was enthusiastically expressed by the English philosopher Herbert Spencer, who claimed in *Social Statics* (1951) that progress is 'not an accident, but a necessity'. Spencer believed that 'surely must evil and immorality disappear; surely must men become perfect'.[19]

In its initial phase, this modernist estrangement from the past did not necessarily mean disrespecting it. Many leading liberals, such as J.S. Mill, wrote at length about the achievements of human civilization and understood that they were the beneficiaries of its legacy. Even the Social-Darwinist Spencer regarded the legacy of the past as an important resource for promoting progress in the future. He wrote that for the individual,

> influences that have acted upon preceding generations; influences that have been brought to bear upon him; the education that disciplined his childhood; together with the circumstances in which he has since lived; have conspired to make him what he is. And the result thus wrought out in him has a purpose.[20]

Spencer recognized that the influence of the past gave people a purpose and provided them with a sense of meaning. The influence of the past provided individuals with the moral resources to engage with the future. He wrote that the individual is not only 'a child of the past' but also 'a parent of the future'. He explained that the moral sentiment that was rooted in the past 'was intended to be instrumental in producing further progress; and to gag it, or to conceal the thoughts it generates, is to balk creative design'.[21]

At the time that Spencer penned his thoughts in the mid-19th century, Sir Isaac Newton's phrase 'standing on the shoulders of giants' – which recognized the contribution of great thinkers from the past to contemporary science – was widely used, indicating a respect accorded towards them.

Phase two: The past as an obstacle to progress

During the late 19th century, there was an important shift from regarding the past as no longer relevant to perceiving it as an obstacle to further progress. Commentators and intellectuals associated with the American Progressive movement most consistently articulated this sentiment. Their belief reflected an outlook that felt deeply estranged from the past. As the economist E.R. Seligman noted in 1903, 'The American of the future will bear but little resemblance to the American of the past.'[22] From his standpoint, there was little to value in the past; on the contrary, it was a burden to be discarded. The American philosopher John Dewey interpreted Darwin's theory of evolution as a call to 'transfer interest from the permanent to the changing'. From this standpoint, as Dorothy Ross wrote, Dewey concluded that it was necessary to 'discard the whole past two thousand years of philosophical discourse, with its search for a permanent and unchanging reality'.[23]

As noted previously, the belief that the past constituted an obstacle to progress gained powerful momentum during the aftermath of the First World War. This catastrophic event was widely perceived as the outcome of ideals and values rooted in the moral universe of the past. Progressive thinkers argued that overcoming the obstacles represented by old ways of thinking was essential to re-educating young people to embrace new values and attitudes. By the 1920s, these sentiments strongly resonated with members of the cultural establishment and the professional classes. They took it as given that the values and customs of their parents and grandparents were outdated and an obstacle that stood in the way of realizing the potential provided by science and technology.

Some educators avowed that the traditional curriculum was not only irrelevant but also positively harmful to the well-being of young people. The sociologist Helen Lynd observed that:

> Hitherto the college has educated people in a knowledge of the past, in the belief that it will have some relevancy for the future. Now it is beginning to recognize that too much immersion in possibly outworn patterns, far from being a help, may actually hinder adaptation to a changing world.[24]

From this perspective, a traditional humanist college education was unhelpful because it could diminish the capacity of undergraduates to adapt to a constantly changing world.

At the time, the German philosopher Edmund Husserl wrote about how Western society was caught up in the 'spell' of 'our times'. He feared that the powerful mood of presentism, which had overtaken society, had led to a 'cultural breakdown, weariness of spirit and disintegration'.[25] The American social scientist Lawrence Frank personified this trend in his condemnation of the harmful effects of traditional forms of socialization:

> It must be recognized . . . that if we examine our traditional ideas and beliefs and find them no longer valid or credible in the light of our newer knowledge and insights, and if, in addition, we find that they are productive of the social disorder and of personality distortions that constitute our major social problems, then we must courageously undertake to create the new concepts, the new patterns, and the new sanctions to meet the persistent tasks of life.[26]

The tendency to regard the ways of the past as an obstacle to progress gained renewed momentum in the aftermath of the Second World War, where this terrible episode was often blamed on the destructive influence of outdated attitudes. This sentiment was forcefully voiced by the Canadian psychiatrist Brock Chisholm, the first director of the World Health Organization, who claimed that the survival of humanity required ridding itself of the obstacles constituted by the past. He warned that:

> In many of the most important questions of life it is evident that the minds of large numbers, indeed almost all, of the human race are not freely open to consider how true or untrue old ideas are, or to consider any advantages which might be found in new ideas.

Chisholm, like many of his colleagues running the newly established, post-Second World War international institutions, regarded one of the virtues of their global organization as helping to remove the obstacle represented by 'untrue old ideas'.[27]

Phase three: The past as principally malevolent

Back in the 1880s, the German sociologist Ferdinand Tönnies pointed to the tendency of modernist technocratic institutions to react to the customs and traditions of community life with 'veiled hatred and contempt'.[28] This point was confirmed in 1972, by the America political scientist C.J. Friedrich, who in his fascinating review of this development observed that 'in the twentieth century tradition became a pejorative term'.[29] Since the end of the Second World War, and especially since the 1960s, this sentiment of intolerant anti-traditionalist scorn has become increasingly directed towards those who have refused to move along with the times and adopt a post-traditional identity. This attitude was explicitly committed to morally distancing itself from the past and rupturing the links that bind society to its historical traditions.

Since the authority of adults is so closely linked to the authority of the past, it is not surprising that its status now appears as a continuous decline. In their classic sociological study *The Lonely Crowd*, originally published in 1950, the social scientists Davis Riesman, Nathan Glazer and Reuel Denney drew attention to the unravelling of adult authority in the late 1940s and 1950s. Their 1969 preface noted that 'since 1950 the decline in the weight and authority of adults chronicled in *The Lonely Crowd* has proceeded even further'. They wrote of the 'loss of inner confidence among adults', which they perceived as 'a worldwide phenomenon'. They remarked that the 'young react to the loss of adult legitimacy with even greater mistrust, confusion, and rebellion'.[30] Mistrust towards the past had almost effortlessly redirected itself towards the status of adulthood.

During the 1960s and the 1970s, the loss of cultural continuity had its greatest impact on the customs and conventions that guided everyday interpersonal relations and people's personal and private lives. The Marxist historian Eric Hobsbawm described this process as a veritable 'cultural revolution'. He wrote of 'the breaking of the threads which in the past had woven human beings into social textures'. Hobsbawm stated that 'what children could learn from parents became less obvious than what parents did not know and children did'.[31] Not surprisingly, the confusion surrounding intergenerational relations was paralleled by an explosion of obsession with people's identities. By the early 1970s, one commentator could write that the terms 'identity' and 'identity crisis' had become 'the purest of clichés'.[32]

Phase four: The past as a clear and present danger!

In recent years, the pathologization of the past has gained such a powerful presence that it has become a taken-for-granted outlook permeating Western society's educational and cultural life. The past is frequently portrayed not only as an obstacle to progress *but also as principally a threatening influence on the present.* Historical continuity is frequently represented by its opponents as a curse. Many Western institutions regard breaking with the past as a cultural imperative. This sentiment even dominates the teaching of history, where anything that precedes the end of the Second World War is often portrayed as the 'bad old days'. From this standpoint, 1945 is Year Zero, and anything that precedes it is interpreted through the prism of cynicism and malevolence.

It is frequently claimed that the misdeeds and injustices of the past continue to contaminate the contemporary world. Advocacy organizations devoted to politicizing their identity often assert that past injustices continue to harm their people. Group causes are often justified on the grounds that certain historical experiences have inflicted emotional damage on the people they represent. Historic misdeeds are held responsible for causing injury to the self today. It is frequently suggested that experiences such as slavery or the Irish Potato Famine have inflicted trauma on subsequent generations. It is often claimed that because of these experiences, people whose group has been historically victimized often suffer from low self-esteem. This argument is regularly advanced by the national campaign that aims to compensate African Americans for what their ancestors had to endure. According to one supporter of this campaign, 'slavery fostered low self-esteem among blacks that has led to today's high teen-pregnancy and crime rates'.[33]

The transformation of the harms of the past into a live contemporary issue has, in practice, led to the erosion of the temporal boundary separating the present from the past. In effect, the evils of the past are often rendered contemporary and a focus for political activism. The past has become a terrain on which, increasingly, political conflicts are fought out. Protesters demanding the pulling down of old statues on the grounds that these symbols of past injustices harm their mental health illustrate the ease with which mentally temporal boundaries can be crossed.

Exacting revenge on the past has acquired a ceaseless momentum. As a result, virtually any symbol linked to the past can become a potential target of protest. What is fascinating about the decolonization movement is that its target is often not simply a specific statue but any old monument. That is why, for example, supporters of Black Lives Matter have vandalized statues that have no direct link with racial oppression. The sin of such historical objects is that they symbolize the past.

The impulse to negate the past has helped transform hatred towards it into a cultural resource that can be used by movements claiming to be its historical victims. As a result, hostility towards the past has acquired a quasi-ideological form. It is frequently blamed for many of the problems faced by people today. This weaponization of the idea of a malevolent past has led to the conflicts of the present being fought out through the prism of the past. Protest movements have targeted their anger at symbols of the past, such as statues and the reputation of historical figures who personify values to which they take exception. *The unstated, and often unconscious, motive driving these protests is to bring the past up to date!*

In contrast to the modernist attitudes expressed in the 19th and 20th centuries, the current reaction to the past is not guided by a positive and future-oriented commitment to progress. At times it even appears that the current revolt against the past is influenced by impulses that are distinctly backward looking. Yet, its impulse to rid the world of the symbols and values of the past suggests that it is striving to forge a Year Zero culture – one where the new identities created and in play are entirely detached from the negative influences of the past.

Final reflections: Readjusting the past

For over a century, modern, powerful voices and interests have sought to detach society from the past. On numerous occasions, the past has been declared irrelevant or an obstacle to change. Yet, despite so much energy devoted towards neutralizing its influence – particularly over the young – it continues to be perceived as a problem, and 'the bad old days' are frequently denounced as exercising a malign influence on contemporary society. Paradoxically, references to the past and the demand to settle scores with it have acquired an unprecedented presence in public life in the Western world.

There has never been a time in living memory when so much energy has been devoted to attempting to readjust the past, to question and criticize historical figures and institutions. There is even a cultural trend towards exacting revenge against the past, and the misdeeds committed centuries ago. At times, it seems as if the boundary between the present and the past has disappeared as sections of society casually cross over it and seek to fix contemporary problems through readjusting the past.

The impulse to exact revenge on the past as if it were a living phenomenon was strikingly illustrated during the protests surrounding Black Lives Matter in 2020. Protesters self-consciously targeted historical symbols of Western culture as if these statues constituted a clear and present danger to their well-being. They were denounced as living figures responsible for the many ills inflicted on the world. On numerous occasions, protesters were quoted as saying that the sight of an offending statue threatened their mental health. At Oxford University, as noted in chapter 1, numerous Rhodes Must Fall campaigners asserted that walking past Rhodes' statue was traumatic.[34] While toppling statues, many protesters acted like they were striking a blow against a living person. The mentality of exacting revenge was at work while pulling down the statue of Edward Colston in Bristol in June 2020. The protesters were not simply interested in toppling the monument but also sought to humiliate it. The statue was rolled to the harbour before being thrown into the water. It was almost as if what was being drowned was a corpse rather than a statue.[35]

The paradox of the past – its rejection and obsessive embrace – is understandable since even with the best effort, it is impossible to abolish it and entirely leave it behind.

The past is not a phenomenon external to individuals or the community they inhabit. Children become humanized and socialized from the point that they become aware that what preceded them has an important bearing on who they are. The past is an integral element of human consciousness, and society's reaction to it is communicated through the way it ascribes meaning to experience.

Despite their best efforts, people who attempt to start from scratch to make the world anew soon become aware of the futility of their enterprise. They fail to comprehend that in reflecting and reacting to the past, they are, in effect, positioning themselves in relation to it. As Dorothy Ross stated, 'We do not make the world, we find it and remake it.'[36]

3

The Ideology of Year Zero

Those who make calls to break with the past and its legacy often argue that it is necessary as an overdue corrective to society's reluctance to accept the consequences of the evils perpetrated by previous generations. They believe that the negative features of the past greatly outweigh the positive ones. They are disposed to be cynical and sceptical of the centuries-old stories that have inspired communities about their past. In particular, they dismiss the historic achievements that European societies have claimed as their distinctive legacy. Their moral condemnation of what were hitherto considered the achievements of humanity has encouraged the production of a genre of entirely negative histories. In these accounts, any of the inspiring dimensions of previous historical experience are downplayed or called into question. The Australian historian Geoffrey Blainey has characterized it as the 'Black Armband' view of history.[1] From this perspective, the past is haunted by evil; its influence is malevolent, and the sway it exercises over present-day society is implicated in oppressive and exploitative behaviour.

According to an American proponent of this school of Black Armband history, 'The United States does not yet have the stomach to look over its shoulder and stare directly at the evil on which this great country stands.'[2] This genre of negative or accusatory history encourages cultivating a gloom-ridden social memory, one where the past possesses few redeeming qualities. The unfolding of history is interpreted through the medium of a *teleology of evil*. From this perspective, the past is the source of much of contemporary evil. This narrative posits the constant reproduction of malevolent practices from historical times to the present day. It is an interpretation of history that depicts the United States as standing on the foundation of evil rather than on the hard-fought achievements of its citizens, and it points to the conclusion that it is essential to cleanse the present from the influence of the past. Recently, this view has evolved to the point that it calls for not just the need to break from history but also to exact revenge on it.

The impulse to break with history while seeking revenge on it expresses the paradox of the past that we discussed previously. Typically, the impulse to break with the past coexists with its apparent opposite: an obsession with it. This sensibility is most systematically advocated through Year Zero ideology. What I characterize as Year Zero ideology is driven by twin objectives: both breaking with the past and denouncing the historical memory associated with it. This orientation is particularly directed at the legacy of Western civilization, which is condemned and whose protagonists are retrospectively tried, found guilty, and imaginatively punished.

To be sure, the terms 'Western civilization' and 'Western culture' are contested because they are recently invented attempts to construct a sense of ideological superiority over other cultures.[3] That these terms gained currency in the 19th century by attempting to project a unique vision of civilizational identity is not in doubt. Nor is the historical journey that led to elaborating the concept of Western civilization and its meaning. It refers to the perception of a shared cultural outlook grounded in the Greco-Roman world's philosophical and religious legacy, the Judaeo-Christian tradition, the medieval Christian experience, the ideals of the Renaissance, the Scientific Revolution, and the Enlightenment. Though the wide usage of the terms 'Western civilization' and 'Western culture' stems from the 19th century, they refer to an historical tradition that goes back to the times of the ancient Greeks and evolved through the centuries that followed. The legacy of these diverse traditions – which are very real and not invented – constitutes the main target of Year Zero ideology.

The notion of a Year Zero, based on the claim that a radical break with the past is necessary, has been a recurring feature in the history of modernity. However, this has taken different forms at different times. In modern times, society's notion of temporality is, in some instances, explicitly organized around a variety of zero points. In Germany, the end of the Second World War in 1945 was often expressed through the term *Stunde Null* or zero hour. For many German commentators, *Stunde Null* serves as a reminder that a dramatic break is required to atone for the sins of Germany's past, which had to be rejected and overcome. In Japan, the bombings of Hiroshima and Nagasaki were often described as zero points, while the site of the September 11 bombing of the World Trade Center was named Ground Zero.

In previous centuries, in many instances, the affirmation of Year Zero did not simply refer to a radical break with the past but also called for the birth of something new. As the historian Adrian Paylor points out, 'The term Year Zero denotes the idea that a society can be reborn and made anew with all the vestiges and heritage of its previous incarnation completely eradicated. In other words, it maintains that a society can be started over and its past completely eliminated.' In general, 'The decimation of a society's history is not an end in itself.' Rather it is represented as 'a necessary first step in the establishment of a completely new socioeconomic and political framework that is designed to secure a more desirable society and propagate new norms, values, cultural practices, hierarchies, and traditions'.[4]

Advocates of Year Zero frequently practise what the Romans characterized as *damnatio memoriae*: the erasure of history. This is achieved by trying to rid society of the visible traces of the past. The ritualistic destruction of images, inscriptions, and even coins was a recurring theme throughout the history of ancient Rome. The term *damnatio memoriae* translates as the 'condemnation of memory'. According to the artist Tucker Neel, *damnatio memoriae* 'refers to a practice associated with ancient rulers who called for the erasure of their predecessors from the historical record; their likeness removed from statues, monuments, coinage and texts. It was a punishment the ancient Romans viewed as worse than death.'[5]

The practice of *damnatio memoriae* had a more restrictive focus than the modern aim of establishing Year Zero. It was directed at the erasure of the existence and reputation of specific individuals, usually associated with the regime that preceded the existing one. In recent times, the renaming of streets and public buildings and the tearing down of statues and symbols of the past express a wider aspiration to establish Year Zero. Paylor noted that 'social spaces, government buildings, and even whole cities were renamed after the Russian Revolution'. In instances such as this, 'the extensive renaming that occurs under a regime that is attempting to implement Year Zero generally focuses on replacing names that are strongly associated with the former political system or culture'.[6]

But unlike *damnatio memoriae*, it also seeks to target the very memory of a nation's past.

The attempt to rid the world of its past was imaginatively expressed by the invention of Year One in the 18th-century French Revolutionary Calendar and by the proclamation of Year Zero by leaders of the Khmer Rouge in Cambodia in 1975. According to the historian Andrus Ers, the founding of the United States was accompanied by an idealistic, if not utopian, belief in the possibility of creating a world anew. He writes that the 'mythology of the American Revolution' was premised upon the idea of a zero point, which received its most striking formulation in Thomas Paine's oft-cited statement in *Common Sense*.[7] In this text, Paine enthused about how the American Revolution would lead to the establishment of a new world through a radical break with the past. He wrote that, 'We have it in our power to begin the world over again. A situation, similar to the present, hath not happened since the days of Noah until now. The birthday of a new world is at hand.'[8] Paine's utopian vision of creating the world anew is totally different from the ethos of Year Zero's contemporary ideology. Today's advocates of Year Zero ideology are much more preoccupied with the project of exacting vengeance on the past than with assisting the birth of a new world.

In numerous instances, Year Zero ideologists have promoted the spirit of exacting vengeance on the past. We live in an era where statues of historical figures who have been the subject of society's veneration for centuries are casually vandalized, disfigured, or toppled. Sympathetic commentators frequently assert that acts of iconoclasm are an understandable response to specific acts of oppressive violence, such as the murder of George Floyd, which led to the rise of the Black Lives Matter movement. However, attacks on symbols of the past have occurred before this tragedy, and, certainly, the animosity against the past that drives contemporary iconoclasm transcends reactions to specific events. The death of George Floyd brought to the surface trends already in play. A tendency to imagine the worst about the values, attitudes, and behaviour of historical figures in the past is integral to the spirit of our time. The physical removal of statues is paralleled by subjecting the individuals they represent to retrospective character assassination.

In the present era, the impulse to exact vengeance on the past has in some instances acquired a disturbing and irrational dimension. One of the most sinister examples of this trend is the irrational burning of books because they are old, outdated, and associated with the unacceptable values of the past. In September 2021, in the province of Ontario in Canada, books featuring so-called 'outdated content' were ceremoniously burned as a goodwill gesture to Indigenous people.[9]

Historically, burning books is associated with the intolerant behaviour of zealots venting their hatred of inanimate objects. This time, the book-burning ceremony organized by an Ontario francophone school board was promoted as an act of reconciliation. This sinister act against civilized cultural norms was labelled a 'flame purification ceremony'!

Lyne Cossette, a spokeswoman for the school board responsible for this ceremony, claimed that burning books struck a blow against outdated norms and benefited the local environment. She added that, 'Symbolically, some books were used as fertilizer.' Cosette explained that the ritual was titled *Redonnons à la terre*, 'give back to the earth'. She added that it sought 'to make a gesture of openness and reconciliation by replacing books in our libraries that had outdated content and carried negative stereotypes about First Nations, Métis and Inuit people'.[10]

The justification for the burning of books was that they contained outdated content. As we noted, 'outdated' is a favourite term of contempt hurled at opponents by zealous culture warriors. In their eyes, any publication – particularly history books – that promotes the classical outlook of Western civilization is 'outdated' and, therefore, conveys views that constitute a form of secular blasphemy. Now that the outdated books have turned to ash, the libraries can boast that the remaining books on their shelves have 'positive and inclusive messages about the diverse communities within our schools'.[11]

In some – thankfully rare – instances, Year Zero ideology encourages barbaric and violent practices. Year Zero ideology in action is demonstrated by a video depicting zealous Islamic State (ISIS) activists destroying the city of Nimrud, in Iraq, including the Northwest Palace built in the 9th century BC by the Assyrian King Ashurnasirpal II. The video shows ISIS militants using sledgehammers, a bulldozer, and explosives to destroy the ancient ruins.[12]

Footage showing ISIS militants bulldozing, destroying, and looting ancient shrines reveals passions that are outwardly ancient but resonate with the Year Zero spirit of our time. The vandals of Nimrud appealed to ancient customs and traditions. They justified their behaviour by insisting that they were 'destroying idols' and emulating Muhammad, who cleared out idolatrous statues in Mecca. Yes, the worship of idols contradicts Islam's teaching, as it does Judaism's. Yet, for many centuries, Muslims in the Middle East had no problems distinguishing between ancient ruins and idolatrous insults to their religion. In the past, ancient artefacts created by civilizations of the Middle East were a source of wonder and not the target of acts of Year Zero vandalism.

It is not past customs and traditions but the passions and motives of our time that have led ISIS vandals to smash and destroy artefacts and statues in Iraq and elsewhere. Many commentators have rightly noted that these acts of destruction represent an attempt to eliminate an important chapter in the historical legacy of humanity. They certainly do that. But ISIS was in the business of not just destroying the past but also wreaking vengeance on it.

Some readers may conclude that the toppling of the statue of Edward Colston by angry protesters or the burning of outdated books by earnest Canadian censors cannot be compared with the violent crimes that ISIS militants have inflicted on the historical heritage of the territories they occupied. Certainly, the project of settling scores with the past in Western societies appears relatively restrained compared to the nihilistic barbarism of ISIS. Yet the atmosphere of mass hysteria that sometimes surrounds acts of iconoclasm in the Western world serves as testimony to the spirit of intolerance that fuels its behaviour. Indeed, the horrific events played out in Nimrud warn of the threat to civilizational values posed by the War Against the Past.

Today, there is little left of the future-oriented idealism of the version of Year Zero ideology associated with the French and American Revolutions. Often, it appears that this ideology merely encourages a break with the past. In the Culture Wars that prevail in the West, opponents of its past do not cultivate a sense of societal rebirth and renewal. Their lack of interest in the future contrasts sharply with their single-minded preoccupation with the erasure of the past. Yet this emphasis on rupture coexists with the opposite tendency of being overwhelmed by the past. As Ers notes, the 'proclamation of a new Year Zero – beyond its overt claim to be cutting ties with history – involves an opposite movement: a fixation on history'.[13]

Advocates of the War Against the Past in the Western world are in thrall to the spell of the past and show very little interest in ensuring that the creation of a new world succeeds in a break with history. Their version of Year Zero Ideology is distinctly modest compared to the ambitious projects proposed by their modernist predecessors. They regard the influence of the past as a curse, and they wish to create a world that has been liberated from its legacy.

What is distinct about 21st-century Year Zero ideology?

Unlike the self-conscious declaration of Year Zero by French Revolutionaries or post-Second World War German commentators, the current manifestation of *damnatio memoriae* is rarely articulated explicitly. Contemporary iconoclasts may wish to cancel the influence of the past, but their project has not yet acquired a coherent and systematic form. It endows the past with a teleology of evil, but the malevolent influence it wishes to eradicate is typically diffuse and free-floating.

In most instances in history, advocates of the constitution of a Year Zero were clear about which aspects of the past they wished to break from and which of its influences they wished to eliminate. The invention of a Revolutionary Calendar that communicated an unambiguous declaration of a new beginning in 18th-century France was justified by the necessity of annihilating the influence of the *Ancien Régime*. As Paylor explained, the Taliban targeted 'Afghanistan's pre-Islamic heritage as well as elements that do not adhere to their strict interpretation of Islam'. In contrast, the Korean Workers' Party in North Korea sought to eliminate 'capitalism and, later, all American, and to a lesser degree foreign, influences'.[14] In 1945, German proponents of Year Zero wished to begin anew after breaking with the legacy of their nation's Nazi past.

Today, the War Against the Past is driven by an expansive but inarticulate dynamic and is underwritten by the assumption that the past itself is the source of contemporary evils. In some instances, it attacks the influence of Western colonialism, in others that of patriarchy, rationality, or capitalism. Year Zero aspirations tend to converge around the theme of removing the influence of Western culture and, more specifically, that of whiteness, patriarchy, racism, and slavery. In his book *The War on the West* (2023), author and journalist Douglas Murray argues that the target of culture warriors is the West itself. It is that, but it is also much more than that since it is about the neutralization and elimination of the influence of the past in general. That is why a variety of seemingly unconnected customs and practices – from grandparental advice to gardening and mathematics – are dismissed as outdated and sometimes as pernicious. The War Against the Past is just that: a war against the past.

Take the case of the classics. Often, the classics are denounced simply because they are the classics: that is, because they are too old. Back in 1990, more than 190 Australian composers, directors, and musicians signed a 'call to action' to remove sexism and gendered violence from operatic works.[15] One commentator supporting this stand wrote, 'Opera is stuck in a racist, sexist past.' She took exception to the fact that even today, the operatic canon is based on 'dead composers' like Mozart, Puccini, Verdi, Wagner, and Rossini.[16] In condemning composers because they lived long ago, she assumed that her comments would resonate with cultural entrepreneurs committed to belittling the artistic and cultural achievements of those often caricatured as 'pale, male, and stale'.

The decolonization movement is the most prominent and successful vehicle for the advocacy of Year Zero Ideology. Its success is, to a considerable extent, due to its focus on de-authorizing the legacy of Western culture by rendering it toxic and shameful. Supporters of the decolonization movement have been able to draw on pre-existing narratives that have called into question the legitimacy of the Western past and the values associated with it. This movement has gone a step further and reduced the history of the West to an ugly story of ceaseless oppression and domination. From the standpoint of the decolonization movement, the contemporary Western world stands on the foundation of racial oppression and white supremacy.

The assertion that Western civilization is inherently racist and is founded on racial oppression and brutal practices such as slavery and colonialism is central to the dogma of Year Zero ideology today. The decolonization movement and its intellectual advocates promote an outlook that seeks to racialize every dimension of experience, including humanity's past. That is why virtually all the civilizational achievements of the West – from philosophy to science – are represented as contaminated by a racist logic and are, therefore, suitable targets of decolonization. These targets go as far back as antiquity. Supporters of decolonizing the study of classics are committed to tainting the positive achievements of Greek civilization so that it ceases to legitimize the West's cultural authority.[17]

Arguments for decolonizing the legacy of ancient Greece are based on the simplistic and ahistorical notion that the ideals and practices of this civilization are an early version of the racist and oppressive practices of modern Western imperialism. The tendency to read history backwards and assess Greek civilization according to the standards of the contemporary world is widespread. Numerous commentators interpret Greece through the prism of racialization and have devoted themselves to digging up material as evidence of the racism of the most influential philosophers of this era. Aristotle is frequently denounced as such. Matthew Sears, a professor of classics at the University of Brunswick, goes so far as to characterize him as the father of scientific racism.[18] The impulse to settle scores with this ancient father of philosophy is sometimes justified because he apparently continues to exercise a pernicious influence on contemporary society. Bryan W. Van Norden, the James Monroe Taylor Chair in Philosophy at Vassar College, claims that we 'need to remember that among our students are people who have felt first hand the continuing practical consequences of Aristotle's more heinous views'.[19] To assert that racial oppression is the practical outcome of Aristotelian philosophy is an irrational fantasy. Yet such thinking resonates in an academic culture dominated by an ideology of racial determinism.

Criticism of racism in ancient Greece is particularly misplaced for the simple reason that the members of this civilization were not interested in developing relations of oppression and hatred based on skin colour. As the American classicist Mary Lefkowitz explains: 'Although the Greeks knew the Egyptians to be what we would now call "people of color", they did not think less or more of them (or any other Africans) on that account.' Why? Because for the Greeks the 'salient fact was that these other people were foreigners'. The Greeks distinguished themselves from all foreigners, and foreigners were regarded as '*barbaroi*, people who speak unintelligibly'.[20] For the Greeks, 'culture was a far more important factor in human behavior than skin color or other "racial" characteristics'.[21] Racism, racial oppression, and racialization had no meaning in an historical context where the important line of differentiation was between native and foreign or fellow citizen and stranger.

Condemning Aristotle's 'heinous views' as if he was a 21st-century Grand Wizard of the Ku Klux Klan says more about the uneducated imagination of the decolonizer than it does about Aristotle's philosophy or his place in history. As far as decolonization activists are concerned, the real crime of Aristotle is that he is regarded as one of the founding figures of Western civilization through the ages. Taking him down by contaminating his reputation is not unlike the 'condemnation of memory' by Roman practitioners of *damnatio memoriae*.

The hostility towards the foundational values of the West drives the campaign to delegitimize the achievements of ancient Greece. The focus on origins is important for this reason. If it can be shown that Western civilization was flawed from its inception, then everything that follows is implicated in this original sin. This is why the attempt to demonize the West has sought to pathologize its foundation in antiquity.

At times, the project of decolonizing antiquity seems to caricature itself. Archaeologist Rennan Lemos asks, 'Can we decolonize the ancient past?' before answering in the affirmative. How? According to Lemos, through a 'better understanding' of how 'antiquity as a whole has been entangled with present-day structural inequalities'.[22] It appears that grievance archaeology trumps real archaeology, and anything that lies buried in the past can be cast as a suitable subject for decolonization.

The War Against the Past has recently focused on condemning the very foundation of the Anglo-American world. The beginnings of Australia, Britain, Canada, and the United States have become a subject of great interest to decolonizers, a trend most coherently expressed by *The New York Times*' 1619 Project. This project asserts that the United States was founded to entrench slavery and that, to this day, this nation is dominated by this legacy.

The 1619 Project casually calls into question the historical fact that the United States actually began in 1776. Through self-consciously distorting America's history, this project claims that 1619 and not 1776 constitutes the origin of the United States, for it was in that year that African slaves first arrived in Jamestown. According to this tendentious version of the past, the American Revolution was not so much a war of independence but a selfish act of preserving exploitation and racial oppression. In this way, the contribution of the American Revolution to the development of the Western ideal of freedom is erased from history. This nation's Declaration of Independence and – for the time – its remarkably advanced liberal and democratic Constitution are implicitly renounced as a slave-owners' charter.

Most significantly, the 1619 Project is designed to contaminate the tradition and foundation that underpins the American way of life. This attempt to vandalize the tradition of a nation and its historical memory is far more toxic than the toppling of a statue. Indeed, one of the main authors of the 1619 Project, Nikole Hannah-Jones, was in no doubt that her objective was to plunder the past to undermine the moral authority of the present-day United States. She responded to critics who claimed that she had distorted history by stating: 'I've always said that the 1619 Project is not a history. . . . It is a work of journalism that explicitly seeks to challenge the national narrative and, therefore, the national memory.'[23] Hannah-Jones made no attempt to justify her contribution because it was an attempt to reinterpret or even revise real history. Her interest was to project present-day concerns back into the past to construct a teleology of America's evil identity.

Hannah-Jones's explicit conflation of the present and the past should be seen not as an innocent disregard of fundamental temporal boundaries but as a project devoted to the contamination of the past to delegitimize US institutions in the here and now. Her construction of evil origins has a clear ideological mission of taking down the moral authority of America's founding.

By providing a simplistic but highly evocative script for members of the public, the authors of the 1619 Project have attempted to seize control of America's national narrative. Hannah-Jones has little inhibition about promoting a script that regards the Founders of the United States, along with all members of the white race, with contempt. As she noted in a letter to Britain's *Observer* newspaper, 'The white race is the biggest murderer, rapist, pillager, and thief of the modern world.' Her reference is not simply to the white people who settled America in the 17th and 18th centuries. She added that the 'descendants of these savage [white] people pump drugs and guns into the Black community, pack Black people into the squalor of segregated urban ghettos and continue to be bloodsuckers in our community'.[24] An unceasing record of wickedness connects the white settlers who arrived on the shores of America in 1619 with their descendants today.

In a different world, the denunciation of an entire race would be interpreted as not a million miles from racist prejudice. However, in the contemporary era, scripts like the one promoted by the 1619 Project are strongly supported by many of society's cultural and educational institutions. It was, after all, *The New York Times* – once the widely recognized paper of record in the United States – that promoted and endorsed Hannah-Jones's narrative of hate towards the nation's past. And to demonstrate that she enjoyed the moral support of the commentariat, she was awarded the prestigious Pulitzer Prize. Hollywood celebrities rushed in to show their support for the Project. Predictably, Oprah Winfrey and the global content platform Lionsgate teamed up with Hannah-Jones to bring her work to an even wider audience.[25]

The embrace of the 1619 Project by celebrities, online influencers, and leaders of America's cultural industry highlights one of the most important developments that encourages the cancellation of American culture. The most significant feature of the War Against the Past in the Anglo-American world is the complicity of cultural institutions and their leaders in estranging society from its traditions and history. The dark side of history is always elevated to represent the framing of the past.

It is not merely universities that promote a vision of the nation's past as one that people should view with shame. The claim that contemporary society and its cultural institutions bear the burden of guilt for the crimes committed by their ancestors is widely internalized by America's cultural establishment. Their playbook shows Western history as a story of unremitting violence and greed. There are no 'good old days' that can serve as a focus for redemption and nostalgia. The current regime promotes a vision of the past as 'the bad old days' in place of nostalgia and incites a demand for revenge, encouraging Americans to feel guilt, shame, and self-loathing. This corrosive orientation towards one's history invites atonement and the apology ritual. The ceaseless ritualization of remorse towards the events of the past is one of the important accomplishments of this movement.

The founding of Canada has been recast as a crime against humanity. Instead of celebrating Canada Day, the detractors of this nation call for mourning. 'This Canada Day, let's remember: this country was built on genocide,' writes Mumilaaq Qaqqaq, an Indigenous Parliamentarian.[26] In a quasi-medieval act of self-flagellation, the Canadian Parliament unanimously agreed to a motion demanding that the federal government recognize the 'genocidal' nature of Indian residential schools.[27] This was a gross miscategorization: while these schools adopted crude and sometimes cruel methods to assimilate native Canadian children, it is an act of calumny to apply the term 'genocide' to their behaviour. Genocide refers to the deliberate killing of people from a particular nation or ethnic group with the aim of destroying that people. Indian residential schools in Canada sought to turn those in its care into members of mainstream society. No doubt, this was a short-sighted and, at times, oppressive policy, but it did not seek to destroy indigenous Canadians.

The origins and foundation of Britain have also become the subject of *damnatio memoriae*. It is frequently asserted that Britain was built on racism and slavery. Some academics go so far as to argue that the British Empire was worse than Nazi Germany. Writing in this vein, Professor Kehinde Andrews posted a tweet that asserted that the British Empire lasted far longer than Nazi Germany and 'did more damage and in many ways paved the way for the Nazi's [*sic*] and their genocidal ideology'.[28] If this grotesque characterization of Britain's past is even remotely correct, then the only course of action is to rupture our connection with it and boldly declare a new Year Zero.

One of the most disturbing practices of Year Zero ideologists is the casual manner in which they manipulate the memory of the Holocaust and the horrors of the Nazi era to legitimate their argument. Colonialism is frequently reinterpreted as the precursor of the Holocaust.[29] Others suggest that 'colonialism was worse than Nazism'. One Sri Lankan commentator declares, 'Imagine Nazis, but for centuries. That's our experience.'[30] The moral status of the foundation of Italy has also been called into question by the 'just like the Holocaust' brigade of revisionist historians. The reputation of the process of Italian reunification – the *Risorgimento* – in the 19th century has been tarnished by the claim that the armies of the North behaved in a barbaric manner. Terms like 'genocide' and even 'Holocaust' have been used to call into question the traditional positive rendition of the *Risorgimento*. Garibaldi, the father of Italian reunification, who is regarded as the personification of 19th-century liberalism, is dismissed by revisionist thinkers as merely a talented, jumped-up bandit.[31] The attacks on the foundation of Italy are driven by an outlook which is not unlike that of the decolonization movement.

Contemporary Western culture – particularly in the Anglo-American world – is hospitable to the worldview of decolonization. Significant sections of these societies have adopted the attitude of thinking the worst about their nation's history. These sentiments are often transmitted to schoolchildren, and many youngsters grow up estranged from their communities' past. According to a survey by the London-based Policy Exchange think-tank, almost half of young people between the ages of 18 and 24 agreed that schools should 'teach students that Britain was founded on racism and remains structurally racist today'.[32] Their reaction is not surprising since 42 per cent of 16- to 18-year-olds have been taught that 'Britain is currently a racist country'.[33]

The acceptance of the view that Britain was founded on racism is based on a pre-existing cultural predisposition in Western society to devalue its past morally. It ignores the complexities of historical experience and transforms racism into an omnipresent force that transcends its historical context and development. Racial thinking and imperialist domination emerged in the 18th century, came into their own in the 19th century, and continued to persist in much of the 20th century. But even during these three centuries, there was far more to British history than the idealization of racism.

Arguably, one of the most significant achievements of the War Against the Past is to racialize the origins of Western civilization and, by implication, subject contemporary society to a racialized imperative. As a cultural practice, the racialization of society has cast its net wide so that the most unlikely normal aspects of life can be deemed a manifestation of white privilege. Even the names of plants and animals have been brought into the frame of decolonization.

Dr Brett Summerell, the chief scientist of the Australian Institute of Botanical Science, has decried the fact that the 'names of effectively all Australian plants were defined by white – primarily male – botanists'. He observed that many plants were 'named using Latinised terms to describe features or locations, and a number are named after (usually white male) politicians or patrons'. As an illustration of the problem of allowing white male scientists to give plants a name, Summerell points to the plant genus *Hibbertia*, named after George Hibbert, a man 'who made his fortune from slave trading'.[34]

Others object to the names of animals linked to individuals who affront their sensibility. From their standpoint, 'decolonizing' species names is no less critical than toppling the historical statues of figures from the past whom they decry. According to one account, species names are far too often enmeshed with colonialism, paternalism, sexism, and racism. The journalist John R. Platt pointed out that the small, bright North American bird the Townsend warbler was named *Setophaga townsendi* by the American naturalist John Kirk Townsend.[35] Since Townsend was implicated in contributing to the development of 19th-century scientific racism, a new name for the little warbler had to be found.

Is there any point in changing the name *Setophaga townsendi*? Decolonization advocates believe it is essential to detoxify the name of this bird. They assert that 'just like toppling statues in Bristol Harbour or removing Cecil Rhodes' name from public buildings, renaming things is important and necessary if we are to right history's wrongs'.[36]

Obsessing about the names of plants and animals has more to do with finding new issues about which to feel offended than with liberating a plant from being associated with a name invented by an imperialist scientist. The management of London's world-famous Kew Gardens has also embraced grievance archaeology. A 10-year manifesto published by Kew is paradigmatic in this respect. Its five key priorities include 'having honest conversations about its links to imperialism and colonialism, and helping to tackle the biodiversity crisis'. That's another way of saying that Kew will do its best to expose as many examples of imperialist misdeeds within the world of plants as possible to demonstrate its commitment to the cause of decolonizing its collection. The head of Kew Gardens, Richard Deverell, has vowed to decolonize this institution. He stated that there is 'no acceptable neutral position' on the history of colonialism and racism'.[37]

Deverell is absolutely right to argue that it is morally wrong to adopt a neutral position on the history of colonialism and racism. But his call to decolonize Kew has little to do with history or a genuine commitment to learning from the past. As is the case with all examples of grievance archaeology, it is about condemning contemporary Western society by blaming it for the behaviour of imperialist biologists two centuries ago.

In effect, Deverell has decided that Kew should take the knee to demonstrate that this institution is 'on the right side of history'. When gardens and plants become the target of politicization, it is evident that what's at issue is external to what's happening inside Kew. In a world where grievance archaeology has become a growth industry, it was only a matter of time before the naming of plants was brought into the frame.

Placing the taxonomy of plants and animals under a linguistic microscope is a project vigorously pursued by practitioners of grievance archaeology. Grievance archaeologists examine names and words that cause them offence and then proceed to cancel them. At times, their zealous commitment to finding offence acquires the form of a self-caricature. Take the example of the gypsy moth – a pesky insect that chews through the leaves of trees. It is unlikely that most people feel offended by the term 'gypsy' when applied to a moth; however, the Entomological Society of America (ESA) has decided to 'remove' it from its list of approved names, just in case,[38] as part of a broader review into insect names that 'may be inappropriate or offensive'.

From now on, the gypsy moth will be identified by the newly invented term 'spongy moth'.[39] Predictably, the term 'gypsy ant' has also been abolished just in case it causes psychological damage to a member of the Roma community. Instead, until a new English name can be agreed upon, this commonly used term will be replaced by its scientific name, *Aphaenogaster araneoides*. And there is more to come. The ESA has asked the public to help draw any potentially offensive insect names to its attention. It has also mobilized experts to assist its new cause. Its Better Common Names project will assemble working groups that include experts who study the species and people from the insect's native regions to decide on a new, truly decolonized offence-free appellation.[40]

It is not just the ESA that has become committed to devoting resources towards mining the past for offence. In 2020, Sadiq Khan, the Mayor of London, announced the establishment of a commission to review the city's statues, plaques, and street names, which largely reflect the rapid expansion of London's wealth and power at the height of Britain's empire in the reign of Queen Victoria.

Khan stated that some statues would have to be removed. He justified his endorsement of iconoclasm on the grounds that'our capital's diversity is our greatest strength' and 'yet our statues, road names and public spaces reflect a bygone era'.[41] Khan's statement offers a textbook illustration of the outlook of Year Zero ideology. It takes for granted the belief that anything that smacks of a 'bygone era' is inherently flawed. The suggestion that public spaces that reflect a bygone era need to be altered or eliminated is a roundabout way of stating that London must be insulated from the symbols of its past. Khan's pathologization of a bygone era would remove all traces of the past and, in effect, impose his version of Year Zero on London. A city where all traces of the past were eliminated so that it no longer reflects a bygone era and no longer breathes the passions of the past would turn into a grotesque no-man's land.

King Charles has signed up to support the mission of grievance archaeology as well with the announcement of his support for a study into the Royal Family's slavery links. The Church of England has also promised to examine its links to slavery, with a review of the presence of statues and memorials linked to it.[42] It announced that it would set aside a fund of £100 million to address the 'shameful past' of the slave trade.[43]

The British Parliament has launched a probe to make its art collection 'more representative of diversity'.[44] One of the first high-profile casualties of this inquisition has been the 18th-century conservative philosopher and Member of Parliament Edmund Burke. Even though Burke opposed the practice of slavery and was a fierce critic of the excesses of the British Empire in India, his statues and portraits in the Palace of Westminster have been targeted by members of the review board because, according to Parliamentary documents, his younger brother made money from Caribbean plantations. It seems that even someone who, by the standards of the time, was an enlightened critic of slavery can be retrospectively taken down because of his brother's sins.

The most fascinating feature of the numerous reviews and audits of the past is their speculative character. They resemble the behaviour of would-be gold diggers hoping to discover a seam of the precious mineral. In this case, supporters of grievance archaeology seek to discover nuggets of offence that can be used to delegitmize the status of contemporary institutions. The numerous universities that have launched audits of their past are assiduously mining their archives for the misdeeds of their ancestors.

Take the case of Durham University. It has launched two projects to review its past. According to the university's Pro-Vice-Chancellor for Equality, Diversity, and Inclusion (EDI), Shaid Mahmood, similar projects are taking place in universities across the county as part of a broader shift in the sector geared 'towards rectifying omissive histories'.[45] The word 'omissive' conveys the implication that some aspect of the past has been wilfully neglected or overlooked. Yet what is fascinating about Durham's review of the past is that it claims ignorance about the omissive object of its quest. What is at stake here is a speculative search for bad news stories.

Mahmood stated that the projects 'may well uncover positive stories, but there is also the possibility of finding out some uncomfortable truths'. Given the prevailing Black Armband orientation towards the past, it is likely that Durham will discover 'uncomfortable truths' rather than positive stories. Why? Because the very motivation for the projects is to justify the practice of decolonization. As the Head of EDI at Durham, Rachel Archbold, stated, 'Developing our understanding of the University's involvement in colonialism and historical slavery is critical to our ongoing enriching and diversification work.' That's another way of saying the project is inspired not by a disinterested commitment to historical truth but by a quest to endorse Durham's 'diversification work'. This point is also echoed by the university's archivist, Jonathan Bush, who noted that the research will be 'helping to inform and address any structural inequalities which may be embedded within the institution'.[46] His objective requires the discovery of the uncomfortable truths in Durham's history to inform its supposed structural inequalities today.

The impulse to find new targets for decolonization appears to possess a frenetic quality. It resembles a veritable witch-hunt against the failings of the past. Even school desks in a classroom can become fair game in the zealous quest to discover something to decolonize. Britain's largest teachers' union, the National Education Union (NEU), contends that school classroom layouts are shaped by colonization. It states that there is an 'urgent' need to 'decolonise' the classroom layout'.[47] Others call for the decolonizing of colour and interior decorating.[48]

It is evident that the term 'decolonization' has acquired a diffuse and expansive dynamic. Initially, decolonizers sought to eliminate the influence of colonialism and racism on contemporary society. In recent times, decolonization has been embraced by various claim-makers who wish to remedy a supposed injustice they face. In Wales, the Association of Local Government Archaeological Officers Cymru has suggested that the memory of the English as the oppressor should be considered when glorifying colonialism and slavery. This organization suggests that monuments and buildings associated with English oppressors should be nominated for inclusion in anti-racist guidance prepared by the Welsh government 'about whether councils should pull down, move, destroy or retain statues showing contentious individuals or events'.[49]

The idea of decolonization resonates with the contemporary zeitgeist. It communicates the objective of undoing pre-existing harms by eliminating the influence of the colonizer. The cause of decolonization has become detached from its original emphasis on breaking away from the influence of Western colonialism and racism. Of course, it is still principally associated with the cause of settling scores with the historical injustice perpetrated by Western racism and imperialism. However, decolonization has mutated into a stand-alone rhetorical idiom that can be applied to just about any phenomenon. There has been a veritable explosion of causes that communicate their goals through the idiom of decolonization. The following list of randomly selected books published on this subject indicates that decolonization has become an all-purpose warrant for justifying action:

- Linda Tuhiwai Smith (2013) *Decolonizing Methodologies*
- Sarah Travis (2014) *Decolonizing Preaching*
- Ali Neghji (2021) *Decolonizing Sociology*
- Robbie Shillam (2021) *Decolonizing Politics*
- Clare Land (2015) *Decolonizing Solidarity*
- Edgar Villanueva (2021) *Decolonizing Wealth*
- Randy S. Woodley (2020) *Decolonizing Evangelicalism*
- Miguel A. De la Torre (2021) *Decolonizing Christianity*
- Kris Clarke (2020) *Decolonizing Pathways Towards Integrative Healing In Social Work*
- Katheryn Batchelor (2014) *Decolonizing Translation*

I selected these ten books to highlight the ease with which decolonization can attach itself to literally any subject. But there are hundreds of other publications to choose from. What they have in common is the ambition to gain legitimacy through invoking the moral appeal of decolonization.

Though decolonization often works as a form of cultural affectation that enjoys the validation of powerful political, cultural, and educational institutions, it also provides a warrant for settling scores with the past. Many of the leading advocates of decolonization make little attempt to hide their aspiration for revenge. As Ibram X. Kendi points out in his book *How to Be an Antiracist* (2020), 'The only remedy to racist discrimination is antiracist discrimination. The only remedy to past discrimination is present discrimination.'[50]

When decolonization can serve as a warrant for discrimination, it is only a matter of time before it will be used to justify more extreme forms of behaviour. As the atrocities committed against Israeli civilians on 7 October 2023 showed, even their mass murder could be justified on the grounds that it represented decolonization in action. In the aftermath of these atrocities, the very mention of the term 'decolonization' works as a magical incantation to appease the conscience of those who may otherwise be upset by the sight of murdered children, women, and the elderly, whose bodies are viciously humiliated and violated by Hamas terrorists. Those who still retain a vestige of moral instinct and react with revulsion to these celebratory videos produced by Hamas are swiftly informed that this is what decolonization looks like.

Since the anti-Jewish pogroms in Israel, numerous pro-Hamas academics have gone to great lengths to explain that decolonization is not simply a nice theory but also a liberating practice of revenge. They took to social media to point out that 'decolonization is not a metaphor' but the violence that Hamas has inflicted on Jewish civilians. Walaa Alqaisiya, a research associate of the London School of Economics, assumes a tone of contempt towards colleagues who have only now woken up to the real meaning of decolonization. He posted on Twitter:

> Academics like to decolonize through discourse and land acknowledgements. Time to understand that Decolonization is NOT a metaphor. Decolonization means resistance of the oppressed and that includes armed struggle to LITERALLY get our lands and lives back![51]

Numerous academic apologists frequently echoed the phrase 'decolonization is not a metaphor' for Hamas violence. Three researchers attached to the University of Sussex's Institute of Development Studies declared:

> In the long term, it is crucial to underscore that decolonisation is not a metaphor, and the time is now to recognise Western imperialism, Israel's settler colonial project – and the cycle of violence that these precipitate – is the crucial backdrop to the horrifying events reaching international headlines this week.[52]

Sarcastic reminders to academics who hesitated before giving Hamas a standing ovation communicated the sentiment that unless you were prepared to applaud the behaviour of this jihadist group, you were on the wrong side of history. As one professor from St Lawrence University posted:

> Faculty colleagues: if you think 'decolonization' is fine for your syllabus, your curriculum, or your classroom, but not for actual colonized people in Palestine, then you've never understood decolonization. Please stop using the term until you take the time to educate yourself.[53]

The call on faint-hearted academics to educate themselves did not mean 'go away, read some books, and study the politics of the Middle East'. It simply meant 'fall in line and agree with our unquestioning support for Hamas's revenge against the Zionist colonizer'.

In his message to academic colleagues, Sandeep Bakshi, who describes himself as a 'Queer vegan of colour academic. Committed to decolonial inquiry. Postcolonial and Queer Studies. Université Paris Cité', was unambiguously clear:

> All scholars who've even once used the term 'decolonisation' for the advancement of their careers, please note that now is the time to show solidarity with Palestine. Stand with Palestine. End all occupations.[54]

Ameil Joseph, a social work professor at McMaster University in Canada, also used social media to encourage the faint-hearted to get real. He stated, 'Postcolonial, anticolonial, and decolonial are not just words you heard in your EDI workshop.'[55] His message was clear: anything decolonial is sacred and beyond criticism. So, when the decolonial was acted out by the perpetrators of the atrocity inflicted on music-festival-goers in Israel, they were only following the script of decolonization.

That tenured academics in Western universities have learned to live with a barbaric atrocity on the grounds that it advances the cause of decolonization highlights the disturbing consequence of allowing free rein to the impulse of exacting revenge on the past.

The curse of continuity

The crusade to decolonize society has made such rapid headway mainly because Western societies already possessed a fragile and insecure sense of the past. As we noted in the previous chapter, the existential and moral crisis that unfolded in the aftermath of the First World War ruptured a sense of continuity with the past and forced society and its individuals to ask 'who they were'. The sense of continuity across time is, as the psychologist Roy Baumeister stated, one of the defining criteria of identity. 'That criterion is hard to satisfy if the continuity is that of process of change rather than that of a stable component,' he wrote.[56] As the sense of discontinuity prevailed over that of continuity, the conditions were created for the historical emergence of what would be referred to as a *crisis of identity* in the 1940s.[57] This absence of a sense of continuity undermined the capacity of the ruling classes to find meaning in the customs and values that previous generations of elites upheld. In such circumstances, they were not intellectually prepared to genuinely internalize the ideals associated with the historical legacy of their societies. With the passing of time, they also proved to be increasingly ineffective in transmitting those values to the younger generations.

At the time, Kingsley Davis, a prominent American social scientist, warned about the consequences of the failure of adult society to transmit the values and the traditions of the past to the younger generations. Davis wrote that if 'many fundamental customs', dismissed as 'anomalous and worthless', were 'eliminated', society would be left 'strangely incapable of maintaining itself'.[58] In 1940, the explicit rejection of historical continuity was confined to the progressivist intelligentsia and sections of the cultural elites. It would take several decades for this sentiment to gain influence over the mainstream of society.

The weakening of a consciousness of historical continuity intensified in the aftermath of the Second World War, when a yearning for Year Zero was evident. Naturally, many reacted to the catastrophic scale of destruction and the utter barbarism of the war. After the Holocaust, many people questioned their faith in humanity. With the bombing of Hiroshima and Nagasaki, the nuclear age had arrived. Many thinking people believed that the origins of these momentous events lay in the past. They concluded that they had no choice but to renounce their connection to their history. As discussed above, many were drawn towards regarding their era as their Year Zero.

Understandably, the rejection of the past and the cultivation of Year Zero history was and remains particularly powerful in Germany, where memories of the catastrophic Nazi experience haunted many members of the post-Second World War younger generations. Calls for an absolute break with the Third Reich and the preceding past were expressed in the concepts of *Stunde Null* or *Nullpunkt*, Zero Hour or Zero Point. In 1945, there were frequent 'declarations by members of a younger generation decrying the bankruptcy of the older generation and indeed of the entire German cultural tradition'.[59] Though at the time this response was most prevalent in Germany, the cause of making a radical break with the past gained adherents in many European countries, notably Italy, and in other parts of the Western world. As we discuss below, Year Zero history became the official doctrine of the European Union.[60]

In Germany, a sense of estrangement from the past gathered pace through the decades and retains its momentum to this day. The need to rupture society's connection with its past is widely taught in schools and has acquired the status of conventional wisdom. As the historian Konrad Jarausch explained, 'The notion of a *Sonderweg* (German deviance from Western norms), popularized by the youth revolt, motivated a more fundamental attack on the continuity of authoritarian patterns in Germany.' According to Jarausch, a consensus was forged that constructed a 'straight line into perdition from Luther through Frederick the Great and Bismarck to Hitler'.[61] A publication by historian Peter Wiener titled *Martin Luther: Hitler's Spiritual Ancestor* (1945) captured the tendency to posit the origins of Nazism in the very distant German past. In numerous accounts, German Protestantism is charged with directly or indirectly paving the way for the ascendancy of the Third Reich.[62] Forced attempts to situate Germany's original sin in its distant past provide the ideology of Year Zero with a plausible argument for rupturing historical continuity.

Not all accounts of the European past are as negative as that of Germany, but within Western culture – popular and high – positive accounts of a nation's history are conspicuously rare. Using the term 'Victorian Values' or 'Victorian morality' in Britain often conveys the connotation of narrow-minded and bigoted attitudes, a rigid social code of conduct, an unhealthy culture of sexual restraint, and the scandal of child labour. Former Prime Minister David Cameron articulated this sentiment in February 2012 when, in response to a racist incident, he stated, 'We will not let recent events drag us back to the bad old days of the past.'[63] His use of the phrase 'bad old days' constituted more than a response to a single ugly incident. It suggested that as far as he was concerned, there was little of worth to 'conserve' from Britain's past.

Some historians have gone so far as to claim that the people of Europe have become psychically distanced from the past to such an extent that they no longer need history to cultivate their identity or to make sense of who they are. 'Clearly Europeans have a sense of themselves as survivors of a history they have left far behind them; they do not see history as their origin or the foundation on which they stand,' argues the German historian Christian Meier. He adds:

> History is not something they desire to carry on (in a better way if possible), Hence they feel no gratitude to their forebears for what they achieved with so much labor; on the contrary, they are fixated on all the things they don't understand (and are making an effort to understand), such as wars, injustice, discrimination against women, slavery, and the like. They feel uncoupled from their history, the seriousness of which they are, generally speaking, less and less able to imagine.

As evidence of this trend, Meier cites the attempt of the European Union to distance itself from Europe's historical past. 'Thus, as far as I can see, the European Union is emerging as the first political entity of the modern era that has no need for its own history and for a historical orientation,' he stated.[64]

Up to a point, Meier is right to highlight the tendency of European federalist ideology to detach the continent's societies from their national history. To a significant extent, the project of European unification was driven by the understandable impulse to start afresh and leave the 'bad old days' behind.

When does history begin?

In the 1940s and 1950s, the main emphasis of the outlook of the founders of European unification was to draw a moral contrast between its vision of the future and the grim events of the past that led to the outbreak of two world wars. Their version of the foundational narrative of the new Europe was based on drawing a moral distinction between itself and the destructive politics of nationalism. The image of a disunited and conflict-ridden old Europe served as the negative counterpoint to a unified and harmonious post-national continent.

The narrative that emerged in the 1950s told a tale of how the original member states of what was to become the European Union (EU) emerged phoenix-like from the ashes of the war to renounce nationalism as a basis for conducting relations between states. According to this version of events, European unity was responsible for transcending the nationalist conflicts that had led to numerous wars and for creating the conditions for economic prosperity in the post-Second World War decades. From this standpoint, the achievement of European unity was portrayed as a secular equivalent of historic redemption. In this story, European federalism symbolized a sacred cause, while nationalism was assigned the role of Antichrist.

One of the predictable consequences of this myth of redemption was that it went beyond the renunciation of the dark era of 1914–45 to the repudiation of much of the past. Europe's pre-1945 past was increasingly depicted in negative terms. In part, this attitude was a reaction to the abuse of history by politically motivated nationalist historians during the previous two centuries. It also expressed the concern that delving too closely into the pre-1945 era would exacerbate conflict between member states and other European nations.

The EU's cultural and educational initiatives constantly peddled a simplistic account of history that made little attempt to educate people to understand the legacy of European civilization. Consequently, any young person embarking on studying the past could easily gain the conviction that Europe was born in the aftermath of 1945.

In all but name, EU-phile historians and policy-makers have settled on 1945 as Europe's Year Zero. Periodic attempts to dig deeper into the past and draw on its legacy are quickly abandoned because of apprehensions about the divisions and conflicts they are likely to provoke between member states. The debate on the Draft Treaty for establishing a Constitution for Europe in 2004 illustrates the danger of probing the legacy of the past. Politicians from different parties and nations clashed on whether Christianity should be evoked in the document as part of Europe's heritage. After a long debate, the authors decided not to include a reference to Christianity in the Preamble to the constitutional document.[65] From the standpoint of Year Zero history, erasing Christianity from Europe's official memory was a small price to pay for avoiding coming to terms with a complicated past.

Following the script outlined by advocates of Year Zero ideology, the EU encouraged its institutions to hide some of the values central to Europe's historical legacy. Take the erasure of Christianity from the EU's narrative of European values. It is worth noting that back in the 1950s, it was still possible for the founders of European integration to acknowledge Christianity as one of the continent's core values. Robert Schuman, who is proclaimed as one of the 'Founding Fathers' of European integration, was in no doubt about the foundational role of Christianity for this project. In 1958, he proclaimed: 'We are called to bethink ourselves of the Christian basics of Europe by forming a democratic model of governance which through reconciliation develops into a "community of peoples" in freedom, equality, solidarity and peace and which is deeply rooted in Christian basic values.'[66]

Even Jacques Delors, the former president of the European Commission, spoke in July 2011 of the 'Europe of values', in whose Constitution 'Catholicism, or rather Christianity more generally, played a major role'. However, by the time Delors made his statement, the political elites associated with EU integration had become reluctant to explicitly associate their values with Christianity or, for that matter, with many of the historical traditions associated with the legacy of Europe. In response to this anti-traditional European federalist political culture, Delors observed that 'today we have hidden our shared values'. As an example, he pointed to the EU's Lisbon Treaty drawn up in 2007, in which 'several heads of governments refused to have these roots alluded to'. He added, 'This was very sad, because we need to know where we have come from.'[67]

In his lament, Delors explicitly criticized the leadership of the EU and argued that its failure to uphold Europe's values would have drastic consequences in the future. He warned that 'all those values that go to make up a society are being done away with; day after day they are being destroyed', and he added that 'if the values of Europe are in decline, then it is Europe that suffers'.[68]

Conclusion

In effect, the EU's leadership did not need to bother to declare the arrival of Year Zero. Instead, as Delors argued, it simply hid the foundational values of European societies. The ideology of Year Zero was already deeply entrenched years before the eruption of the Culture Wars and the subsequent emergence of the decolonization movement. The cultural and political elites running Western societies were neither able to hold the line against the opponents of the cultural legacy that they were meant to represent, nor were they interested in doing so. The dominant cultural ideal was oriented towards the prevailing need to detach society from the past and to exult the cult of the new. Frequently, the prevailing EU narrative signalled that it was not just estranged from but also ashamed of its past.

Year Zero ideology is the antithesis of historical continuity in the current era. This ideology has fostered a climate hospitable to the practice of accusatory history. Accusatory history ceaselessly denounces the past and reduces history to successive episodes of misdeeds and acts of ignominy. Its negative orientation towards the past stems from its pessimistic view of the human condition in general. Unlike the modernist Year Zero ideologies of the past, the current version does not seek a rebirth or call for social transformation that can create a world anew. The classical modernist sensibility of breaking with the past has been subverted by growing disenchantment towards the future.

Jarausch has drawn attention to the prevalence of temporal negativity in relation to the outlook of the EU. Writing about the coexistence of negative memories of Europe with the absence of positive values, he has remarked that the consequence of this development is that 'Europe has become a kind of insurance policy against the repetition of prior problems rather than a positive goal, based upon a shared vision for the future'.[69]

What is noteworthy about the negative vision projected by the supporters of Year Zero ideology is that their passivity towards the future parallels an activist practice towards the past. Society is continually lectured about past misdeeds and warned that it must devote its energies to overcoming its baneful effects. The prevailing obsessive impulse to settle scores with the past is underpinned by a narcissistic tendency to evaluate history from the standpoint of contemporary cultural conventions. A kind of ritual of self-flattery seems to be at work when important historical figures are taken down a peg or two and exposed as morally inferior to the highly sensitive and aware outlook of Year Zero idealogues.

Society needs to understand and learn about the past. It needs to evaluate and reject the evils that its ancestors have perpetrated over the centuries. A critical approach towards the experience of humanity over the centuries makes for good history. But the uncritical criticism of the past adopted by Year Zero ideologues makes for bad history. It is a history trapped in the present. It lacks the intellectual resources necessary to investigate and understand humanity's complexities and twists and turns in its journey to the present. Worse still, its anachronistic practice of reading history backwards has desensitized it from grasping the specificity of different experiences along that journey.

According to this imperative of cultural anachronism, centuries-old historical figures and literary characters from the past are castigated for their racism, sexism, classism, or whatever-ism that offends the imagination of the contemporary author. Yet, many of these figures were instrumental in developing the knowledge and insights that have led to the development of the kind of civilized behaviour associated with the moral flourishing of humanity. Paradoxically, the values used today as a stick with which to beat and punish our ancestors were developed by these now-pathologized perpetrators of historical evils.

One of the most unattractive features of Year Zero ideology is its obsessive presentism. This outlook that pervades the current era is the subject of our next chapter.

4

The Present Eternalized

In what might seem a bizarre twist of logic, the War Against the Past is pursued by engaging with individuals and communities from the past as if they were our contemporaries.

This eternalization of the present requires the erosion of temporal boundaries and coincides with the sensibility of presentism. At first sight, the projection of the present onto the canvas of the past appears to contradict our previous discussion on Year Zero ideology, an outlook that exhorts the necessity for breaking with the past. However, as in many other wars, the War Against the Past is pursued through invading the territory it contests. In this war, the territory of bygone years is treated as an extension of the contemporary world.

In George Orwell's nightmare world of *1984*, Winston Smith, the book's main protagonist, explains, 'History has stopped. Nothing exists except an endless present in which the Party is always right.'[1] It was a prescient observation in a novel published in 1949. It is also very pertinent to this chapter, which is about the interaction of an endless present with the assault on the authority of the past.

Anachronism

The cultural anachronism discussed in the previous chapter rests on the foundation of the all-pervasive zeitgeist of presentism, which prevails in the contemporary era. *The Oxford English Dictionary* defines anachronism as an 'error in chronology; the placing of something in a period of time to which it does not belong'.[2] Anachronistic thinking loses sight of temporal distinctions and sees in the past a reflection of itself. It often attributes something that does not belong to a period of history. Promoters of the politicization of identity are consummate practitioners of anachronism. Reading history backwards, they seize on traces of historical experience that can be turned into evidence that their identity existed across the ages. For instance, they are determined to discover manifestations of sexual and gender politics in the ancient world and tend to look at every instance of discriminatory and oppressive behaviour as an early version of their account of contemporary transphobia, homophobia, or racism.

They find it difficult to distinguish between the meaning that past generations attached to relationships and intimate aspects of life and how the contemporary world makes sense of their experience. That is why they can effortlessly use categories like 'gender', 'identity', 'queering', 'discrimination', or 'intolerance' to interpret events 2,000 years ago. Yet the connotations conveyed by these categories were alien to pre-modern societies. For example, historically, even discrimination was not associated with the negative connotations it possesses today since, in bygone days, discrimination was accepted and non-contested and even regarded as a mark of cultured behaviour. It was an unquestioned and all-pervasive norm. It had none of the negative associations that it has in our time. On the contrary, it was the failure to discriminate that violated the conventional norms of behaviour.

The self-conscious orientation towards the past invariably leads to the distortion of historical reality. It expresses itself in the constant tendency to invent dubious parallels between contemporary issues and events in the past. Recycling contemporary concerns through the past is used to legitimize claims. For instance, anti-binary advocates of transgenderist ideology have sought to naturalize their standpoint by reinterpreting rituals and practices from ancient times to demonstrate that transgenderism has flourished and been a widely accepted norm throughout history. To reinforce the claim that gender fluidity, rather than sexual binarism, is the natural state of affairs, some ideologues have argued that binary thinking about sex is relatively recent, and that history provides numerous examples of gender-fluid practices.

Through a selective reading of history, anti-binary activists attempt to discover evidence of their *a priori* assumptions. They present instances of supposedly gender-fluid behaviour throughout history to reinforce their claims. Writing in *Psychology Today*, Karen Blair asserts:

> Yet, while the gender binary is certainly well anchored within society and our social mores, there is actually a long history of gender not being viewed in

> such a black and white manner. Indeed, many indigenous cultures around the globe held more fluid and dynamic understandings of gender before encountering Western theories of gender. Even within Western cultures, the characteristics associated with one gender or the other have changed stripes so many times through history that it is almost surprising how adamantly we now argue that heels, wigs, makeup, and the color pink are *only* for women and girls, when all of these things were previously reserved *only* for men and boys.[3]

That men wore wigs, makeup, and heels in the past is not in doubt. However, historical differences in how men and women presented themselves do not undermine the biological binary between people with XX and people with YY chromosomes. Nor can it be assumed that what we associate with a certain style of dress now was associated with a similar identity in a different epoch. The meanings we attach to the identity and the presentation of the self are historically specific.

References to 'the long history of gender' indicate a lack of sensitivity to historical variations in attitudes towards human relations. In previous centuries, gender referred to the classification of different types and nouns that may be divided, such as noble/ignoble. According to the genealogical account of gender provided by *The Oxford English Dictionary*, using the term 'gender' to classify and sort need not have any connection with sex.[4] Gender – at least in its modern sense – does not have a long history. It was first used in 1955 by the sexologist John Money to refer to sexual identity.[5] It was during the decades that followed that gender became politicized and endowed with a radically different meaning.

Once gender is eternalized as possessing a 'long history', it can be used to interpret the behaviour of historical figures through the narrative of 21st-century concerns with sexual identity. The anachronistic temper fuelling the retrospective insertion of gender identity into the past is strikingly illustrated by the attempt to represent France's national heroine Joan of Arc as a confused young woman 'questioning the gender binary'. In its wisdom, London's Shakespeare's Globe theatre decided to produce a play that invested Joan of Arc with a non-binary identity.[6] This interpretation of Joan of Arc through the medium of 21st-century gender theory imposes on the 15th century an outlook that is totally alien to it. Undoubtedly, there were many women in the 15th century whose behaviour diverged from the prevailing norms of femininity. Joan of Arc may have sported a cropped hairstyle and worn armour and men's clothing. However, her appearance had nothing to do with pursuing a non-binary lifestyle but arose from her allegedly divinely inspired mission of defeating the English army. In this instance, anachronism does not merely distort the past but also retrospectively unwomans a female hero.

An essay by trans activist historian Kit Heyam that was released to accompany the Globe's production insisted that to portray Joan as a woman would be to 'deny the historical existence of trans experience'. In the same essay, Heyam also suggested that Queen Elizabeth I could have been trans or non-binary. Why? Because, in both cases, these women wore men's armour in battle and performed traditionally male military roles.[7] Did people who regarded Joan as a woman throughout the centuries choose to deny the historical existence of trans experience? Or have supporters of 21st-century trans ideology reinvented Joan in their own image?

The journalist Lauren Smith uses the term 'trans-washing the past' to capture the growing trend towards constantly reinventing individuals from the distant past as possessing transgender identities.[8] If the practitioners of the trans-washing of history are to be believed, then non-binary identity has flourished through the ages. The ancient Egyptian pharaoh Hatshepsut, who died in 1458 BC, is often cast in the role of the first 'fully documented transgender figure in history'.[9]

Speculation has transformed into magical thinking, such as when theologian Joshua Heath declared that Jesus could have been transgender. Heath concluded that the paintings he saw of Jesus suggested that Christ had a trans body.[10]

'1,000-year-old remains in Finland may be non-binary iron leader,' wrote a journalist in *The Guardian*. The article cited researchers who asserted that the body was buried in feminine attire with swords. Whatever this person's gender identity was, it requires an imaginative leap to suggest that the analysis 'challenges long-held beliefs about gender roles in ancient societies' and that 'non-binary people were not only accepted but respected members of their communities'.[11]

Others, too, are delighted that 'long-held beliefs' about the novelty of transgender identity are under challenge. According to the same article, 'Archaeologists and historians also backed the findings, saying it was "exciting" to see new work engaging with questions of gender and identity.' Leszek Gardeła of the National Museum of Denmark stated that the study showed that early medieval societies 'had very nuanced approaches to and understandings of gender identities'.

Like Gardela, many supporters of transgenderist ideology are determined to read back into ancient societies current notions of gender identity. It does not occur to them that the idea of gender, particularly gender identity, had no meaning in ancient times. On the contrary, they insert a timeless, ahistorical version of themselves into ancient times. For example, advocates of academic 'queer archaeology' assert that ancient human remains should be labelled non-binary. They insist that ancient bones should not be classified as male or female because, regardless of the physical differences between male and female bone structure, we do not know how these people would have *identified* themselves.[12] Queer archaeologists are so wrapped up in their presentist universe that they can take the recently emergent concept of 'I identify as' and apply it to a world where it simply could not make any sense. Their attempt to prevent the application of the categories of male and female to ancient bones arrogantly displaces the meaning and significance that communities attached to these categories. It imposes on the lifeworld of ancient communities values totally alien to them.

There is now a veritable scramble to reinvent characters from the past as gender-fluid, and numerous cultural institutions have adopted the grotesque practice of dropping conventional pronouns when referring to historic figures. For example the North Hertfordshire Museum decided to be 'sensitive' to the 'pronoun preferences' of the 3rd-century AD Roman emperor Elagabalus, treating him as a transgender woman and referring to him as 'she'. The museum claimed that according to one classical text the emperor asked to be referred to as a 'lady'. In contrast, some historians take the view that these accounts were likely to be motivated by the goal of undermining the character of this figure.[13] As classics professor Shushma Malik explained: 'The historians we use to try and understand the life of Elagabalus are extremely hostile towards him, and therefore cannot be taken at face value. We don't have any direct evidence from Elagabalus himself of his own words.' She added that 'there are many examples in Roman literature of times where effeminate language and words were used as a way of criticising or weakening a political figure'.[14]

What is striking about the attitude of the individuals supporting the trans-washing of a Roman emperor is the ideological certainty with which they insist that Elagabalus identified as a woman. Councillor Keith Hoskins, an executive member for Enterprise and Arts at North Herts Council, had no doubt that 'Elagabalus most definitely preferred the "she" pronoun and as such this is something we reflect when discussing her in contemporary time'. He added: 'We know that Elagabalus identified as a woman and was explicit about which pronouns to use, which shows that pronouns are not a new thing.'[15] Anyone who is familiar with Latin knows that pronoun usage was far less frequent than in English 'because the subject of a verb is understood rather than stated'.[16] When museums become institutions of propaganda promoting 21st-century fads through presenting them as eternal historical facts, they become complicit in the manipulation of historical memory.

In a similar vein, the attitudes and practices of LGBTQ+ identity groups are often eternalized, and their recent framing is overlooked. One apologist for the eternalization of LGBTQ+ politics claims: 'In ancient societies, there was no distinction made between same-sex and opposite-sex couples as both were equally acceptable.'[17] Once people become so invested in discovering themselves in the ancient past, it is only a matter of time before traces of the rainbow flag will be unearthed within the pyramids of Egypt.

An unabashed practice of anachronism is pursued through the so-called 'queer reading' of history. The queering of history simply means that historical figures are cast in the role of potential, possible, or proven homosexuals. Numerous well-known museums and galleries are in the business of queering their collections. One example is at the Mary Rose Museum in Portsmouth, where curators decided to attribute LGBTQ+ meanings to objects retrieved from Henry VIII's famous battleship.[18] Items found aboard, such as mirrors and nit combs, have been presented in a way that suggests that gay sailors may have owned them. In a museum blog titled 'How we can understand The Mary Rose's collection of personal objects through a Queer lens?', readers are told accurately that men would have used the 'nit combs' discovered on the wreck to remove the eggs of lice (nits) from their hair. However, as if to contextualize, it adds that 'for many Queer people today, how we wear our hair is a central pillar of our identity'.[19] Linking the two statements is curious. Why would the practical use of this instrument in the 16th century have any relationship to a manifestation of sexual identity almost 500 years later? The implication of this statement is that since how people wear their hair today is central to gay people's identity, the presence of nit combs on the ship should be interpreted as an indication that this identity flourished amongst the sailors of the *Mary Rose*. The author of the blog appears unaware of the salience of historical context and treats 16th-century sailors as if they are contemporary men cultivating their queer identity through their hair.

Shakespeare's plays have also become the target of the anachronistic temper that aims to reinterpret and rewrite his text in accordance with the ethos of decolonization. Paradoxically, the language of his play *Titus Andronicus* has been altered so that its language is rendered *explicitly* racist. Critics have observed that the play's allegedly racist assumptions are too subtle and implicit, so they must be corrected to make them more obvious. Jude Christian, when directing this play as part of the Globe's repertoire in 2023, explained that the language of the production needed to resonate more clearly with the outlook of a contemporary audience. 'Racism in the play is masked by Shakespeare's language,' stated Christian. He explained that 'what we've done is show clearly what the words meant in Shakespeare's time'.[20] In truth, the company had put words into Shakespeare's mouth and ascribed contemporary meanings to antiquated 16th-century terms such as 'Moor' and 'raven-coloured'. According to Christian, these are replaced with contemporary racial terminology like 'black to expose the attitudes of some of the characters'. Through this text rewriting, 21st-century attitudes towards race are inserted into a 16th-century play, and characters are transformed into racialized figures. The Globe even organized free Anti-Racist Shakespeare webinars to discuss race and social themes in the play.[21] In America's Binghamton university, *Titus Adronicus* and other Shakespeare plays are 'discussed through the lens of Critical Race Theory'.[22]

Anachronistic readings of Shakespeare are far from new. Throughout the centuries, critics have reflected on his plays in accordance with the issues that preoccupied them. In his essay 'Anachronism in Shakespeare Criticism' published in 1910, Elmar Edgar Stoll warned of the problem of the tendency to turn Shakespeare into a contemporary figure. He stated that the 'function of criticism is not to make the poet in question the contemporary of the reader, but to make the reader for the time being a contemporary of the poet'.[23] In this essay, he warned that modern notions are 'read into Shakespeare', and he noted that the critics of his time adopted the fashionable concerns of 'the newer psychology concerning subconscious states, racial distinctions, criminal and morbid types' to interpret his plays.[24] Compared to today, the anachronistic readings of Shakespeare to which Stoll referred come across as careful and restrained. Were he alive today, he would be astonished by the activist-inspired expansion and normalization of anachronistic literary criticism.

It is worthy of note that Shakespeare himself was a consummate and deliberate practitioner of anachronism, deploying it as a literary device. In Act 2, Scene 1 of his play *Julius Caesar*, there is a reference to the clock striking. Brutus tells Cassius to 'count the clock', and Cassius replies that it 'hath stricken three'. In reality, there were no clocks in Julius Caesar's time. Another 1,500 years would pass before the invention of a mechanical clock that could strike on the hour. However, this form of literary licence, often used by creative writers and artists, has a very different objective to the Globe's politically inspired use of anachronism in the 21st century, which is directed at casting Shakespeare in the role of a central figure in the construction of white identity.

Arthur Little, a UCLA professor and Shakespeare scholar, has argued that 'Shakespeare's poems and plays actively engage in "white-people-making"'. According to Little, Shakespeare provided the cultural resources white people have drawn on over the centuries to 'define and bolster their white cultural, racial identity, solidarity, and authority'.[25] Little's edited collection of essays *White People in Shakespeare* (2022) claims that some of the Bard's most famous plays – *Hamlet*, *Romeo and Juliet*, and *Othello* – and his sonnets are about race and the construction of whiteness as a social category. These essays also assert that white people have used Shakespeare to regulate racial and social categories since his era.

The racialization of Shakespeare's work has acquired a perverse dynamic where his plays are carefully scrutinized for examples of dialogue with racist connotations. Farah Karim-Cooper's *The Great White Bard: How to Love Shakespeare While Talking About Race* (2023) is devoted to the racialization of the work of the Bard. The manner in which material is selected to promote this book indicates that the author intends to 'take the playwright down from his pedestal'.[26] Although, unlike Little, Karim-Cooper clearly respect's Shakespeare's genius, having fallen prey to the prevailing obsession about race, she cannot help but interpret his text through the prism of racism and believes he must be engaged with as one of the founding figures of white Anglo-American civilization.

Karim-Cooper's determination to prove her thesis sometimes leads her to impose her pre-existing assumptions on Shakespeare's text. In her representation of *Macbeth*, the atmospheric gloom and the grotesque depiction of the three witches both evoke images of racialized anxieties. From her perspective, the disgust Shakespeare wishes to incite towards these 'Weird Sisters' is a form of displaced racism. However, as Rowan Williams commented on Karim-Cooper's one-sided racialized representation of the three witches:

> Racialising the strangeness of the Weird Sisters and the obsessive nocturnal imagery can distract from some of the central themes of *Macbeth*: the ambiguity surrounding the 'witches' (who are both peasant sorcerers and classical Fates, not the agents of devilish malignity that King James I was losing sleep about when the play was composed); and the agonised compulsion of Macbeth and his wife to seek a place of final lightless security where they cannot be seen. After all, it is not only in Western culture that the absence of daylight is thought of as liminal and dangerous.[27]

Of course, darkness and colour had important symbolic significance in 'the past', as they still do. But the qualities attributed to differences in colour – skin and hair – have as their reference point biologically given differences. And the moral qualities they convey need to be distinguished from the racist categories that emerged in the modern era. The biological differences that underpinned ideas about race in Shakespeare's time are fundamentally different to the institutionalized system of racism that emerged in ours.

The anachronistic representation of Shakespeare as an ideologist of whiteness is not an outcome of a disinterested exploration of his work. Shakespeare is recognized as, arguably, *the* key figure of the Western literary canon. By associating him with the present-day demeaning qualities of whiteness, the reputation of one of the foundational figures of this canon is blemished. In this way, he can be effortlessly pushed off his pedestal, and through this, his entire corpus of work lies compromised.

Shakespeare is not simply racialized but also charged with many other cultural crimes dreamt up by supporters of identity politics. According to *The School Library Journal*, the Bard's works are full of 'problematic, outdated ideas, with plenty of misogyny, racism, homophobia, classism, anti-Semitism, and misogynoir'. One teacher quoted in the journal explains that Shakespeare is banished from her classroom so as to avoid 'centering the narrative of white, cisgender, heterosexual men'.[28]

One of the most frequent and disturbing uses of anachronism is drawing analogies between contemporary events and Germany in the 1930s. As one insightful commentary remarked, in the United States, comparing the election of Donald Trump to the 'doomed Weimar Republic has become pundits' favourite pastime'.[29] The frequent depictions of Trump as a latter-day fascist leader illustrate the trend towards wielding anachronism as a political weapon. 'Thirteen Similarities Between Donald Trump and Adolf Hitler' is the title of one very forced attempt to relocate this American politician to the dying days of Weimar Germany.[30]

The Weimar analogy is so widely used by academics and commentators that it has turned into a veritable cultural affectation as they draw parallels between the behaviour of politicians of the Nazi era and their political opponents during the years following Trump's election. Yale historian Timothy Snyder personified the 'he is just like Hitler' commentariat, even claiming that Trump was deliberately following in Hitler's footsteps.[31] Writing in *The New York Times*, he claimed:

> Like historical fascist leaders, Trump has presented himself as the single source of truth. His use of the term 'fake news' echoed the Nazi smear *Lügenpresse* ('lying press'); like the Nazis, he referred to reporters as 'enemies of the people'. Like Adolf Hitler, he came to power at a moment when the conventional press had taken a beating; the financial crisis of 2008 did to American newspapers what the Great Depression did to German ones. The Nazis thought that they could use radio to replace the old pluralism of the newspaper; Trump tried to do the same with Twitter.[32]

Snyder's forced attempt to link Trump to Hitler ignores the historical circumstance of the 1930s in a way that breaks down essential distinctions between the present and the past.

Dovid Efune, the editor-in-chief of *The Algemeiner*, a news service covering matters of Jewish interest, has criticized the unfortunate tendency to draw parallels between recent and current political developments in the United States and Nazi Germany. He observes that 'references to Nazi Germany – which is obviously the most extreme and dangerous regime in modern history – seem to be the political cudgel of choice that commentators, political pundits, politicians and leaders themselves are quickly reverting to'.[33]

The 'just like Hitler' trope occurs repeatedly. Since the outbreak of the war in Ukraine, both sides of the conflict have hurled 'just like Hitler' allegations at one another. In January 2023, Russia's Foreign Minister, Sergei Lavrov, accused the American-led NATO countries of solving 'the Russian question' in the same way that Hitler sought to implement his 'final solution' of annihilating Jewish communities in Europe.[34] In turn, Russia's President, Vladimir Putin, is often represented as the 21st-century reincarnation of the Führer. Commentaries with titles like 'Is Putin the New Hitler?' readily invite a response in the affirmative.[35]

The practitioners of anachronistic history lose all sense of moral perspective when they exploit the Holocaust for their own political ends. When animal rights activists ask whether it is offensive to compare the Holocaust with the meat industry, they consider this a rhetorical question, to which the answer is 'No'. They then justify their argument by the thought experiment of replacing the animals in any meat production facility with Jews. The casual way Jews can be 'replaced' by animals in discussions of the Holocaust shows how far this event has been decontextualized from history and turned into a transcendental morality play. To the manipulators of this tragedy's memory, it seems an insignificant fact that Jews were the main target of the Holocaust. From this standpoint, replacing Jews with sheep is considered a legitimate exercise in storytelling.

If Jews can be replaced with sheep, why not embryos? This is what Mike Huckabee, the former governor of Arkansas, was getting at when he argued that abortion is just like the Holocaust. It seems that, sooner or later, all campaigns feel tempted to exploit the Holocaust brand. Animal rights activists in Canada refer to a holocaust of seals. In Australia, there is talk about the holocaust against Aborigines. Then there is the African American holocaust, the Serbian holocaust, the Bosnian holocaust, and the Rwandan holocaust.

Indifference to historical context, crucially important to historians, underpins the 'just like ...' quest for historical parallels. From this perspective, ancient Greece can be reframed as the incubator of racism and racial science, and the Renaissance can be associated with a 'moment when race competes for dominance as a system of classification, justifying the rights of individuals and groups to rule over, disenfranchise, violate, and enslave others'.[36] Through the selective and tendentious reinterpretation of historical events, critical race theorists have sought to reframe the glorification of whiteness as an eternal cultural crime. Yet contemporary society's perception of race, racism, and racial categories bears little relationship to how they were understood before the 19th and especially the 18th century. In the 19th century, racial thinking often focused more on social distinctions between classes than colour differences. The journalist Henry Mayhew expressed this approach and regarded England's poor and vagabonds as a different race – 'a "race" apart'.[37] Racial thinkers at that time were more concerned with the threat posed by the lower races in their society than with the distinction between black and white.

Contemporary cultural anachronism travels in two opposite directions. It plunders the past to draw parallels with today to either condemn or legitimate its object. At the same time, it projects contemporary concerns into the past, usually to condemn and discredit its targets. In this way, present-day concerns about the environment provide a script for discovering allegedly parallel issues in the ancient world.[38] In many instances, the fascination of post-1960s Western societies with 'sexual politics' has led to its sighting in the ancient world. Eva Keuls's study *The Reign of the Phallus: Sexual Politics in Ancient Athens* (1993) is an excellent example of reading history backwards. Driven by a powerful animosity towards patriarchy, she interprets social life in ancient Athens through the prism of present-day sexual politics. Yet the very conceptualization of the politics of sex, like that of identity, had no meaning in ancient times. The theme of sexual politics is not one that people in ancient Athens would have understood or recognized.

Environmentalism is yet another issue that is reimagined in epochs when humanity's relationship with nature was dictated by issues that were specific to their times. Thus, the agriculture of ancient Egypt can be represented through the idiom of environmental sustainability – a term that had little meaning to those living around 3100 BC. Articles on 'sustainable agriculture in ancient Egypt' ignore the different values that prevailed in ancient times.[39] It makes no sense to claim that the ancient Maya 'used sustainable farming, forestry for millennia'[40] when they would not understand what it means to require sustainability.

In 1942, the French historian Lucien Febvre – one of the founders of the French Annales School of History – referred to anachronism as the historian's 'sin of sins'.[41] The tendency to uncritically interpret the past through the concerns and values of contemporary society loses sight of the historical specificity of human experience. In practice, it invariably leads to the erosion of the boundary that separates the present from the past. The behaviour and attitudes of individuals who lived centuries ago are regarded as those of our contemporaries. The problems of 21st-century society are projected back into distant times with little regard to the very different experiences of our ancestors. That is why, according to the imperative of cultural anachronism, centuries-old historical figures and literary characters from the past can be so readily castigated for their racism, sexism, classism, or whatever offends the imagination of the contemporary author. Academics at the University of Lincoln adopted this approach when they branded the 19th-century poet laureate Alfred Lord Tennyson as problematic. The university went so far as to erect a plaque stating that this renowned poet had 'failings' to be 'regretted'.[42] His support for British imperialism during the 19th century is considered an unacceptable character flaw today; therefore, Tennyson must be reprimanded and put in his place.

When Lucien Febvre referred to anachronism as a historian's sin, he understood that it is always tempting to interpret the past from a contemporary standpoint. And, to some extent, it is inevitable. However, there is a fundamental difference between using our present-day insights as our point of departure and uncritically discovering ourselves and our current values in the past.

Today's academic embrace of anachronism resonates with a wider development: the ascendancy of presentism as a dominant cultural outlook. Presentism has become integral to the spirit of our time. As numerous scholars have noted, this sensibility of the ever-present has encroached on the past and the future, thereby gradually eroding conventional temporal boundaries.

The French historian François Hartog importantly observed that the present has '*extended* both into the future and into the past'.[43] This territorial expansion of the present has significant implications for contemporary society's meaning of both the past and the future. It has not only de-authorized the past but also closed off the future. Hartog pointed out that the 20th century 'combined futurism and presentism. It started out more futurist than presentist, and ended up more presentist than futurist.'[44] In effect, presentism coincides with the erosion of Western society's positive orientation towards the future.

As we noted in the previous chapter, Year Zero ideology possesses a distinct lack of interest in projecting a better world into the future. Since modern times, until the late 20th century, the future was frequently perceived as a source of enlightenment. Today, as Hartog explained, 'enlightenment has its source in the present, and the present alone'.[45]

The reorganization of society's sense of temporality can be understood from two – seemingly opposite – perspectives. On the one hand, it can be interpreted as the eternalization of the present as it expands into the past and the future. At the same time, it appears as if the present is a temporal state divorced from the past and the future. This development was highlighted by the sociologist Zygmunt Bauman when he wrote:

> With the present cut off on both sides – from the past, now denied the authority of an accredited guide, and from a future that already ignores the commands and immolations of the present and treats them with a negligence not unlike that with which the present treats its past, the world appears to remain perpetually in *statu nascendi* – in a 'state of becoming'.[46]

Interestingly, the expansion of the present coincides with society's detachment from its past and its disconnection from its future.

The emergence of presentism as the unending now is the cumulative outcome of decades of disparagement of the legacy of the past. As Hartog put it in an article with fellow French historian Gérard Lenclud, to grasp the paradoxical way presentism presents itself, we need to undertake 'the task of accounting for two opposing movements at work' before our eyes: 'first, the mutation of the present into the past; and second, the mutation of the past into the present'. [47]

Presentism

An anachronistic orientation towards the past leads to its inevitable distortions. Instead of grasping the past in its unique specificity, it becomes a medium for recycling contemporary concerns. Its integrity is undermined once the past is framed as a cultural appendage of the present. We lose sight of the principle of historical specificity when bygone events are interpreted as earlier versions of developments today. In this way, hindsight acquires the character of a teleology in reverse.

In an important statement, 'On Presentism', Lyn Hunt, a former President of the American Historical Association, eloquently explained the problem posed by what she characterized as 'temporal superiority'. She wrote:

> Presentism, at its worst, encourages a kind of moral complacency and self-congratulation. Interpreting the past in terms of present concerns usually leads us to find ourselves morally superior; the Greeks had slavery, even David Hume was a racist, and European women endorsed imperial ventures.

She argued that 'we must question the stance of temporal superiority that is implicit in the Western (and now probably worldwide) historical discipline'.[48]

The presentist sensibility dominating Western culture looks at the past with a patronizing glare. Instead of learning from history, it strives to teach the past a lesson. Presentism encourages a narcissistic mode of consciousness that flatters its practitioners for being enlightened and 'aware', unlike those who inhabited the 'bad old days'. Ancient and pre-modern societies are not simply represented as different but also as morally inferior to ours. The drawing of an unfavourable moral contrast between the present and past serves to legitimize the presentist outlook. That is why presentism sustains itself by constantly revisiting its malevolent construction of the past.

As noted previously, contemporary Western culture has become deeply estranged from its traditions and history. The past is often represented as a very dark place where human degradation, abuse, victimization, and genocide are normal features of daily life. One aim of this type of sanctimonious history is to create and extend a moral distance between the present and the legacy of the past. The other objective is to convert the injustices of the past into a moral currency that can be used as a resource for claiming attention, respect, and authority today.

If one judges the past by the current moment's norms, values, and sensibilities, then what people did in the last century or the preceding ones will be almost perfunctorily looked down upon. This disdainful attitude towards the world of our ancestors makes no allowances for the historical circumstances within which they lived. Nor does it appreciate the long and difficult journey on which humanity embarked thousands and thousands of years ago. Instead of seeking to understand the different historical experiences that taught humanity to develop our current attitudes and behaviour, individuals and communities are condemned for their superstitious, tradition-bound, and oppressive behaviour.

Through reading history backwards and treating ancient, medieval, and early modern societies in accordance with the experiences and values of the contemporary world, people from the past are contemptuously dismissed as moral inferiors who lack the awareness of their 21st-century critics. It is a self-flattering practice which reinforces the cultural zeitgeist. A presentist sensibility leads to a form of historical amnesia where temporal distinctions are overlooked, and the difference between different historical moments becomes erased.

In effect, presentism diminishes society's sense of historical consciousness. It inevitably leads to a failure to grasp different historical moments in their specific context. At the same time, it encourages a mood of indifference to the integrity of the cultural achievements of the past. This is why contemporary critics engage with a play by Shakespeare as if it were a 21st-century political statement. Similarly, interest in the integrity and quality of 19th-century novels gives way to a political assessment of how they measure up to the values that prevail in 21st-century university literature departments.

Of course, one can condemn ancient Egyptian pharaohs for mistreating their slaves or the numerous warlords and kings who, through the ages, have massacred their prisoners. But, since condemning individuals and their behaviour in the distant past changes nothing, it is, at best, a performative accomplishment. All it can possibly do is make us feel personally better about ourselves, which is precisely its purpose: it attempts to convey a sense of moral superiority. However, those who read history backwards to demonstrate their moral superiority over the behaviour of people in the past evade the question of how to gain moral clarity in response to the challenges facing society today. Setting right the injustices that confront us in our time will not be done by confusing them with waging war against past misdeeds.

The dramatization of change

As a cultural sensibility, presentism is underpinned by the dramatization of change. Since the rise of modernity, societies have been under the spell of the appearance of constant change. In recent decades, the assumption that the pace of change has accelerated and is likely to accelerate further has acquired the status of conventional wisdom. At times, the consciousness of rapid change has led to an outlook that obliterates the past or, at the very least, renders it irrelevant. Warnings that, in the future, change will increasingly accelerate are frequently asserted and rarely interrogated. In recent times, the term 'New Normal' is frequently used in obituaries about the past. The author of *Organizing for the New Normal* (2021) claims that 'in today's world, everything seems to be happening much more quickly'. He argues that since the world is changing 'exponentially', companies must be ready to embrace the new constantly. 'There is no time to rest, no time to admire their efforts, no time to think,' he concludes.[49] When the mantra of 'there is no time to think' turns into a dogma, reflections on the past become a luxury we cannot afford.

Scholars have characterized the hyper-consciousness of rapid change and its widespread institutionalization as the 'acceleration of history'. This term was first advanced by the French historian Daniel Halévy in 1948.[50] He concluded that modern society's dominant and permanent feature has ceased to be permanence and continuity but change. Drawing on Halévy's work, François Hartog elaborated the concept of 'presentism'. According to Hartog, presentism is 'the sense that only the present exists, a present characterized at once by the tyranny of the instant and by the treadmill of an unending now'.[51] The cultural imperative of presentism profoundly influences the attitude of Western society towards the past. Presentism encourages a shift in the site of legitimation from the past to the future. It promotes an attitude of indifference, even disdain, towards historical precedents and the legacy of the past. Pierre Nora writes of an 'increasingly rapid slippage of the present into a historical past that is gone for good'.[52]

As a cultural outlook, presentism reflects a temporal orientation that cannot or refuses to draw nourishment from the past. At the same time, it finds difficulty investing its emotions in the future. What follows from its detachment from the past and lack of confidence in the future is a retreat into the present. That is why a loss of respect for past traditions can coexist with a dramatic decline of utopian ideals about the future.

If, indeed, change is so rapid that nothing can be taught, and all that can be done is to learn to react, then the future becomes our permanent present. In all but name, history comes to an end. This sense of terminus, which invariably characterizes presentism, has as its symptom profound confusions about temporality. The German sociologist Hartmut Rosa invented the concept of *frenetic standstill*, which refers to a social condition where there is 'the sense that, while everything seems to change faster and faster, real or structural social change is no longer possible'.[53] Back in the 19th century, the German philosopher Friedrich Nietzsche voiced this sentiment when he wrote that European culture was 'moving towards a catastrophe, with a tortured tension that is growing from decade to decade, relentlessly, violently, like a river that wants to reach the end'.[54]

Presentism is underpinned by a theory of rapid change – an acceleration of time – that cuts off the present from the past and collapses the distinction between the present and the future so that the problems projected onto the future become our own. Therefore, instead of ourselves influencing the future, the future shapes our lives today. The constant expansion of the present into different temporal domains desensitizes society from cultivating a conscious relationship with the past and the future. A state of frenetic standstill implies that the present is becoming increasingly isolated from what preceded it and what will follow it.

The idea that the present has become detached from the past due to the acceleration of history was first raised in the 19th century. The French writer and historian François-René Chateaubriand wrote in the preface to an essay in 1826 that 'events moved faster than my pen'. In 1831, he noted that he was writing ancient history while modern history knocked on his door, and it 'thundered past'.[55] In the United States, Henry Adams elaborated the theory of the Law of Acceleration. According to Adams, events move so fast that 'every past example is always too late'. In his study, published in 1919, Adams concluded that the rapid pace of change meant there was little point in teaching the young about the past facts. He stated, 'All the teacher could hope for was to teach [the mind] reaction.'[56]

Being caught up in the spell of the present has acquired an unprecedented influence since the end of the Cold War. The conviction that rapid change renders the past irrelevant has acquired the status of dogma within the political and cultural establishment. Presentism has exercised a powerful influence on educational and social theory. David Inglis's comment on 'The Death of History in British Sociology' speaks to the cultural condition of historical amnesia that prevails in the social science university departments of the West.[57]

The sense of terminus accompanying presentism particularly gained a hold in the 1970s when the future-oriented ideologies of modernity became exhausted. Utopian visions and even idealistic views about the possibility of positive social transformation gradually gave way to a more downbeat, even dystopian, view of the future. A loss of enthusiasm about the possibility of future progress has encouraged the flourishing of strong presentist impulses, which have led the present to encroach more and more on the past. Estranged from the past and now alienated from the future, Western societies unconsciously adopted presentism as a way of life.

The erosion of temporal boundaries

In effect, presentist cultural influences encourage society to relive the present in the past and the past in the present. Numerous students of society's consciousness of time write of a temporal crisis where 'we can no longer clearly distinguish between the temporal registers of present, past, and future'. In her study *Is Time out of Joint?* (2020), literature professor Aleida Assmann remarks that 'what historians view as an utterly necessary condition for their work – namely, the separation of these temporal registers – has since given way to their complete entanglement with one another'. She observes that because of temporal confusions, 'the past and the future are said to have lost their functions; they no longer represent the virtually sacred dimensions of the objective real (the past), or the expected not-yet (the future), but rather something created in, and suited to, the (actual) present'.[58] Assmann concludes that we lack the normative foundation for distinguishing the present from the past.

The entanglement of the different temporal states is intertwined with the loss of temporal boundaries. As discussed in my study *Why Borders Matter: Why Humanity Must Relearn the Art of Drawing Boundaries* (2020), Western societies have become estranged from affirming the traditional boundaries that have historically guided their affairs. As a result, the distinction between the different temporal states becomes blurred. The imperative of distancing the present from the past is often closely linked with the impulse to expand the present into the past to settle scores with it.

The Manifesto of the V21 Collective systematically pursues this borderless sense of temporality. This contemporary collective of Victorian studies scholars is self-consciously devoted to the breaking down of the temporal boundaries separating the 19th century from the 21st. They claim that because of the timeless impact of 19th-century imperialism, 'we *are* Victorian, inhabiting, advancing, and resisting the world they made'. As far as they are concerned, 'presentism is not a sin' because 'the Victorian period is a survey of empire, war, and ecological destruction', and 'insofar as the world we inhabit bears the traces of the nineteenth century, these traces are to be found not only in serial multiplot narrative, but in income inequality, global warming, and neoliberalism'.[59]

An approach like that of the V21 Collective was adopted by a thematic discussion paper presented for discussion at the International Centre for the Study of the Preservation and Restoration of Cultural Property (ICCROM) General Assembly in 2019. ICCROM, a global institution coordinating the activities of museums and heritage centres, devoted its discussion to how to decolonize the collections held by its member institutions. After noting that there 'are so very many remnants of colonial times: from street names and statues that glorify people responsible for massacre and genocide, to objects in museums taken from their original owners to the human remains of unidentified people held as collection artefacts', the authors of the paper concluded, 'Coloniality is in many different ways more present than past.'[60] Its perception that 'coloniality' is more present than past highlights the borderless sense of temporality that turns decolonization into a timeless project.

Luke Syson, the director of the Fitzwilliam Museum in Cambridge, voiced a similar sentiment when referring to its 2023 exhibition 'Black Atlantic: Power, People, Resistance', exploring the city's connections to the slave trade. He stated that 'reflecting on the origins of our museum, the exhibition situates us within an enormous transatlantic story of exploitation and enslavement, one whose legacy is in many ways as pervasive and insidious today as it was in the seventeenth, eighteenth or nineteenth century'.[61] His claim exemplifies the presentist disposition to wilfully ignore the distinction between the present and the past.

The conviction that we remain Victorians or that what we do should correct past problems has encouraged the habitual and effortless criss-crossing of what were hitherto rigid temporal boundaries. French historian Henry Rousso has pointed to the tendency to regard the past as a territory to be acted upon by contemporaries. This activist perspective towards the past has influenced social memory and the language we use to communicate our engagement with this temporal state. Rousso has drawn attention to the 'desire to define the crimes of the past in legal terms and to atone for them in accordance with the standards and values of the present'.[62]

This is an approach which cannot be detached from the exercise of moral anachronism. It is a form of anachronism explicitly directed towards applying the standards and ideals of contemporary moral judgements to the past. The philosopher Gerald Dworkin uses the term 'moral anachronism' in relation to the act of evaluating the behaviour and sentiments that prevailed in the past. He points out that it is 'easy enough to look back to the beginning of the century and see many ethical views that we now believe to be profoundly mistaken'. He poses the question of to what extent it is legitimate to judge people in the past who acted by beliefs that we now deem to be wrong: 'When does the fact that our current understandings and commitments were not historically present in an earlier period get people off the hook for behavior that, today, would be universally viewed as outrageous?'[63]

Dworkin's usage of the term getting people 'off the hook' is interesting, for it highlights the presentist tendency to react to historical figures in the same manner as if they were our contemporaries. Of course, we can decide to 'nail' someone like the German philosopher Immanuel Kant, the father of the Enlightenment, for stating that 'humanity has achieved its greatest perfection in the white race'.[64] Or we can 'let him off the hook' for his nuanced understanding that differences in appearance and skin colour did not contradict the universality of humanity. But isn't it more productive to assess his intellectual legacy and the significance of his philosophical contribution instead of treating him as one of our 21st-century peers?

Moral anachronism breeds an interventionist approach towards the behaviour of historical figures. It assumes that, at the very least, the past can be morally acted upon. Hungarian historian Zoltán Simon, in his *History in Times of Unprecedented Change* (2019), drew attention to various campaigns such as the Rhodes Must Fall protests to bring down the statue of Sir Cecil Rhodes in university campuses in South Africa and Oxford and efforts to ban the comic book *Tintin in the Congo* in Belgium. Simon asserted that the 'sheer act of demanding removal and the sheer act of demanding the ban tacitly implies a sense that "we", in the present, are no longer those people who could reasonably erect a statue to Rhodes and write or read a comic book like *Tintin in the Congo*'.[65] Moral anachronism often expresses itself through virtue signalling. From this standpoint, people who despise Tintin are morally superior to characters in the Bible who owned slaves, or to Moses, who, in Numbers 31, encouraged the Israelites to take female captives. For the advocates of moral anachronism, history serves as an instrument for narcissistic self-flattery.

The erosion of temporal boundaries expresses itself in an outlook that regards the past as a territory that can be managed and acted upon. As Rousso writes, 'To judge political crimes sometimes half a century old, temporal justice systems have been turned into "tribunals of world history".' Increasingly, the problems of the past confront us as our own. Rousso argues:

> In the public mind, in ordinary language, the past has become a problem to be solved. It is now common to hear that societies, groups, or individuals must 'face up to', 'confront', or 'cope with' the past or that one must 'come to terms with' or 'master' the past. It is a strange metaphor when you think about it, since, literally, it means either that we put the past in a place that is in principle not its own, namely, in front of us; or that we constantly have our backs turned to the future in order to face the past.[66]

Engaging with the past on our terms has become a cultural imperative that constantly energizes the War Against the Past. The past is imagined and managed as if it were morally inferior territory that must be colonized by enlightened crusaders intent on saving it from itself.

The tendency to judge the past as morally inferior fundamentally extinguishes the reverence that previous generations possessed towards it. Rousso declares that 'history no longer unfolds in the first place as traditions to be respected, legacies to be transmitted, knowledge to be elaborated, or deaths to be commemorated, but rather as problems to be "managed", a constant "work" of mourning or of memory to be undertaken'. In effect, the past becomes 'a substance that can and even must be acted upon, adapted to the needs of the present'. Rousso concludes that the past is 'now a realm of public action'.[67] Hartog echoes Rousso's view of the presentist tendency to render the past contemporary and highlights the 'desire to relive the past in the present', or, alternatively, to fix the past.[68] 'Many critical projects seek to fix or heal the past, perhaps through monetary reparations, affirmative action, decolonization, or a juridical "Truth and Reconciliation Commission",' notes the Victorian literature scholar Eleanor Courtemanche.[69]

The politicization of presentism

The War Against the Past draws on the prevailing presentist zeitgeist, which now enjoys significant support in the Academy. Presentism has been adopted as an intellectual outlook by many professional historians as a medium through which identity politics are communicated. Sections of the current cohort of Anglo-American professional historians reject one of the central principles of modern historiography, which is the commitment to interpret events in history in their terms rather than through the prism of present-day moral and cultural norms. This approach is alien to their disciplinary tradition, which until recent times considered anachronism an illegitimate way to deal with the past. This belief was forcefully articulated by Eric Hobsbawm, who warned in 1997 that 'the most usual ideological abuse of history is based on anachronism rather than lies'.[70] It is only in recent decades that Hobsbawm's warning about the distorting effect of anachronism has been challenged by professional historians and other scholars reflecting on the past.

Today, presentism is zealously supported by activists within the Anglo-American Academy. Advocates of presentism reject a rigorous version of historical scholarship that aspires to objectivity. The historian Alexandra Walsham decries that the term 'presentism' has become 'a term of abuse, a slur conventionally deployed to describe an interpretation of history that is biased towards and coloured by present-day concerns, preoccupations and values'. Walsham takes a different view and questions the wisdom of studying the past for its own sake rather than to advance a presentist agenda. She writes:

> The instinctive suspicion of presentism that prevails among many historians is also a legacy of the lofty ideal of objectivity that we have inherited from the positivists who placed the discipline of history on a professional footing in the nineteenth century. It is a function of the conviction that we should study the past for its own sake and not in order to advance other agendas.

She supports the presentist agenda and asks, 'Can students of the past avoid seeing it through the prism of the present?'[71]

Walsham's statement implies that there is something flawed about the commitment to study the past for its own sake. Of course, the study of the past is always mounted from the present, and no historian can or should avoid approaching their work from the standpoint of the present. However, there is a fundamental difference between presentism and its anachronistic attempt to render the past contemporary with an approach that uses the insights gained over the centuries to acquire greater knowledge about the past. In this way, the specificity of historical experience can be grasped and understanding the past for its own sake allows us to comprehend its variations and our distinct circumstances. In contrast, presentism constitutes a form of cultural imperialism that attempts to colonize and impose its agenda on the past.

Supporters of presentism openly acknowledge that their approach of projecting the present back into the past is motivated by their political and social commitments. Historian Miri Rubin contends that 'engaging concepts and posing ethical questions is the most honest – and perhaps the only – way of making history that does justice to the past and is accountable in the present'.[72] Making the past accountable to the present offers a clear expression of moral anachronism. The assumption that present-day academics should hold the centuries-old actions and beliefs of individuals and communities to account is perverse. It sets up presentist activists as the grand inquisitors of the past, who enjoy the prerogative of condemning people living thousands of years ago in circumstances very different to theirs. Holding to account those who have been dead for centuries and cannot understand the concerns of their present-day inquisitors represents a grotesque mockery of justice.

Rubin justifies the arrogance of presentism on the grounds that 'we know a great deal about their world of which they were ignorant' and 'we have learned to understand texts beyond an author's declared aims'.[73] The condescending notion that we understand the meaning of historical texts better than the authors who wrote them communicates a sense of trans-historical elitism and contempt towards our ancestors. The language of contemporary cultural elitism suggests that we are more 'aware' than previous generations of authors whose understanding of their text was deficient compared to ours.

Presentist historiography belittles the past to legitimate its determination to intervene to remedy the error of its ways. The cultural politics of identity is the principal driver of this intervention. Rubin notes:

> Some historians are intent on recovering experiences of people marginalized in their own times and since, women and peasants, those conquered, enchained or silenced. They do so for a host of reasons, often spurred on by the discontents of contemporary life, embedded in the historian's personal and professional formation, and thus inescapably in ethical and political environments.[74]

Understandably, historians, like other people, are influenced by the discontents of contemporary life and their ethical and political environment. Political and social activism is an honourable enterprise when directed at the injustices of our time. When this activism crosses over a temporal boundary and directs its energies towards holding the past to account, however, it becomes a caricature of itself. Presentist historians are not disinterested scholars committed to understanding the integrity of historical experiences. They have turned into grievance archaeologists whose work confirms their *a priori* assumptions.

The American sociologist John Torpey warned that 'we need to be aware, as we seek to mend the damage from the past, that a politics of the past may crowd out or replace a vision of progress'.[75] We can go a step further than Torpey and conclude that when so much effort is devoted to mending 'the damage of the past', a vision of progress has already been extinguished. Judging and acting on the past has become a displacement activity pursued by activists who would rather declare war on the past than engage with the problems that lie ahead.

In effect, the presentist version of the past works as a blank screen on which to project contemporary preoccupations. Some go so far as to reject an historical reading of the past explicitly. One literary scholar, Ewen Fernie, argues for 'the crucial importance of Shakespeare *now*'. He claims that his essay 'reflects on presentism: a strategy of interpreting texts in relation to current affairs which challenges the dominant fashion of reading Shakespeare historically'. He writes that 'where new historicism emphasizes historical difference, presentism proceeds by reading the literature of the past in terms of what most "ringingly chimes" with "the modern world"'.[76] From this perspective, what matters is not what Shakespeare wrote or intended to communicate through his text but what it tells us now. In this way, a play written in the 16th century mutates into a 21st-century drama.

From a presentist standpoint, Shakespeare's *Titus Andronicus* can be represented as a play that, according to literature scholars Cary DiPietro and Hugh Grady, 'speaks to us of our own twenty-first-century experience of terrorism'. They acknowledge that their 'approach can be seen as anachronistic, but it is an anachronism that opens up the play to its full meanings as a work of art in the twenty-first century'.[77]

Critics are entitled to focus on what Shakespeare means to them. In many instances, the fact that Shakespeare speaks so directly to a 21st-century audience confirms his universal message. The problem is not dwelling on what Shakespeare says to us in the here and now but confusing this with what the playwright set out to achieve. So long as we acknowledge that *Titus Andronicus* has nothing to do with global terrorism, there is no harm in imaginatively attaching an anachronistic 21st-century meaning to a very old play. Anachronism only becomes a problem when it is politicized and turned into a weapon with which to attack the past.

Presentism fuels Cancel Culture

Since the War Against the Past is committed to eroding temporal boundaries, it relies on an anachronistic outlook to underpin its project. That is why it is intensely hostile to anyone who dares challenge its version of the past. Since it heavily relies on drawing historical analogies to argue for its cause, it is fervently hostile to critics of the 'it's just like Weimar' approach. As far as they are concerned, questioning the projection of the present back into the past and the rediscovery of the past in the present constitutes a heresy against their cultural ideals.

At first, it looked like an obscure academic dispute over teaching history. But the humiliation of James H. Sweet, a professor of history at the University of Wisconsin and the president of the American Historical Association (AHA), at the hand of a mob of academic heresy hunters in 2022 shows that what is at stake is who gets to decide how we view our past.

Sweet came under fire for daring to challenge what he described as the 'trend towards presentism' in academic history. Particularly in the United States, presentist academic history treats events in the past as if they are statements that accurately reflect today. It reads history backwards to recycle its contemporary concerns through the past. This history gives voice to a powerful cultural trend that condemns the past for failing to live up to the causes and values of the contemporary cultural establishment.

In an article for the AHA's *Newsletter*, titled 'Identity Politics and Teleologies of the Present', Sweet tried to gently remind his colleagues of the need for historians to respect the boundary that divides the present from the past. He questioned the widely adopted practice of reading history backwards and complained that for many of his colleagues, the past only mattered when read 'through the prism of contemporary social justice issues – race, gender, sexuality, nationalism, capitalism'.

Sweet asked 'if history was little more than "short-term . . . identity politics defined by present concerns, wouldn't students be better served by taking degrees in sociology, political science, or ethnic studies instead?'[78] As he discovered, the simple posing of this question is forbidden by an intemperate academic clerisy patrolling university history departments.

Anachronistic historians are devoted to the mission of imposing a non-negotiable party line on the way that the past is discussed. They are intolerant of dissident interpretations of the past, and historians who do not toe this line face ostracism and punishment. The fanaticism with which dissident views are punished bears all the hallmarks of the spirit of the Inquisition. The dogmatic zeal with which the presentist version of the Western past is policed was on full display in the explosion of unrestrained hatred directed against Sweet in August 2022.

Sweet's commentary about the subordination of academic history to the imperative of ideology led to a veritable explosion of condemnation of his professional status and integrity. The venomous hatred directed at him by supposedly educated academics highlighted the spirit of fanaticism that has engulfed many cultural institutions. He was mobbed on social media and condemned as a heretic for daring to question the presentist turn of the American history profession. Sweet's inquisitors denounced him as a racist for questioning the concerns of minority advocates of the cultural politics of identity.

Sweet was condemned for being a 'white man' who had no right to interrogate or criticize how black or African history is interpreted. His statement was denounced because it supposedly adopted an approach that resembled those of right-wingers and Nazis, who worked 'in the service of 'white supremacism and misogyny'.[79] These days, the very posing of a view that questions the imposition of a presentist dogma is casually equated with white supremacism and/or fascism.

The reaction of the historian David Veevers was illustrative of the mean-spirited contempt directed at Sweet. 'One of the worst things about this absolute twaddle is that this guy thinks societal issues like race, gender, and sexuality are "contemporary" and somehow did not exist in the past. How the hell did he get beyond his undergraduate degree, let alone become President of the AHA?,' Veevers posted on Twitter.[80]

As it happens, contemporary issues such as the obsession with transgenderism and sexuality were conspicuously absent in many societies in the past. But to make this obvious observation about historical variations in societal concerns about race and gender is to court the charge of heresy. Sadly, but predictably, under massive pressure on social media, Sweet issued a forced apology for the 'harms' that his statement caused.

Sweet's use of the word 'harm' is significant. Anyone who understands how Cancel Culture works knows that it insists that criticism and offensive words cause harm. Cancel Culture validates its demand for the policing of language by claiming that criticism and words that offend can traumatize and damage people's mental health. The medicalization of speech forces people to watch their words, especially when involved in an argument or dispute touching someone's identity. The mere questioning of such conventions is often portrayed as damaging and harmful, which is why Sweet felt obliged to state that 'I apologize for the damage I have caused to my fellow historians, the discipline, and the AHA'.[81]

How can a commentary disputing a version of academic history damage historians? The answer lies in how therapeutic censorship has turned robust verbal exchange into a medical problem. From this standpoint, criticism is not simply questioning an idea or an intellectual perspective but an attack on the identity of the person whose view is challenged. Thus, the questioning of presentism itself is represented as an assault on the identity of the historians who subscribe to its tenets.

In an unfortunate act of self-abasement, Sweet stated, 'I hope to redeem myself in future conversations with you all. I'm listening and learning.'[82] The tone of abject humiliation with which Sweet promised to re-educate himself came across as an American version of a Maoist Struggle Session. Sweet's hope for redemption is likely to be dashed because the War Against the Past does not forgive its opponents. These days, an apology invites a metaphorical slap in the face and a gloating expression of contempt.

In a practice reminiscent of the forced confessionals of the Stalinist era, the response to an apology is to demand further acts of contrition. Sweet's apology was swiftly denounced as insincere and condemned as a 'faux-apology'. Under Stalin, such a response to a confession would have led to a one-way ticket to the Gulag. Sweet is lucky; he only faces ostracism and marginalization within the academic profession.

Exacting vengeance on the past

The vengeful attack on the reputation of an academic who dared criticize the growing tendency of reading history backwards is constantly replicated by individuals motivated to exact vengeance against the past. At times, participants in the War Against the Past behave as if they have crossed over into a different temporal territory to attack historical figures. A banal illustration of this behaviour occurred in Broadstairs in Kent, where Ian Driver, a former local councillor for the Green Party, defaced the Charles Dickens Museum with graffiti denouncing the author as 'racist'.[83]

Driver, who scrawled the words 'Dickens Racist, Dickens Racist' on the walls of the Victorian cottage housing the museum, was so proud of his deed that he publicly admitted he was behind the vandalism on his blog, where he published photos of himself carrying it out. He stated he did not mind being arrested because he was certain he had a strong defence under current equality legislation. He defended his action because it was brought about by 'informed duress' in which he feared minority groups would suffer immediate threat unless he acted.[84]

What is fascinating about the justification for this act of vandalism is a narrative that validates it on the grounds that attacking a building that symbolizes a 19th-century author is likely to be endorsed by current equality legislation. Reliance on current equality legislation to seek vengeance on 19th-century literary figures indicates that some culture warriors believe they can use recently enacted laws to indict and punish the past. This interweaving of two different temporal domains is strikingly demonstrated by the sense of urgency that demands that action be taken to protect minority groups who otherwise 'would suffer immediate threat'. Driver's quixotic battle against the threat posed by the past is one illustration of the numerous ways the War Against the Past is enacted. The claim that the Charles Dickens Museum constitutes a clear and present danger to the lives of minorities is absurd. Still, such absurdities inevitably flourish when the sight of temporal boundaries is lost.

This incidence of vandalism did not make national headlines. It comes across as a relatively minor and even idiosyncratic affair. But the matter-of-fact manner with which it was reported indicated that the vandalizing of a building devoted to remembering one of England's greatest literary figures did not merit an expression of outrage. It is as if the legacy of the past has become fair game for any intemperate activist seeking to vent their anger on it.

5

Identity and the Past

Although today's presentist zeitgeist is deeply embedded and sustained by decades of historical experience, its intellectual and cultural expression is fuelled by the politicization of identity. When James Sweet titled his controversial critique of presentism 'Identity Politics and Teleologies of the Present' in August 2022, he correctly made a connection between identity politics and the presentist approach towards historiography. The moral anachronism immanent in identity politics aims to politicize the past through imposing a specific ideological agenda onto it. From this perspective, the politicization of the past is informed by two seemingly contradictory perspectives: to validate the identity of some groups and types of people while stigmatizing the identity of others. One way that identity politics attempts to consolidate its current status is by seizing control of the narrative of the past. Through finding representatives of their views and prejudices in different historical epochs, the current elite seeks to ensure that its view of the past acquires hegemonic status.

The relationship of identity politics with the past is ambivalent. Like numerous movements throughout history, it looks to it for validation. However, in contrast to most conventional accounts of history, identity politics presents itself as the victim. Its claim to authority is based on its historic suffering. This is achieved by projecting back into the past the injustices it claims to suffer from in the present. For contemporary identity politics, the past provides a rich vein of injustice. With the erosion of temporal boundaries, the past is seized upon as a boundless offering of never-ending opportunities for providing a home for the identitarian version of injustice. The flourishing of grievance archaeology indicates that the War Against the Past will not end anytime soon. From its standpoint, the past is transformed into boundless territory where injustices are waiting to be discovered and the authority of victim groups can be validated.

Yet the current hyper-politicization of identity is itself an outcome of Western societies' estrangement from the past. One of the cultural imperatives of modernism has been to alienate communities from their past. In response to the weakening of the bonds linking the present to the past, the quest for identity has acquired a commanding influence in Western societies. Identity becomes an issue when people struggle to find an answer to the question of who they are. As the American social psychologist Kenneth Gergen explained, a people's 'capacity to achieve moral identity' is intimately linked to its 'relationship with the narratives of the past'.[1] An individual's identity is linked to their community and the identity of that community itself is rooted in its sense of the past. It is when people's sense of identity is dispossessed of the clarity gained through a meaningful narrative of the past that a crisis of identity ensues.

On a close inspection of our individual moral identity, it becomes evident that the past is present within us. As the Scottish-American philosopher Alasdair MacIntyre noted, our inheritance from the past is integral to the particularity of our moral identity:

> I am a citizen of this or that city, a member of this or that guild or profession; I belong to this clan, that tribe, this nation. Hence what is good for me has to be the good for one who inhabits these roles. As such, I inherit from the past of my family, my city, my tribe, my nation, a variety of debts, inheritances, rightful expectations and obligations. These constitute the given of my life, my moral starting point. This is in part what gives my life its own moral particularity.[2]

That the past is present in us does not mean that it will be recognized by those who write off its accomplishment as outdated. When – as now – society encourages the condition of social amnesia, an important connection with our cultural legacy risks being eroded.

The narratives of the past are not the accidental products of nature but are forged through cultural conflicts and engagements about them. People's moral identity is intertwined with a narrative that locates it in relation to a past. As Gergen explained:

> Because individual identity is configured or implicated in historical narratives, so is the achievement of moral being sustained (or impeded) by

> historical accounts. For good or ill, we each live within and are constructed by particular historical narratives – of our people, culture, nation, region, family, and so on. These historical narratives serve as a foreground for achieving moral identity within relevant communities.[3]

The precondition for the rise of the emergence of identity as a stand-alone focus of concern is the diminished sense of connection of individuals and communities with a narrative rooted in the past. The predicament of uprootedness led to the problematization of identity, which in recent decades has been reinforced by its politicization. The War Against the Past is an indirect outcome of this politicization of identity. At the same time, its pursuit of this conflict has made a significant contribution to further dispossess people of their narrative of the past. It directs its energy towards the dissolution of historical and cultural continuity. It calls into question the salience of the legacy of the past and aims to de-authorize the historical foundation of contemporary society. This disruption of historical continuity has led to the unprecedented significance attached to identity and to its politicization. The Culture War against the past undermines people's traditional identities while also creating a demand for new ones. Since these newly invented identities lack an organic relationship with historical experience, they lack firm roots. Therefore, identities that are constructed or invented from a presentist perspective are inherently fragile and transient.

The fragility of 21st-century identities is due to their lack of roots in the past and their weak normative foundation. It is the detachment of identity from normativity that accounts for the obsessive attitude of identitarians towards the past. It is its alienation from moral norms that has lent identity an unstable, arbitrary, and fluid form. Many attempts at explaining this development assert that the fluidity of identity is a consequence of the post-modern condition and the rapid acceleration of change. While these conditions influence the forms that identity assumes, the experience of the past century indicates that the *decisive* influence on the problematization of identity is a lack of clarity about the moral values that underpin the self. As the philosopher Christine Korsgaard pointed out, 'You can't maintain the integrity you need in order to be an agent with your own identity on any terms short of morality itself.'[4] According to Korsgaard, 'normative standards provide the principles' through 'which we achieve the psychic unity that makes agency possible'. Psychic unity with society's moral norms provides the normative resources for what she characterizes as *self-constitution*, the possession of which is the precondition for a dynamic sense of identity.[5] Without a sense of rootedness in the past, the quest for a dynamic and self-assertive sense of identity becomes elusive.

The politicization of identity

Today, when identity has become a constant source of concern and conflict, it is easy to lose sight of the fact that this issue is a relatively recent one. The presentist outlook on the past assumes that a preoccupation with identity has been a constant dimension of the human experience. In numerous instances, commentaries contend that society's absorption with the issue of identity is the contemporary version of an age-old problem. Such assumptions are based on the premise that the search for identity or the impulse to gain validation is an eternal feature of the human condition. From this standpoint, the problem of identity transcends different historical epochs and different cultures.

Most accounts treat identity in an ahistorical manner. The distinguished social scientist Shmuel Eisenstadt asserted that constructions of collective identities 'have been going on in all human societies throughout history'.[6] This tendency to presume that, in every age, identity preoccupies human society also extends to reflections on identity politics. Both supporters and opponents assume that identity politics has an age-old history. One critic claimed that 'before the identity politics of the 1980s and 1990s, there was the identity politics of the 1930s and 1940s'.[7] A fervent advocate of identity politics dismisses the belief that it is a relatively recent phenomenon. He exhorts his opponents to 'pick up a history book', and adds, 'Identity politics is as old as America itself.'[8]

It is important to realize that concern with the self – which is a recurrent theme in history – was not until the post-Second World War era framed through the medium of identity. The German psychologist Erich Fromm, in his *Escape from Freedom* (1941), used the concept of identity in relation to his concern with what he saw as the loss of the individual self in totalitarian societies. However, identity as '*substantive self-definition*, self-definition as *something*, which purportedly determines what I believe and do', came into 'common usage' with the work of the psychologist Erik Erikson.[9]

Erikson wrote that the concept of identity emerged in response to the problems faced by individuals in the interwar era and the early 1940s. 'And so it comes about that we begin to conceptualize matters of identity at the very time in history when they become a problem,' he stated.[10] The problems to which he alluded were particularly noteworthy in the United States, and the social and cultural concerns of this society significantly influenced the way that the crisis of identity was portrayed and perceived throughout the world. This point is confirmed by a fascinating study of the semantic history of identity, which concluded that the formal conceptualization of identity emerged first in the United States in response to a growing concern about what it meant to be an American.[11]

Far from there being a universal concern to 'possess an identity', this issue was absent in public deliberations throughout most of human history. The most authoritative account of the historical specificity of identity is provided by Marie Moran's *Identity and Capitalism* (2015). Moran offers a compelling case for her contention that identity is a very new idea and it 'never "mattered" prior to the 1960s because it did not in fact *exist* or operate as a shared political and cultural idea *until* the 1960s'.[12] She points out that 'until the 1950s, or even the 1960s and 1970s, there was no discussion of sexual identity, ethnic identity, political identity, national identity, corporate identity, brand identity, identity crisis or "losing" or 'finding" one's identity'.[13] My own research into identity-related concepts indicates that insofar as writers referred to national identity in the 19th century, their aim was to underline the sense of moral continuity of a community. As one Scottish clergyman stated in 1844: 'Upon what principle then, can the moral feeling of nations be explained, if not that of national identity which we are attempting to establish?'[14]

In the 19th century, identity was essentially a moral construct and possessed a meaning that is very different to that of today. The search engine Google Ngram Viewer offers a database of literary sources for investigating the context within which the term 'identity' was used in the 19th century. It indicates that at that time concern with the stability and continuity of identity was often captured by the concept of *moral identity*. In its 19th-century usage, this concept linked moral authority to an idea of identity that conveyed a sense of stability and immutability. Moral identity referred to its quality of sameness and continuity. Theologians and conservative commentators used this phrase to underline the importance of historical continuity. As a tract issued in 1827 by the American Unitarian Association indicated, 'The moral identity once broken, all other continuity goes for nothing, all other sameness is illusory.'[15]

Although it is not possible to fix a precise date when identity emerged as an influential concept, the evidence available indicates that it was during the 1950s that it became a rhetorical idiom through which people came to know and understand themselves and construct an understanding of what it means to be a human. This was precisely the time when, under the spell of modernization, the project of freeing society from the outdated traditions of the past gained significant momentum. This was also the moment when the sense of moral continuity of a community gradually gave way to a consciousness of disconnection.

It is not possible to grasp the true significance of Western society's adoption of the rhetoric of identity without situating it within a wider historical context. The current tendency to eternalize this development coincides with a propensity to overlook the specific features of the predicament facing individuals in 21st-century society. As we previously noted, a sensibility of historical amnesia dominates contemporary intellectual culture, which encourages a tendency to read history backwards. That is why so many commentators cannot avoid the temptation of projecting their own identity issues into the distant past. For example, Zairong Xiang's *Queer Ancient Ways: A Decolonial Exploration* (2018) uses the rhetoric of contemporary identity politics to uncover the 'rich queer imaginary' in ancient civilizations that 'has been all but lost to modern thought'.[16] In the same vein, some go as far back as human prehistory to claim early, very early, sightings of queer identity. 'A possible example of homosexual eroticism in the art of the European Mesolithic might be a drawing found in the cave of Addaura in Sicily,' asserts a commentary on 'The Queer History of Art'.[17] In the current presentist climate, the mere mention of the term 'possible' almost seamlessly turns into 'probable', before it mutates into an 'historic fact'. In this way, the Mesolithic Age (10,000 BC–8,000 BC) is updated to fall in line with the outlook of 21st-century queer ideology.

Any analysis that does not attend to the historical dimension of the ascendancy of identity rhetoric will fail to capture those underlying cultural, social, and political trends that have sustained its growing influence. This point was appreciated by Eric Hobsbawm, who sought to specify the historical emergence of identity as a political issue in its own right. Taking a long view of this development, he explained that 'until the 1960s', the 'problems of uncertain identity were confined to special border zones of politics'.[18] Although the politicization of identity has its origins in the 1960s, the term itself only acquired usage in the 1970s.

The Nexis database of newspaper and periodical sources gives an interesting insight into the genealogy of the usage of the term 'identity politics'. The first reference to this specific term was in a news story from *The New York Times* on 24 June 1990.[19] By this time, although the term 'identity politics' was widely used on campuses and by political activists, it had not yet acquired a noticeable presence in mainstream public life. There were 8 references to it in 1992 and 25 the year after. In 1995, the number rose to 143. In 2000, there were 331 hits for identity politics, rising to 1,140 in 2010. From this point onwards, there was a steady year-on-year increase to 8,923 in 2017, after which the number exploded further.

The politicization of identity was in the first instance a response to society's struggle to endow people's identity with meaning. This development was eloquently explained by the sociologist Peter Berger and his collaborators in their classic study *The Homeless Mind* (1974). The authors of this text drew attention to the weakening of what they characterized as the 'identity-defining powers of institutions'. Their emphasis on the difficulty that society's institutions had in providing norms and values through which individuals could lend meaning to their personal values drew attention to what would – with the passing of time – turn into one of the greatest problems facing public life. At the time, they wrote:

> Stable identities (and this also means identities that will be subjectively plausible) can only emerge in reciprocity with stable social contexts. Therefore, there is a deep uncertainty about contemporary identity. Put differently, there is a built-in identity crisis in the contemporary situation.[20]

Half a century later, the 'deep uncertainty' about identity to which they referred has become a far greater source of conflict and tension than the authors could have imagined in the 1970s. Experience shows that it is easier to dethrone the authority of traditional identities than to forge new ones that possess the same weight and status. In a fragmented and destabilized landscape, uncertainty about identity becomes a source of conflict and is one of the main drivers of the War Against the Past.

Homelessness

The phenomenon of uprootedness implied by the metaphor of 'homelessness' refers to the unravelling of the threads that connect people to the generations that preceded them. The past is consequential for the affirmation of identity. The sense of historical continuity plays an important role in the constitution of the self. Understanding where we come from influences and strengthens individuals' sense of who they are. A feeling of continuity with the experience of previous generations lends stability to a people's identity. Continuity across time is mediated through the intergenerational transmission of a community's way of life and its ideals. As we note in chapter 7, the success of this transmission depends on the effectiveness of the prevailing regime of socialization and the institutions through which it is enacted.

It is difficult to develop a sturdy sense of collective identity without a shared memory and a common attachment to conventions or customs that are rooted in the past. Collective identities are intergenerational accomplishments that are cultivated through the absorption of a common cultural inheritance. For socialization to occur successfully, adults draw on the experience of previous generations to provide young people with a meaningful account of adulthood. Erikson remarked that the values with which children are trained 'persist because the cultural ethos continues to consider them "natural" and does not admit of alternatives'. He observed that:

> They persist because they have become an essential part of the individual's sense of identity, which he must preserve as a core of sanity and efficiency. But values do not persist unless they work, economically, psychologically, and spiritually; and I argue that to this end they must continue to be anchored, generation after generation, in early child training; while child training, to

> remain consistent, must be embedded in a system of continued economic and cultural synthesis.[21]

The socialization of children is key to the transmission of this legacy of the past. It is integral to an intergenerational transaction whereby moral norms are communicated by authoritative adults to the young.

Although adulthood and childhood are often discussed as separate and stand-alone concepts, they exist and thrive as part of an intergenerational community where their relationship exists in a common web of meaning. Because both adults and children see themselves as heirs to a common past, adults are able to transfer to the young the cultural resources that they will need to make their way in this world. Through this generational continuity – one that is as much cultural as biological – the organic relationship between a community's present and past is reproduced and reinforced.

Once the moral status of the past is put into question, the achievement of a stable identity becomes fraught with uncertainty. The de-authorization of the past renders the experiences of the older generations redundant. Adulthood becomes compromised by its association with the past, and instead of being able to serve as a model to the young, it ceases to effectively serve that role. Erikson's reference to the 'collective sense of identity' which adults communicate to young people has as its premise the capacity of the older generation to communicate a model of identity to their offspring. However, with the loss of the 'sense of the past', cultural continuity has become disrupted and the capacity of adults to serve as models to the young has diminished.[22]

Cultural continuity is reproduced through community rituals and symbols and narratives that focus on common origins and belonging. In the modern world, the task of ensuring the meaning of such continuity is mainly assigned to family and schools. It is through the education of young people that cultural continuity gains salience. That is why one of the goals of education is the preservation of the sense of the past.

Education needs to conserve the past. Political philosopher Hannah Arendt was unequivocal on this point. 'To avoid misunderstanding: it seems to me that conservatism, in the sense of conservation, is of the essence of the educational activity,' she argued.[23] Arendt's objective to conserve the legacy of the past was not for the sake of nostalgia but because the conservation of the old provided the foundation for renewal and innovation.

The characterization of conservation as the essence of educational activity can be easily misunderstood as motivated by a backward or reactionary political agenda. But the argument for conservation is based on the understanding that, in a generational transaction, adults must assume responsibility for the world as it is and pass on its cultural and intellectual legacy to young people. An attitude of conservation is called for specifically in the context of intergenerational transmission. Until recently, leading thinkers from across the ideological divide understood the significance of transmitting the knowledge and the values of the past to young people. Antonio Gramsci, the Italian Marxist thinker, wrote in one of his *Prison Notebooks*, 'It is believed that the child's mind is like a ball of string which the teacher helps to unwind. In reality, each generation educates the new generation, i.e. forms it.'[24] He assumed that young people's experience of life is insufficient to grasp the workings of the world. They require the assistance of the older generations to gain their bearings.

Writing from a conservative perspective, the English philosopher Michael Oakeshott concluded, 'Education in its most general significance may be recognized as a specific transaction which may go on between the generations of human beings in which newcomers to the scene are initiated into the world they inhabit.' Oakeshott went on to call it a 'moral transaction', one 'upon which a recognizably human life depends for its continuance'.[25]

This socialization of young people through the intergenerational transmission of the legacy of the past forges connections between members of society. It provides young people with the cultural and moral resources necessary to make their way in the world and gain strength from the experience of their elders. A 16-year-old boy who knows that his uncle and grandfather served in the navy has a model of duty available to him even if he doesn't join up when he comes of age. A girl whose mother commits herself to environmental activism grows up oriented towards valuing the planet. This is more than school-acquired knowledge; it is fundamental to the adulthood that children and teenagers envision as they get older. The stories that children hear from their parents, relatives, and neighbours help them to understand who they are, how they are expected to behave in response to the challenges of everyday life, and what kind of person they will be. Through this intergenerational dialogue, the experience of the past is both tested and revitalized.

But during the past century, this natural process of generational transmission has been stymied. Western societies have found it increasingly difficult to socialize young people into the values of the previous generations. In the face of society's estrangement from the past, older generations have lost confidence in the values into which they were acculturated. As things now stand, Western society is estranged from the values that inspired it in previous centuries. It no longer provides adults with a compelling narrative for socialization. And without a compelling narrative, socialization ceases to be an effective medium for ensuring that children are provided with a stable sense of identity. That is why young people find it difficult to resolve their crisis of identity. The unprecedented significance that society attaches to identity serves as an indirect statement about the difficulty of acquiring a meaningful sense of who you are.

The dramatic ascendancy of identity and the prominent role it assumed in public life in the 1970s has served as an invitation to its politicization. This development became codified with the slogan 'the personal is political'. Carol Hanisch's 1969 essay with that title resonated with the mood of the times.[26] The rhetoric of 'the personal is political' and the attachment of the term 'political' to the emotional needs of the self were not simply confined to an individual quest for esteem and recognition. This sentiment was quickly assimilated into group identity. Identities based on wider affiliations, such as those of race, gender, ethnicity, and community, came to be represented through the language of feelings.

This merging of individual identity with that provided by a group would from the 1970s onwards become a key site not only for political affiliation but also for conflict. Since that point, the identities that matter are those between groups rather than between individuals. Individuals tend to be conceptually flattened out once they personify a group identity. Once these differences are politicized, group identities tend to become absolutized.

The tendency to associate the realization of individual identity with the recognition of group grievances has unleashed a constant demand for the affirmation of new group identities. Individuals and groups who have deliberately invented their own cultural identity, rather than acquired it unconsciously through a lifetime of growing up, seem to require constant validation. It is not good enough to celebrate a particular identity occasionally, they need continuous cultivation and recognition through institutional practices and rituals of recognition.

Since the very obsession with identity is a symptom of insecurity, the quest for its validation is a never-ending one. That is why the preoccupation with group injury has acquired an unrestrained, irrational, and often aggressive form.

Once identity became politicized, it was only a matter of time before the past became a terrain on which its disputes were fought out. That is why the War Against the Past is so intimately linked to the politics of identity.

Until recently, the key motif in the rewriting of history was the desire to promote the unique qualities of a particular people or culture. National myths were about heroic deeds and glorious events. Such myths were not simply used as sentimental celebrations of the past. They were mobilized to construct a positive vision of the future. The myth of the American frontier promised a great destiny for that society. British, French, and German national myths were mobilized to provide an optimistic representation of future possibilities. Today, the rewriting of history is driven by a very different impulse. The manipulation of collective memory makes no grand claims on the future; rather, the current version of historic memory serves as a monument to a people's historic suffering. In a perceptive contribution on this subject, Ian Buruma has drawn attention to the tendency of many identity groups 'to define themselves as historic victims'.[27] This reorientation towards a preoccupation with past suffering provides a form of collective therapy that leads to a never-ending search for historical injustices. As Martin Gurri explains, identity politics 'can thrive only so long as injustice advances'.[28] From this standpoint, an injustice can never be put right, which is why the quest for identity leads its practitioners to find new ways of foregrounding their claims of being victims of the past.

Using history to invalidate competing identities

The quest for the validation of the past exists in a symbiotic relationship with its invalidation. In the early stage of identity politics, its focus was on gaining validation and recognition through the imaginative reinterpretation of the past. The 1970s saw a proliferation of projects promoting women's history, black history, and queer history. While these projects were critical of mainstream history and expressed resentment at being excluded from it, their main goal was to use the past to legitimate their identity. They claimed to reclaim their past to take their rightful place on the stage of history. Published in 1977, Sheila Rowbotham's *Hidden From History: 300 Years of Women's Oppression and the Fight Against It* offered an early example of this approach.

From the late 1980s onwards, the hidden-from-history approach gave way to one that was at least as interested in invalidating the identity of its opponents as in reclaiming its own. Since the turn of the 21st century, the emphasis has shifted further to the point that identity politics has become thoroughly invested in the invalidation of the identity of its opponents. This ambition is most systematically and effectively pursued by the decolonization movement. Its campaign of invalidating so-called 'whiteness' and Western identity has been remarkably successful.

The most interesting feature of the ascendancy of decolonization is its reception by the media and cultural establishment as well as the corporate world. Their willingness to positively embrace Black Lives Matter ideology was demonstrated by an enthusiastic willingness to reject the values and identities of their forebears. It is evident that the success of the decolonization movement is underwritten by the willingness of the corporate and cultural elites of Western societies to wholeheartedly embrace its rhetoric and objectives.

As we noted previously, the main forces behind the War Against the Past are not the identity groups committed to the ripping apart of the legacy of Western culture. The political and cultural elites of the West have been more than just willing collaborators in this enterprise. Ever since the cultural turn of the 1970s, they have acquiesced to the countercultural norms of the 1960s, and since the turn of the 21st century, they have zealously adopted them as their own. As I argue in my study *100 Years of Identity Crisis* (2021), their technocratic orientation towards social engineering has merged with the politics of cultural identity.[29]

The speed with which the dominant institutions of Western societies have enthusiastically adopted the project of stigmatizing their own past and invalidating the identities associated with it has been astonishing.

The leaders of the cultural and corporate world have self-consciously distanced themselves from the traditions associated with the past. Corporations are now in the forefront of adopting a form of 'diversity and inclusion' agenda that explicitly rejects the so-called 'outdated ideas' of the past. Those in their ranks who bucked this trend and continued to support traditional marriage were treated as outcasts.[30] It is now commonplace for Anglo-American institutions to launch highly publicized surveys into their past to discover historic misdeeds such as links with slavery. The proliferation of rainbow flags hanging over their buildings indicates their preference over symbols of nation and tradition.

Elite institutions – especially in the cultural and intellectual sphere – are in the forefront of the project of invalidating the traditional image that the West had of itself. Plundering the past with the view to invalidating the identity of Britishness is now widely practised by institutions that have previously sought to preserve and uphold it. Take the example of the National Trust. Founded in 1895, this organization for heritage conservation in England, Wales, and Northern Ireland has recently committed itself to challenging the traditional memory of this heritage. Instead of conserving, it has decided to invalidate important dimensions of this heritage. Its report 'Connections between Colonialism and Properties Now in the Care of the National Trust, Including Links with Slavery' is typical of the 'let's turn the past into a story of shame' approach.

Although this report is ostensibly about the historical association of heritage sites with colonialism and slavery, its main accomplishment is to call into question the legitimacy of British identity. Its interpretation of the past highlights slavery and colonialism as the dominant influence on the heritage it is meant to conserve. As the authors of this report explain:

> The National Trust has made a commitment to research, interpret and share the histories of slavery and the legacies of colonialism at the places we care for. Those histories are deeply interwoven into the material fabric of the British Isles; a significant number of the collections, houses, gardens and parklands in our care were created or remodelled as expressions of the taste and wealth, as well as power and privilege, that derived from colonial connections and in some cases from the trade in enslaved people. We believe that only by honestly and openly acknowledging and sharing those stories can we do

> justice to the true complexity of past, present and future, and the sometimes-uncomfortable role that Britain, and Britons, have played in global history since the sixteenth century or even earlier.[31]

The reference to 'even earlier' is interesting for it indicates that by casting its net so wide as to encompass the pre-16th-century era, the authors have decided to apply the decolonization narrative to an age that preceded British colonialism.

Anyone reading the report will readily conclude that the reference to 'the sometimes-uncomfortable role' played by Britain works as a euphemism. In the report, Britain comes across as the villain of the modern era. That is why a correspondent from Reuters responded to the report with the headline 'Revealed: The Darkness behind the Beauty of Britain's Great Houses'.[32] Almost seamlessly, the great architectural achievements of the previous centuries become tainted by the ugliness of Britain's history.

After outlining the numerous links of heritage sites with colonialism, the National Trust's report notes that its findings should not come as a surprise 'as the practice of enslaving African people was a fundamental part of the British economy in the late seventeenth, eighteenth and early nineteenth centuries'. It asserts that 'the oppression and violence of the slave trade and the legacies of colonialism have played' a central role 'in the making of modern Britain'. The authors' stated aim is to 'make us question our assumptions about the past'. This phrase is a euphemism for communicating the report's aim of guilt-tripping British people for the sins of their forebears.

The questioning of assumptions about the past or indeed any feature of human experience is important for a society that is open to new ideas. However, there is a world of difference between supporting critical thought and advancing didacticism. The report does not raise questions but closes down discussion in offering a view of the past that presents many great buildings in the care of the National Trust as the products of a history of shame.

The report's version of the past is anything but neutral. Undoubtedly, colonialism and the Empire played a significant role in the development of British society. But the assertion that this role is central to British modernity is at the very least a matter of dispute. Such an interpretation overlooks Britain's agrarian revolution, the development of its science and technology, the Industrial Revolution, and this society's relatively forward-looking legal, social, and cultural ideals and norms in the shaping of modern Britain.

The report claims to offer a disinterested story of the past, declaring that 'as a heritage charity, it's our responsibility to make sure we are historically accurate and academically robust when we talk about places and collections in our care'. However, the report did not emerge in response to a disinterested scholarly fascination with the stories behind the great buildings in the care of the National Trust. Nor was it provoked by questions and problems that were internal to its collection. Rather, it responds to a cultural climate in which institutions are expected to subject their collection to a political critique. Instead of acknowledging this, the National Trust dishonestly pretends that the report is merely motivated by public service, claiming that it was 'not intended to make judgments about the past' but is 'presenting information based on research allowing people to explore and draw conclusions for themselves'.[33]

However, readers can be left in no doubt that the report is all about judging the past, finding it guilty, and casting it in a negative light. Take the example of its treatment of Winston Churchill's former home, Chartwell, in Kent, which is one of the properties in the National Trust's care. It is difficult to avoid the conclusion that the purpose of the report's account of Chartwell is to discredit the reputation of Churchill. It is worth citing at length its tendentious and highly selective account of him:

> Sir Winston Churchill (1874–1965), whose family home is Chartwell (NT), served as Secretary of State for the Colonies from 1921 to 1922. He was Prime Minister during the devastating Bengal Famine of 1943, the British response to which has been heavily criticised. Churchill opposed the Government of India Act in 1935, which granted India a degree of self-governance. On 1 July 1947, he wrote to Prime Minister Clement Attlee (1883–1967), arguing that India should not gain independence.

The Churchill portrayed in this account is that of a mean-spirited politician with no redeeming features. Nothing is said of his inspiring leadership and positive deeds, only his misdeeds. In effect, an iconic statesman, who is regarded as one of the most celebrated figures of modern British history, is cast in the role of a heartless and nasty imperialist. Inevitably, the identity and values that he personifies are also morally invalidated.

It is entirely legitimate to point out that Churchill was an ardent imperialist and draw attention to his shortcomings. However, the report provides no historical guidance that situates him in the context of his time. Anyone who has no knowledge of British history could easily conclude that he was just one of many prime ministers with an interest in colonial affairs. His unique role during the Second World War is overlooked, as is the fact that he inspired the Western world with his defence of freedom against Nazi aggression. This attempt to decolonize Churchill and his reputation has little to do with encouraging people to think critically about their war-time Prime Minister and a lot to do with the ideological project of delegitimizing the identity of a national leader most identified with Britishness.

If institutions charged with conserving Britain's heritage can casually disparage the reputation of one of this nation's greatest leaders, it is no surprise that activists in the business of invalidating the identity of Britishness believe that their day has come. Insanely, a man who famously stood up to Hitler and played a key role in Nazi Germany's defeat has been denounced as a Nazi by supporters of the Black Lives Matter movement.

In November 2021, visitors to the London's Imperial War Museum were taken aback by the performance by a group of teenagers of a rap condemning Churchill. The performance, which occurred on Remembrance Sunday, concluded with a speech that attacked the way that Britain remembers its war dead. During the performance, one girl shouted:

> Why, when some remember, do they see the same faces, the white faces from western places. This was the Second World War, yet how many remember that it wasn't only Churchill who fought. The same man who had a hand in famine in 1943, wiping out three million Bengalis, denial, displacement, malnutrition, starvation, without any apologies.[34]

In a similar manner, Mohammed Hijab, a Muslim philosopher, denounced Churchill as a war criminal on a television discussion in November 2023 on the war between Israel and Hamas.[35]

The project of transforming Churchill the war hero into Churchill the war criminal is not simply directed at dishonouring the reputation of one man. It is also about striking a blow against a man who personifies the identity of Britishness. Churchill and Britain's role during the Second World War are understandable sources of national pride. This war-time leader's reputation reflects well on Britain's global image. That is why the take-down of Churchill performed at the Imperial War Museum was principally about discrediting someone who remains a source of pride in Britain's past.

The targeting of Britishness through soiling the reputation of historical figures that personify its heritage is not confined to Churchill. As discussed in chapter 4, Shakespeare, too, has been put into the frame of 'Great British Historical Figures to be De-mystified'. Elizabeth Winkler's book *Shakespeare Was a Woman and Other Heresies: How Doubting the Bard Became the Biggest Taboo in Literature* (2023) aims to uncover the 'real Shakespeare'. The conceit of this book is that because Shakespeare's reputation is fiercely protected by a coterie of critics committed to upholding his unique status, it is time to raise serious doubts about the very existence of the Bard.

According to a favourable review of Winkler's book, questioning the reputation of Shakespeare is 'perhaps the final blasphemy of British culture'.[36] The aim of representing the questioning of Shakespeare's authorship as a form of heresy is to suggest that the defenders of this playwright are principally concerned with preserving the national identity that he personifies. Winkler's interview with the actor and former artistic director of Shakespeare's Globe, Mark Rylance, and his wife, Claire van Kampen, a director and playwright, is illustrative of the tendency to represent the defence of Shakespeare's authorship as an expression of nationalist anxiety. Van Kampen is in no doubt that what is at stake is the association of Shakespeare with Britishness. She told Winkler:

> You can see this with the whole Brexit thing and how powerful people's emotions are about having a British identity. Shakespeare is up there as embodying an idea of something like the heart of Britishness. If you take that away, what is there?[37]

From this perspective, Shakespeare ceases to be one of the greatest figures of Western civilization with universal appeal and becomes a mythical figure who is desperately celebrated by simplistic Brexiteers in search of an identity. Discredit this myth and British identity becomes fatally undermined – after all 'what is there'?

It is entirely legitimate to question the authenticity of Shakespeare's authorship of the numerous plays that he wrote. Indeed, many have done so, and in spite of the claim that it is taboo, the status of these plays is energetically discussed and disputed by scholars. Similar questions have been raised about numerous great literary figures such as Homer and his authorship of the *Iliad* and the *Odyssey*. The aim of serious literary scholarship is to engage with the text and with its historical and cultural context. That is not the approach adopted by some contemporary critics of Shakespeare. They are often devoted to the presentist project of taking down a cultural icon who serves as a source of national pride.

At times, the targeting of Britain's past acquires the character of a caricature. At Cambridge University, some historians seem committed to discrediting the identity of the different nations that constitute Britain by calling into question their sense of the past. Cambridge's Department of Anglo-Saxon, Norse, and Celtic (ASNC) seeks to 'dismantle the basis of myths of nationalism' by asserting the novel and baseless idea that the Anglo-Saxons were not a distinct ethnic group.[38]

According to ASNC, 'There were never "coherent" Scottish, Irish and Welsh ethnic identities with ancient roots.' However, what drives the department's attempt to eliminate Anglo-Saxon origins has little to do with a new historical discovery about ancient roots in the past but is concerned with political ideology Its dislike of the term 'Anglo-Saxon' is linked to its allegation that it is used to support 'racist' claims regarding a native English identity.

The influence that identity politics exercises over the teaching of history is evidenced in a decision in 2019 by the International Society of Anglo-Saxonists to change its name to the International Society for the Study of Early Medieval England 'in recognition of the problematic connotations that are widely associated with the terms "Anglo-Saxon"'. This change followed Canadian academic Mary Rambaran-Olm's resignation from the society. She later condemned the field as one of 'inherent whiteness'. 'The Anglo-Saxon myth perpetuates a false idea of what it means to be "native" to Britain,' she wrote in the *Smithsonian* magazine. She is hostile to the term 'Anglo-Saxon' because she believes that it evokes 'an imagined medieval past that justifies beliefs in white, Western superiority'.[39]

No doubt a particular version of the past can be used to justify racist ideals. But the objective of Cambridge's suppression of the term is to 'dismantle' what it considers to be 'the basis of myths of nationalism' and invalidating the identities founded on it. Whatever the opinion of some Cambridge scholars, from the 8th century onwards, Anglo-Saxons were an integral part of Britain's past. Inevitably, the early medieval era saw the rise of numerous myths about the origins of communities, and many of those myths remain part of Britain's national stories. Myths are based on tradition and offer a narrative for linking human experience to the past. To be sure, there are numerous Anglo-Saxon myths, but the existence of this people is not a myth.

For those motivated to invalidate the image that the West has of itself, there is no better place to start than in ancient Greece. Classical Greece is regarded as the cradle of Western civilization. The culture of the West and its understanding of itself draw on the ideas developed in Greece in the field of politics, philosophy, science, and art. That is why critics of Western civilization invariably subject Greece to a critique that seeks to downgrade its achievements.

The archaeology course 0325 at Brown University titled 'Dead White Guys: Greco-Roman Civilization and American Identity' is an illustration of this. The course guide indicates that its main interest is to explore why Classical antiquity is regarded as the foundation of Western civilization and of American identity. It states:

> Why does Classical antiquity matter? How did a group defined as white and European come to represent America's ancestors? And by emphasizing this 'heritage', who do we exclude? This course turns an analytical eye on the continued appeal of the cultures of Ancient Greece and Rome, and the ways they are used to define America's past, serving as the foundation of 'Western Civilization'.[40]

The mission of this undergraduate course is to question the foundation of Western civilization. The questions posed in the course guide (and cited above) are relatively restrained compared to the denunciations made by others about civilizational claims made on behalf of the West.

The verdict of one journalist is that 'the words "western civilisation" denote a racist colonial project to crush, change, enslave, eradicate or genocidally erase other cultures'.[41] Thomas Patterson's book *Inventing Western Civilization* (1997) regards the civilizational identities as elitist, male, white, and racist. Athens stands condemned for inventing the idea of a barbarian whom it regarded as morally inferior to its citizens.

Ancient Athens is denounced for its oppressive attitude towards women. Patterson observes that 'new hierarchically organized gender relations also emerged in Athens during the fifth century as the traditional male leaders of the local communities sought to retain their authority and maintain the integrity of the community against the incursions of the state'.[42] This implies that women in Athens were subjected to a far harsher regime of oppressions than elsewhere, yet, with the possible exception of Sparta, a sexual hierarchy prevailed throughout the ancient world, and in this respect the record of Athens is unremarkable. Patterson also claims that 'Aristotle expressed fear of diversity in his *Politics*'.[43]

From this standpoint, one of the fathers of Western philosophy turns into a sexist and racist apologist for slavery. By the time Patterson finishes his grim account of Athens, there is little left of the spectacular achievements of this democratic city-state. Even its discovery of democracy is decried because of the prevalence of slavery. Patterson informs his readers that 'by the mid-fourth century BC, democratic Athens was perhaps the major slave-owning state in the eastern Mediterranean'.[44] His association of democracy with slavery is an explicit attempt to delegitimize Athens's reputation for political enlightenment.

Typically, contemporary critics of Greek civilization dwell on the shortcomings of Athenian democracy rather than its achievements. The Greeks are condemned for their ethnocentrism, for practising slavery, and for oppressing women. Why? Because the downsizing of Greek civilization serves to deprive Western identity of one of its most precious cultural legacies.

Identitarians in search of historic injustices in the ancient world have turned the legacy of ancient Greece and Rome into a horror show. A recently published collection, *Toxic Masculinity in the Ancient World* (2023), edited by Melanie Racette-Campbell and Aven McMaster, shows the remarkable convergence of moral anachronism with the politics of identity. The publisher claims that the influence of these toxic civilizations is 'invoked in the construction of toxic masculinity today'.[45]

Spoiling white identity

One point that is often overlooked is that identity politics involves not just the celebration of some identities but also the spoiling of others. In his classic study *Stigma* (2009 [1963]), the sociologist Eric Goffman developed the concept of a 'spoiled identity' to refer to identities that lack any redeeming moral qualities. It is an identity that invites stigma and scorn. In the contemporary era, 'whiteness' provides a paradigmatic example of a spoiled identity.

It is important to note that the very identity of 'whiteness' is not about the sensibility of being white. Nor is it even about the consciousness of white supremacy as expressed by the poet Rudyard Kipling in his 1899 poem 'White Man's Burden'. The category 'whiteness' is the invention of critics who aim to eternalize and naturalize this identity. As an identity, whiteness was invented through the racialization of Western history and the arguments provided by Critical Race Theory.

Critical Race Theory, with its emphasis on White Privilege and Whiteness, serves to indict an entire race of people for their supposed historical complicity in acts of racial oppression. Through the eternalization of white racism, Critical Race Theory has sought to morally devalue those possessing a white skin. It invented the concept of whiteness to attribute a negative moral connotation to those it brands with this sin. Almost effortlessly, the moral devaluation of whiteness has entered the mainstream of society. Hence the growing usage of the terms like 'too white'. In the jargon of the Western elites, 'too white' serves as a synonym for words like 'unpleasant', 'problematic', 'repulsive', or 'toxic'.

Tom Perez, the American Democratic Party's National Chairman, expressed this clearly when he claimed that New Hampshire was 'too white' to have the first primary for the election of a president. He also claimed that Iowa was 'too white' to have the first caucus during the election campaign.[46] According to *The New Republic*, the American Department of Justice is 'too white'.[47] Similarly, a survey of minority businesses in the United States concludes that local chambers of commerce are 'too white',[48] and the same accusation has been levelled at disaster management[49] and American TV.[50]

Television in the UK has also come under scrutiny. When the comedian Lenny Henry observed that it was 'too white',[51] a former head of comedy at the BBC agreed, suggesting that the broadcaster would not commission the iconic *Monty Python* today because of this.[52] There are claims that the UK's green sector is also 'too white'. Former head of Friends of the Earth Craig Bennett insisted that his sector is 'too white' and must leave behind its 'white middle-class ghetto'.[53] Even Extinction Rebellion is indicted for being 'too white, too middle class and lacking in empathy'.[54]

The sense of outrage conveyed by the term 'too white' can attach itself to the most unexpected of targets. Apparently 'dyslexia heroes are too white'![55] Numerous sources insist that classical music is 'too white'.[56] One frequently hears the claim that philosophy is too white. Some would even want to cancel some of the most important philosophers, like Plato and Kant, because they are too white.[57] In fact, virtually every university discipline – from music to mathematics through to history[58] – has been condemned for being 'too white'. Leicester University, meanwhile, announced that it would be dropping Chaucer in favour of modules on race and sexuality.[59]

The current obsession with the identity of whiteness and white privilege is often projected backwards, leading to the racialization of the past. The racialization of the past often vents its fury at the influence of that very strange contemporary phenomenon 'The Dead White Men'. Like the term 'too white', the expression Dead White Men is used to signal condemnation and disapproval of major figures from the past. They are perceived as individuals who personify a past which contemporary commentators perceive as best left behind. At the very least, the use of the term 'White Man' invites a reaction of disapproval. So, when Professor Sarah Maddison of the University of Melbourne stated, 'As Australia publicly struggles once again with the contemporary legacy of our brutal colonial history, we need to ask ourselves, are the white men we choose to commemorate the people we truly want to celebrate?'[60] the response was a resounding NO!

It is remarkable the speed and the ease with which the phrase 'Dead White Men' has become a widely used colloquial term signifying moral disapproval. Ending the hegemony of Dead White Men over contemporary cultural and intellectual life is widely endorsed by public and private institutions. One of its companion terms, 'pale, male, and stale', reinforces the conviction that organizations should put an end to the power of Living White Men, especially if they are middle aged.[61] In a sneering tone, the UK's 'first transgender investment chief' declared that finance is 'pale, male and stale'.[62] 'Pale, male, stale and clueless, why we should send travel TV presenters into exile,' declares train travel expert Monisha Rajesh.[63] The moral devaluation of the identity of the pale white male was in full display in the Irish Parliament during the aftermath of an outburst of violent protest against mass migration in November 2023. Numerous legislators decried their privileged white identity. Ivana Bacik, the leader of the Labour Party, complained that the Parliament looked 'very male, very stale and pale'. Her sentiment was echoed by her party colleague Aodhán Ó Ríordán, whose denunciation of white privilege came across as a consummate performance of self-loathing. He recalled the 'very dull, white, pasty Ireland'[64] that he grew up in, self-consciously lashing out against his country's past on the grounds that it was too white.

The widespread usage of the term 'pale, male, and stale' serves as testimony of the ease with which the identity of the white man was spoiled. The association of white men with staleness offers a striking example of how a very unattractive identity can be constructed through the crusade against the past.

The spoiling of white identity has had a disproportionate impact on the way that Jewish identity is perceived and represented. In a fascinating account of this development, Pamela Paresky has coined the term of the 'Hyper-White Jew'.[65] Jews are often portrayed as a unique, hyper-white community who have far more privileges to check than others. Often this reaction against 'Jewish privilege' meshes with hostility to Israel to produce a unique 21st-century species of anti-Semitism. This is why even though victims are routinely celebrated today, the oppression of Jews and the experience of the Holocaust do not provide contemporary Jews with legitimate claims to victimhood. Indeed, the Holocaust is often turned *against* the Jews, with Israel depicted as the natural heir to Nazi Germany. That at least in some quarters Jewish people are regarded as a hyper-white community was on display in March 2021, on the BBC's flagship politics programme *Politics Live*, which featured a bizarre debate on the topic of whether or not Jews are an ethnic minority. Apparently, this was open to question because *some* Jews have reached positions of power and influence. Thus, at least for some, Jewish people have joined the ranks of the oppressors. From this perspective, Jewish privilege is but an extreme version of white privilege

The message communicated by *Politics Live* was that Jewish identity, that is, the way that Jews perceive themselves, should not be taken too seriously because they have little claim to the status of victimhood. In this instance, the historical experience of the oppression of Jews was overlooked and regarded as not a big deal in comparison to other people's experience of victimization. That the spoiling of Jewish identity has had enormous consequences was highlighted in the aftermath of the 7 October 2023 atrocities committed by Hamas against ordinary Israeli citizens. Numerous celebrities and cultural influencers appeared indifferent to the horrific acts of rape, hostage taking, and murder of children on that day. The American actress Susan Sarandon personified this callous sensibility. At a pro-Palestinian rally in November 2023, she told the crowd that those people who were feeling afraid of being Jewish right now were 'getting a taste of what it feels like to be a Muslim in this country, so often subjected to violence'.[66] Sarandon somehow clearly had no idea that Jews faced more than their share of violence in the past. The condition of social amnesia – discussed previously – comes to mind. More than any other instance of invalidating a people's historical identity, the response to 7 October demonstrated the disturbing consequence of the spoiling of Jewish identity.

Numerous identity-based groups adopted Sarandon's hostility towards the 'hyper-white' Jew. The #MeToo movement, which always springs into action to defend women facing violence, appeared to switch into silent mode in response to the scenes of barbaric violence against Jewish women. It appeared that for many feminist activists, the idea of sisterhood did not apply to Jewish women.[67] Some went so far as to deny what had happened. For example, a rape crisis centre at Canada's University of Alberta signed onto an open letter that asserted that calling Hamas terrorists was Islamophobic and denied that Israeli women were raped by Hamas.[68]

Validating identity

Invalidating some identities runs in parallel with validating others. The controversy surrounding Netflix's 2023 docudrama *Cleopatra* indicates that contemporary identities are heavily invested in how this ancient Egyptian monarch is perceived. When Netflix introduced Adele James, who is black, as Cleopatra, a debate broke out about the historical accuracy of the series. Egypt's Minister of Tourism and Antiquities, Zahi Hawass, took immediate offence and argued that Cleopatra 'had light skin' and Greek features. He insisted that Cleopatra 'was many things, and well deserving of having her story told to modern audiences, but one thing she most definitely was not was black'. Hawass accused Netflix of cultural identity theft and his reaction to the programme indicated that the dispute about Cleopatra's skin was an identity-related matter.[69] That the colour of Cleopatra's skin matters to members of the Egyptian government is not in doubt. However, it also matters to members of the African American community who feel that a black Cleopatra validates their identity. Shelley Haley, a retired professor of classics and Africana studies who took part in the show, recalled that her grandmother told her, 'I don't care what they tell you in school, Cleopatra was Black.'[70]

That the colour of a very ancient historical figure can matter so much to members of our society brings to the surface the role of the past in validating contemporary identity. Decades before the production of the series, the colour of Cleopatra's skin had already become a matter of controversy. In 1993, Shelley Haley suggested that 'white, mainly male authors concealed Cleopatra's true identity as a black woman'. She recalled that, 'I began to see and still am arriving at seeing that Cleopatra is the crystallization of the tension between my yearning to fit in among classicists and my identity politics.'[71] As noted previously, a politicized identity is constantly in search of recognition and often draws on historical injustices to validate itself. A story of white authors conspiring to conceal Cleopatra's skin colour and thereby depriving African Americans of a great role model is one that readily appeals to grievance archaeologists.

It was Haley's identity politics that stimulated her search for black role models in the ancient world and influenced how she represented the past. Haley wrote that

> when we say in general that, the ancient Egyptians were Black, and more specifically Cleopatra was Black, we claim them as part of a culture and history that has known oppression and triumph, exploitation and survival. ... Even as a 'Greco-Egyptian', Cleopatra was a product of miscegenation. How is she not Black?[72]

The very posing of this rhetorical question is significant because it indicates that the matter has been settled.

Validating identity through the imaginative rewriting of history is an integral component of 21st-century politicization of identity. The rebranding of Cleopatra as a black monarch is connected to a wider project of revising history so that an African Egypt rather than a European Greece serves as the cradle of ancient knowledge and civilization. Afro-centrist commentators wish to assert 'both African priority and Greek inferiority'.[73] Some of them have developed a theory that claims that the Greeks stole Egypt's intellectual heritage and claimed it as their own. According to Halford Fairchild, a professor of psychology and black studies at Pitzer College, the story of stolen legacy has a 'transforming effect' on African Americans. He observes that 'learning that the early Greek philosophers' did their 'most important research' in Africa 'empowers black people to reclaim their rightful place as equal players in contemporary society'.[74]

The claim that whites purloined black achievement is based on a story that asserts that Greek civilization was stolen from Africa. From this perspective, Aristotle is assigned the role of a thief. He is charged with robbing the library of Alexandria. As classicist Mary Lefkowitz explained, Afro-centrist supporters of the thesis of white theft seek to 'remove the ancient Greeks from the important role they have previously played in history, and to assign to the African civilization of Egypt the credit for the Greek's achievement'.[75]

Identity politics has no respect for temporal distinctions, and in a narcissistic manner uses the past to discover reflections of itself and its concerns and predicaments. It unthinkingly applies 21st-century racialized categories to the ancient era. From this perspective, the binary cultural and political contrast between black and white of our era and the prevailing racialized narrative acquire a timeless character. This approach requires overlooking historical distinctions and imposing concepts and categories to the ancient world which are alien to itself. Mary Lefkowitz and Guy MacLean Rogers argue against this anachronistic history and state 'that the attempt to assign the people of the Nile Valley to "Caucasoid" or "Negroid" categories is an arbitrary act and wholly devoid of historical or biological significance'. They continue:

> It would be inaccurate to describe the ancient Egyptians as either black or white; the population of ancient Egypt was one of mixed pigmentation. Essentially, the Egyptians were the Egyptians. To describe them otherwise promotes a misconception about the ancient Egyptians, with racist undertones, that reveals much more about those who wish to make such attempts than about the ancient Egyptians themselves.[76]

The impulse to draw on the distant past to validate a group's identity is normal and understandable. It is, however, regrettable when the people and cultures of the past are turned into an historical caricature. It is also regrettable that this story of supposed civilizational theft dispossesses ancient Greece of its important historical achievements.

In some instances, the drive to validate identity leads to the construction of a veritable fantasy representation of the past. Numerous racial entrepreneurs now argue that Britain was a black country a long time before white people arrived on its shores. The publication of the children's book titled *Brilliant Black British History* by the Nigerian-born British author Atinuke, asserts that 'every single British person comes from a migrant' but 'the very first Britons were black'. Turning history on its head, this reframing of the nation's past contends that Stonehenge was built by Black people, while Britain was a Black country. This book was highly praised by numerous cultural institutions, who all echoed its thesis. The Book Trust claimed that 'Britain was a black country for more than 7,000 years before white people came'.[77] A similar claim is asserted in a video titled 'Been Here from the Start', which portrays a black actor dressed as a caveman singing that 'for 10,000 British years some Brits have looked like me'.[78] The purpose of associating the origins of Britain and its people with the colour black is to validate and celebrate black identity in the 21st century.

Sweden, too, has been subjected to a campaign promoting the claim that black people or people with dark skin were the original inhabitants of this nation. The thesis of black Vikings is supported by what is best characterized as hypothetical history. Speculation about 'whether or not the Vikings intermingled with people from Africa' is justified on the grounds that while 'there is no concrete evidence of mixing', it is 'not impossible'.[79] The use of the word 'possible' constantly recurs in discussions about an African presence in Scandinavia. One commentator, for example, has noted that 'according to one theory, it is possible that some Africans were present in Scandinavia as part of the origins of the Scandinavian people who came from the Nile Valley region'.[80] This possibilistic orientation towards the rewriting of the past helps break down the boundary between historical facts and fantasy.

SVT, Sweden's national broadcaster, has invested heavily in the possibilistic representation of the nation's past. Its mega-series *Historien om Sverige* (*the History of Sweden*) is its biggest history investment ever. The clip advertising it shows early Nordic hunters lying in wait for their prey – played by Africans. There is nothing objectionable about black actors playing white characters, but the educational campaign promoted by SVT aims to make a political point about Swedish identity. In particular, it seeks to suggest that 'early Swedes did not in fact look anything like today's light-skinned Swedes but more like sub-Saharan Africans'.[81]

Every identity group has adopted the strategy of rediscovering itself in the most improbable of settings. There is now a discernible tendency on the part of educational and cultural institutions to rearrange the past in such a way that it responds to the demand for validation on the part of competing identity groups. The work of the Heritage Fund, responsible for the distribution of National Lottery Funds to voluntary organizations across the UK, is an example of this.

The Heritage Fund, in detailing its investment in LGBTQ+ heritage, explains that it makes it 'mandatory' that all projects it funds involve a 'wide range of people involved in heritage', and boasts that since 1994 'we've invested over £12million across the UK in sharing stories of LGBTQ+ (lesbian, gay, bisexual, transgender, queer and other identities) heritage, creativity, activism and much more'.[82] In short, this organization's funds are distributed according to the exigencies of identity politics.

As noted above, museums are often in the forefront of reorganizing the past to reflect the imperative of identity politics. The Pitt Rivers Museum in Oxford is devoted to 'queering and questioning' its collection. It has organized a project, 'Beyond the Binary', to demonstrate its solidarity with LGBT+ communities. The aim of the project is to legitimate LGBT+-related identities by endowing them with the authority of the past. One of its stated aims is to contest any notion that LGBT+ lives are a 'western' invention, a 'new trend', or that queer people do not have history.

To realize its objective of eternalizing LGBT+ identity, the Pitt Rivers Museum has decided to turn its collection into a resource for identity validation. According to a statement outlining this project, the 'museum's collections have been made available to communities with LGBTIAQ+ lived experiences to help them uncover and narrate their own stories, challenging the erasure of queer voices'.[83]

The imperative of providing LGBT+ communities with a history has led 'Beyond the Binary' to emulate the narrative of the decolonization movement. The authors of this project explicitly link its quest for a usable past that can be harnessed to support LGBT+ identity with colonialism. Out of nowhere, it links colonialism with the historical injustices perpetrated on LGBT+ communities. The statement outlining the project and its accompanying exhibition declares that the Pitt Rivers Museum 'is rooted in colonialism and some histories and voices have for too long been ignored, erased or omitted. We hope this exhibition is a positive step in tackling oppression, which LGBTIAQ+ communities often feel in spaces such as this one.'[84]

The 'Beyond the Binary' project plays fast and loose with its representation of the past. In its discussion on the organization of the exhibition, it notes that there are

> a range of historical and contemporary objects featuring well-known mythological and religious figures that can be used to tell LGBTIAQ+ stories. This includes figures that might not have been considered queer originally but have been claimed by the community. Creating this type of heritage is not a new practice. LGBTIAQ+ communities and individuals have always made connections with historical and fictional figures who reflect their identity.[85]

This statement is not simply about rewriting the past but also about reimagining it to create a storyline that supports its project. What are we to make of the reference to 'figures that might not have been considered queer originally but have been claimed by the community'? This retrospective attribution of queerness to historical and fictional figures turns the past into a hunting ground for its early traces. Since historical figures who are queered are not able to offer an account of themselves, the version offered by 21st-century activists cannot be challenged.

Take the case of Queen Elizabeth I, whose sexual preferences are the subject of constant speculation. One commentator asks,'Was she a lesbian?', before replying: 'The truth may never be known, but one thing is certain – Elizabeth was definitely not straight.' The commentator's certainty about the private life of one of England's greatest monarchs displays an arrogance that is truly breath-taking. When he asserts that 'whether or not Elizabeth was actually queer, she was certainly not straight',[86] he relies on language that would have been totally alien to the culture of the 16th century, when Elizabeth reigned. She would not have known the cultural connotation of either straight or queer. The words 'definitely not straight' reflect the imperious attitudes towards people in the past that resembles the Pitt Rivers Museum's assertion that LGBT+ identity can be attributed to whomever it chooses to include in its 'heritage'. There is violence in a language that imposes contemporary labels on people who because they have been dead for centuries cannot speak for themselves.

The retrospective assignment of a recently invented identity on historical figures is fast becoming an accepted practice within leading Western cultural institutions. Individuals who lived in the past and whose behaviour was unaffected by the politicization of their personal behaviour are often cast in the role of identity heroes by commentators who possess little sensitivity to the moral and cultural climate of former times. The high-handed assumption by cultural entrepreneurs that they can speak for the dead actually dispossesses historical figures of their agency.

The London-based National Gallery decided to use the gender-neutral pronoun 'they/them' to refer to an 18th-century French spy known as Chevalier d'Eon who apparently lived as a man for 49 years and a woman thereafter. The panel displaying portraits of Chevalier d'Eon states: 'We cannot be certain how d'Eon would have chosen to describe their gender as they had fewer options during their lifetime than we have today. We have chosen to use language available to modern audiences in this display.' In other words, the gallery decided that it possessed the authority to update the past and attribute to d'Eon an identity that would certainly had made no sense to this individual. It justified this act of anachronistic distortion by declaring that 'd'Eon's success and bravery in expressing their gender identity is remarkable for the late 18th century'.[87] Yet d'Eon would certainly not have understood the meaning of the concept of gender identity, and the attempt to portray the way this spy appeared in public as a blow for gender fluidity bears all the hallmarks of an arrogant presentism.

The retrospective reassignment of gender to people living in the 18th century may appear to be a harmless performative act. But the patronizing and unrestrained and yet casual manner with which the past is colonized is unprecedented. Even revolutionary movements in France, China, and the Soviet Union did not reinvent historical figures in their image. The Stalinist regime may have extolled the rising of slaves led by Spartacus but it refrained from portraying him as a would-be communist commissar.

In the heart of darkness

The grievance archaeology practised by culture warriors justifies their projects on the grounds that the past injustices they unearth are consequential for the lives of numerous identity groups today. The politicization of identity is often presented as part of a struggle to correct hitherto unrecognized wrongs and to allow people to express themselves through the lifeforms appropriate to their culture. Jürgen Habermas, a leading German social theorist, interprets these struggles as representing demands for the 'recognition of lifeforms and traditions which have been marginalized'.[88] However, this interpretation tends to read history backwards and overlooks the distinct features of contemporary claims for recognition by identity entrepreneurs. The demand for recognition has acquired its own imperative. Why? Because the diminishing capacity of contemporary institutions – formal and informal – to confer and affirm identity fuels the demand to be recognized.

The idea that past identities and injustices have been consciously hidden from history, waiting to be discovered and acknowledged, is premised on both an ahistorical and naïve conceptualization of the problem. Identities emerge through the practices and arrangement of community life. They are cultivated over time and not discovered through an archaeological excavation of the past. On the contrary, the project of excavating the past is itself motivated by the *a priori* perception of a problem that needs the validation of history. The sociologically naïve conviction that those who hitherto have lacked a voice centuries ago now possess a new willingness to talk and confront the past represents a form of collective self-flattery.

It is important to recall that the act of remembering represents an attempt to engage with the past through the idiom of the present. Concern with historical injustices is informed by the self-consciousness and cultural values of contemporary society. The historical quest for the validation of identity can never be entirely satisfied. The search for validation rarely provides long-term answers. The very search for validation is a symptom of an insecure and unconfident disposition which encourages a heightened sense of suspicion and sensitivity towards the behaviour of others. Identity entrepreneurs are easily slighted and interpret innocent acts of miscommunication or misrecognition as a serious insult to their identity. At the same time, identities based on being the victims of historical injustice and marginalization can never let go of the circumstances that gave rise to their predicament. That is why they so often cross over temporal boundaries to rejuvenate their identity by drawing on the injustices of the past.

Identities based on being the victim of past injustices easily become entrenched in the perpetuation of their condition of suffering. As the political theorist Wendy Brown argues, 'politicized identity' becomes 'attached to its own exclusion' because 'it is premised on this exclusion for its very existence as identity'.[89] That is why the recognition of a past wrong can never prove satisfactory for those who seek restitution. History can never be reversed, and an identity based on the experience of victimization, injustice, and trauma cannot be 'reconciled' to its fate without annihilating itself. Consequently, the demand for recognition of past injustice can never be effectively met. The War Against the Past must continue.

6

The Struggle to Control Language

Language has become an important site of cultural conflict. Various commentators have drawn attention to the emergence and institutionalization of the policing of language throughout society. Censorship coexists with a growing tendency to discredit words that have been integral to the traditional vocabulary. Numerous words have become the target of the language police on the grounds that they are 'problematic' or outdated. New words are invented constantly and unrelenting pressure is placed on the public to accept their use. The discussion on the politicization of language often overlooks one of the most important drivers of semantic engineering: that the assault on traditional language is closely linked to the War Against the Past. As words that meant something important to generations of people are declared null and void, then the capacity of communities to remember their past significance diminishes. They are quite literally rendered 'speechless'.

When words are declared to be unacceptable or outdated, the meaning that they expressed and communicated over the years becomes increasingly difficult to keep in mind. The forced transformation of the vocabulary implicitly calls into question the cultural values that the now delegitimized words expressed. When even a word like 'woman' is displaced by a gender-neutral term, an historically significant distinction between male and female can lose its salience. If unchecked, the ideologically motivated transformation of language will significantly consolidate the condition of social amnesia.

From the standpoint of identity politics, the language of the past communicates a set of assumptions that are antithetical to its view of the world. That is why since its inception the politicization of identity was often conducted through challenging linguistic conventions. Words such as 'female' are targeted because they do not fit into the worldview of trans ideology. A self-appointed language inspectorate continually warns people against using the word 'female' to refer to women. 'Stop calling women "females",' warns the headline of the *Daily Nexus*, the student newspaper of the University of California at Santa Barbara.[1] In case you have doubts about the necessity for ceasing to use this term, *BuzzFeed* offers '6 Reasons You Should Stop Referring To Women as "Females" Right Now'.[2] But before providing an explanation for excising the use of this word from the vocabulary of everyday life, readers are told: 'Simply put, it's rude and it's weird'! Most normal human beings who have used 'female' and 'woman' interchangeably throughout their lives would be surprised to discover that they had behaved rudely and weirdly. However, for the supporters of the crusade against traditional language, abolishing the usage of the word 'female' from everyday conversation is mandatory because they insist that 'not all women are biologically female', whereas when 'you use "woman", you include all people who identify as women'.[3] According to those opposing the usage of the word 'female' as a synonym for woman, 'not everyone who was born female is a woman, and not every woman was born female'.[4]

It appears that the reason why 'female' must go is because it does not fit in with the logic and outlook of trans activists. This word, which has been in constant usage since the 14th century, has, according to *The Oxford English Dictionary*, a self-evident meaning. It defines female as 'simply: a woman or girl'. The problem that trans activists have with female is that, as another definition offered by the *OED* explains, it refers to a 'person of the sex that can bear offspring: a woman or a girl'.[5] Since abolishing the traditional connection between women and the bearing of a child is one of the aims of trans activism, the word 'female' must give way to a gender-neutral alternative. A word whose first recorded usage was around 1350, and was presumably used and made sense to people for centuries before that, can now be summarily dismissed as rude and weird by supposedly enlightened commentators Theirs is not simply an intellectual argument against the use of the word 'female'. Nor do they merely exhort people to alter the use of this word but they also condemn all those people in the past who 'wrongly' used the word to refer to women. If the word 'female' is deemed discriminatory today, then presumably it also played the same role in the past.

Under the banner of promoting a new 'inclusive language', linguistic engineering seeks to change public language with a view to transforming prevailing cultural attitudes and norms. It does not merely police the use of language and censor and abolish words it finds objectionable, it also re-engineers the meaning of words and introduces terms that communicate its ideals and norms. In particular, it targets words that intrinsically reflect what it considers to be outdated human relationships. It is especially hostile towards classical kinship terminology – mother, father, grandfather, grandmother, sister, brother, wife, or husband – and seeks to replace it with a supposedly neutral-sounding terminology. In this way, the traditional normative status of kinship-related language becomes deprived of its cultural authority. As one commentator lectures his readers: 'Families have evolved. Now language must too.'[6]

Anti-traditional language strives to deprive intimate relationships of their unique normative status. Consequently, words like 'husband' and 'wife' no longer possess the cultural authority that they enjoyed five or six decades ago. In some instances, kinship terminology has become neutralized and so divested of its unique relational meaning. For example, in many UK hospitals, instead of relatives being referred to by their specific relationship (e.g. son, mother), all become 'carers' in an effort to extend inclusivity.

The significance of this development was brought home to me when my dying mother lay in our local hospital in 2007. It was at this moment that I realized that my relationship to her was now regarded as outdated. As soon as I heard that she had had a stroke, I went to see her at the hospital. Upon arrival, I introduced myself to the nurse with the words, 'I'm Frank Furedi, I'm Clara's son.' The woman looked up at me and said, 'Are you her "carer"?' 'No, her son,' I responded. But she was insistent: 'No, you are her carer.' I assumed at first this was to identify that I was responsible for her care. However, later a hospital administrator explained to me that they used the word 'carer' because it included all – apparently not every patient has a close relative to look after them. She claimed that they had a preference for 'carer' because it is a very inclusive word.

The word 'carer' may be inclusive, but if a special connection between mother and son is transformed into a bureaucratic typology, something very important has been lost. The relationship between patients and their family, friends, and paid professional help all involve care but convey fundamentally different meanings to the people concerned. Of course, people have every right to refer to themselves as carers, but so should everyone have the right to use an intimate kinship-based terminology to refer to themselves. The term 'partner', too, is inclusive, but it does not possess the same normative content as 'husband' and 'wife'. The use of a neutral and administratively informed language has the merit of not discriminating between different people and relationships. But the price we pay is that cultural sensitivity to the particularity conveyed by terminology that has evolved over the centuries is undermined and, in some cases, becomes lost.

Some of the most taken-for-granted, everyday expressions that relate to our family and community lives are now excluded from the new 'inclusive language guides'. Titles like 'mum' and 'dad', 'homeless', 'ladies' and 'gentlemen', 'ex-pat', and terms like 'deprived neighbourhoods', 'second generation', 'lifestyle choices', and 'economic migrant' are now deemed unacceptable by the authors of the *Inclusive Language Guide*, published by the Local Government Association (LGA) of England. As a 'positive' alternative to 'mum' or 'dad', the LGA suggests using 'birthing parent'.[7]

Even traditional institutions are prepared to delete from their discourse words that have been used for thousands of years. According to the Archbishop of York, Stephen Cottrell, the opening words of the Lord's Prayer, recited by Christians all over the world for 2,000 years, may be 'problematic' because of their patriarchal association. Consequently, he questions the use of the words 'Our Father', to avoid any association with abusive earthly fathers.[8]

The aim of language guides is not to explain the conventional usage and meaning of the vocabulary in currency. Its objective is to alter and re-engineer traditional vocabulary to distance society from its pre-existing use of language. By challenging traditional language usage, the meaning attached to it in the past is called into question and de-authorized. In this way, the words and the attitudes they reflect are disparaged and condemned. The linguistic assault on the language of the past has important implications for how society perceives itself since, as the philosopher John Locke explained, 'speech is the great bond that holds society together'. In his 'An Essay Concerning Human Understanding' (1689), Locke explained that it is through language that 'knowledge is conveyed from man to man and down the generations'.[9]

The words we use today have evolved through centuries – if not millennia – and through their use, they have helped people gain meaning about their place in the world. They have bound different generations together in a common language community. Locke was aware that the manipulation of language could be a serious problem, which is why he insisted that it should not be regarded as a form of private property. He wrote:

'For words, especially in languages already formed, are no man's private possession, but rather the common measure of commerce and communication, so no one is at liberty to please himself about what to mean by them.'[10] From Locke's standpoint, the use of specific words makes up a language that is underpinned by a semantic and moral compact between members of civil society.[11]

Locke's sentiments resonated with the widely held belief that a nation's elite should serve as the guardian of the language that had organically evolved through the experience of a community. The poet and philosopher Samuel Taylor Coleridge, who developed the concept of the Clerisy in the 19th century, saw language as a living phenomenon which was always in the process of becoming. His vision of a national Clerisy was underwritten by the belief that language was a civilizational accomplishment that required nurturing by the most gifted members of the elite. He wrote:

> The care of the national language I consider as at all times a sacred trust and a most important privilege of the higher orders of society. Every man of education should make it the object of his unceasing concern to preserve his language pure and entire, to speak it, so far as in his power, in all its beauty and perfection. . . . A nation which allows her language to go to ruin is parting with the last of her intellectual independence, and testifies her willingness to cease to exist.[12]

When it came to the task of preserving the national language, Coleridge was more idealistic and fervent than most. Nevertheless, a commitment to preserving the integrity of a received language and the cultural values associated with it was widely shared by the Victorian elites. Respect for a community's linguistic inheritance continued well into the 20th century. The new words and slangs that gained public usage emerged out of the experience of a community rather than from the heads of anti-traditionalist cultural elites.

Coleridge's Clerisy adopted an orientation towards language and culture which is the polar opposite to the practice of semantic engineering today. The Clerisy and successive generations of elites took seriously the authority of pre-existing linguistic conventions. They understood that language was a living phenomenon and accepted that new words would enter the vocabulary, but they did not see themselves as semantic engineers who were in the business of manufacturing new expressions and words. Very importantly, they were not in the business of policing language and forcing people to change their vocabulary.

The words used by members of a society signal what values and attitudes society deems to be important. The Culture Wars today are so intertwined with conflicts over words because language reflects the norms and beliefs that underpin culture. Of course, language is always changing, and so it should. But there is a fundamental difference between the spontaneous evolution of a community's vocabulary, one that is organic to its experience, and the external imposition of new words. The latter represents a political project designed to alter people's view of the world. Unlike the spontaneous evolution of language that is organic to the experience of a community, the new, politicized vocabulary relies on the artificial re-engineering of language.

Opponents of traditional language often use the term 'outdated' to refer to words and concepts that they find objectionable. The branding of a word or an expression in this way represents an implicit call for its invalidation. As we explain below, the term 'outdated' conveys a moral statement about the inferiority of the past. It is for that reason that the charge of being outdated frequently serves as a weapon in the struggle over language.

The moral pathology of the outdated

Terms like 'outdated' and 'old' are used to repudiate the past. As the historian J.C.D. Clark observed: 'Effective disparagements within popular American discourse are now the phrases "that's old" and "that's history".' He added: '"That's old" does not mean "that originated some time ago", but "that is vexatious". "That's history" does not mean "that is important because it has made us what we are"; it means "that it is laughably irrelevant to us".'[13]

The *OED* defines outdated as 'out-of-date, obsolete; old-fashioned, antiquated'.[14] It is still used this way in certain sectors, for example in supermarkets, where the use of this term conveys the meaning of a food product being out of date in the sense of beyond a date when it may be sold. However, in general usage, outdated is no longer used simply to characterize the age of an object. In recent times, its meaning has mutated from a term of description to a statement of condemnation. It is used to provide a negative framing of language, behaviour, and cultural practices from the past. From this perspective, outdated does not refer only to forms that have ceased to have relevance but also to their negative status. That is why the very coupling of 'outdated' with the attitudes and behaviour of older generations conveys the sense of moral and intellectual inferiority. In intergenerational discussions and arguments, the response to the views of older people is often the put-down statement 'They don't get it.' The implication of this phrase is that they don't get it because they are old and under the spell of views which, because they are 'outdated', are irrelevant and ought not be taken seriously. Instead, they can be legitimately vilified and condemned.

'Outdated' is invoked as a form of criticism of attitudes and language expressed by people. Its casual use as a term of condemnation has become mainstream in public discourse. Most people who use this term are not consciously making a statement about the past. However, the constant invocation of 'outdated' as a negative phenomenon serves as a reminder of the moral failings of the values and practices of people in the past. That it has become such a taken-for granted negative concept indicates how language itself has adapted to the moral devaluation of history.

The term 'outdated' is also used to discredit individuals and their behaviour. *The New York Times*' response to the death of Britain's Queen Elizabeth's was to adopt a pompous, sanctimonious tone and lecture the world about Britain's supposedly shameful past. In an essay titled 'Mourn the Queen, Not Her Empire', Harvard academic Maya Jasanoff reminded her readers not to be misled by Elizabeth's benevolent public persona. In her view, she was complicit in the 'bloody history' of imperial decolonization in the 1950s and 1960s. According to Jasanoff, the Queen's public reputation and moral authority obscured the truth and allowed Britain to retain its 'outdated fantasies' about its benevolent imperial past.[15]

The endowment of the concept 'outdated' with normative content is a recent phenomenon. And the current frequently used term 'outdated language' as a form of condemnation is also relatively new. A search of the Nexis database of newspaper publications in 2023 indicated that the current, morally charged usage of 'outdated language' was unknown until the end of the 20th century. One of the first appearances of the contemporary usage of this turn was in 1996 when university professors in Salt Lake City called for the removal of outdated offensive language, 'such as the word "handicapped"'.[16] It was not until three years later that its current usage began to gain currency.

Public figures are often taken to task for making 'outdated comments'. For example, Greg Clarke, a former Chairman of the English Football Association, was forced to apologize for using the term 'coloured' when describing people of Black, Asian, and Minority Ethnic (BAME) backgrounds during an appearance before a Parliamentary Select Community.[17] In Bolton, a Liberal Democrat local councillor was also forced to apologize after using 'outdated language' to describe disabled people. He made the error of writing about the illegal parking of 'invalid carriages'.[18] The frequency with which the charge that something is outdated leads to a demand for an apology highlights a lack of willingness to defend and uphold traditional forms of behaviour and language usage.

Another case of forced apology was witnessed by fans of crime fiction at a festival of the genre in Bristol in May 2023. Sections of the audience at this CrimeFest used social media to attack the host's speech, which he introduced with the statement 'my personal pronouns are grammatically correct'. Several social media posts responded to his words with a sense of outrage. People described feeling 'shocked and saddened' and decried the 'offensive and outdated' tone of the speech. The criticisms levelled at the host associated the comments with the outdated values of the past. Crime fiction adviser Graham Bartlett stated: 'I was at the dinner where I was shocked and saddened by the toastmaster's speech which was outdated and offensive. I raised it with the organisers the next day who took my comments on board wholeheartedly.' Predictably, the organizers apologized for the 'hurtful and discomforting comments made during the event'.

TV journalist Roger Corke posted on Twitter: 'I thought I was one of the least woke people I know until I heard that speech. People may get offended too quickly these days but that speech sounded as though it was written in the last century and was really inappropriate.'[19] The assumption that what was written a century ago is no longer acceptable and morally inferior to the more enlightened values of our time underpins the negative representation of outdated. The mere hint that a point of view is outdated serves as a signal that it need not be taken seriously. It can be legitimately vilified and condemned. And the more that the negative usage of 'outdated' gains momentum, the greater the psychic distance between the present and the past.

'Outdated' and 'offensive' are used interchangeably. At Durham University, a student society was condemned for a statement that was described as 'outdated and malicious'. This was a response to a light-hearted statement issued to explain that due to COVID restrictions a summer ball would be cancelled. The statement indicated that the cancellation occurred because 'because somebody in Wuhan ate a bat in late 2019'.[20] The linkage of this supposedly malicious statement with it being outdated is curious. Presumably the university's offence inspectorate concluded that this comment was in bad taste. But why should this attempt at a joke have anything to do with the state of being out of date?

These days, references to 'outdated' views and comments need not have anything to do with their temporal status, they may refer solely to their offensive and socially unacceptable quality.

Often outdated practices, particularly words, are diagnosed as a cause of harm or of potential harm. Even words that were penned a long, long time ago can be represented as a source of harm to the contemporary reader. The American Library Association organized a webinar in 2021 entitled 'Decolonizing the Catalog: Anti-Racist Description Practices from Authority Records to Discovery Layers'.[21] The aim of the webinar was to discuss efforts to 'remap problematic, outdated, and offensive' catalogue subject headings. In line with this approach, the library at Columbia University issued a statement in the same year that warned library users about the 'outdated and harmful language in Library of Congress subject headings'.[22]

The association of harm with outdated words was also highlighted by a statement from representatives of the National Archives and Records Administration (NARA) in Washington. Rather than referring to the age of the language used in documents in its collection, the point of NARA's statement was to warn that its 'Catalog and web pages contain some content that may be harmful or difficult to view'. It continued: 'NARA's records span the history of the United States, and it is our charge to preserve and make available these historical records. As a result, some of the materials presented here may reflect outdated, biased, offensive, and possibly violent views and opinions.[23]

That NARA felt the need to remind its readers that its collection of historical documents might reflect outdated views is interesting. What else should one expect when inspecting centuries-old documents? Whatever the motive for publishing this statement, its effect is to underline the moral distance separating its enlightened authors from the outdated and harmful views expressed by the authors of the documents of yesteryear.

It is not only the term 'outdated' that is fixed to words like 'malicious', 'harm', and 'offensive', the word 'problematic' is also used in the same way: to discredit traditional language. 'Problematic' serves as an opaque signifier of something that is not quite right. When linked to 'outdated', it hints at the diffuse, negative, and unacceptable quality of its target. This sentiment is conveyed by the authors of 'Six Ways to Fix the Army's Culture'. The objective of the authors is to help the US army prepare for the long-term future, and to realize this, they recommend that it changes those 'elements of the Army's self-identity that are problematic, outdated, or both'.[24] This call to detach the military's self-identity from a supposedly 'problematic' past represents an explicit demand to change a way of life and thinking to the one recommended by the authors, which is presumably superior because it is 'up to date' and so *un*problematic.

Even in everyday communication, the couplet is used casually to identify a phenomenon that is inherently troublesome. 'Can you still love a book despite its problematic or outdated content?' asks one reader on Reddit.[25]

There is a hint of what is problematic about 'problematic terminology' in the guidance offered by the University of New Hampshire's 'Bias-Free Language Guide'. It uses the couplet of 'problematic/outdated' as a contrast to the category of 'preferred words'.

When a word is deemed problematic because it is outdated, it clearly signifies a negative orientation to the language of the past and the values that underpin them. The University of New Hampshire's guide offers a vivid illustration of how the problematic/outdated couplet works. It has usefully published a list of words that are 'problematic' and should therefore cease to be used.

> **Preferred**: people of advanced age, old people*
> **Problematic/Outdated:** older people, elders, seniors, senior citizen
> *Old people has been reclaimed by some older activists who believe the standard wording of old people lacks the stigma of the term 'advanced age'. Old people also halts the euphemizing of age. Euphemizing automatically positions age as a negative.
> **Preferred**: person living at or below the poverty line, people experiencing poverty
> **Problematic/Outdated**: poor person, poverty-stricken person
> **Preferred**: person of material wealth
> **Problematic**: rich
> Being rich gets conflated with a sort of omnipotence; hence, immunity from customs and the law. People without material wealth could be wealthy or rich of spirit, kindness, etc.
> **Preferred**: people of size
> **Problematic/Outdated**: obese*, overweight people
> **Preferred**: person who is blind/visually impaired
> **Problematic**: blind person, 'dumb'
> **Preferred**: US citizen or Resident of the US
> **Problematic**: American
> **Preferred**: White people, European-American individuals
> **Problematic**: Caucasian people
> **Preferred**: Folks, People, You All, Y'all
> **Problematic/Outdated**: Guys (when referring to people overall)
> **Preferred**: Other Sex
> **Problematic/Outdated**: Opposite Sex
> **Preferred**: Children who are gender non-conforming, Children who are gender variant
> **Problematic/Outdated**: Girlie or Tomboy[26]

Numerous critics derided or drew amusement from this language guide when it was published in 2016. However, since then, similar guidance has proliferated and the contrast between preferred and problematic/outdated has shifted to mandatory versus problematic and outdated. Often language is no longer a matter of preference and there is pressure to use the officially approved words.

Over the past decade, the attacks on so-called 'outdated' language and practices have escalated and, in some jurisdictions, even criminalized them. In British Columbia, Canada, a tribunal has ruled that misgendering a person – not using the correct pronouns – is a violation of their human rights.[27] The use of a wrong pronoun can lead to a loss of employment. In July 2023, Michigan's House of Representatives passed a hate speech bill which criminalizes causing someone to feel threatened by words, including the misusing of pronouns. Someone guilty of the felony of misusing a pronoun can face up to five years in prison and a $10,000 fine.[28]

Outdating: The project of nullifying the past

The constant demoralization of what has gone before through discrediting the outdated is a recurrent theme in the War Against the Past. From the issuing of language guidelines, through to the censoring of texts and ridding libraries of so-called 'problematic' books, cultural and educational institutions have participated in the activity of outdating. By 'outdating', I refer to the practice of delegitimizing words, forms of behaviour, and cultural works on the grounds that they belong to a bygone era. The practice of outdating is based on the premise that the language and attitudes of previous generations are likely to be 'problematic' simply because they are old. In effect, outdating renders the activities and accomplishments of previous generations morally subordinate to people living in the here and now.

In the sphere of education and culture, the practice of outdating draws attention to the supposed threats posed by attitudes and behaviours from the past and seeks to protect people from being offended and harmed by them. This is the purpose of a cautionary note the publisher Penguin Random House attached to the latest edition of Ernest Hemingway's classic novel *The Sun Also Rises* raising concerns about Hemingway's 'attitudes' and 'language' in his writings as well as his 'cultural representations'. The disclaimer explains that the publisher decided not to censor the work but makes clear that this does not constitute an 'endorsement' of Hemingway's original text. That publishers see themselves as responsible for endorsing or not endorsing the great literature of the past is troubling enough, but what is particularly chilling about the note is its warning that 'this book was published in 1926 and reflects the attitudes of its time'.[29]

Works of literature tend to reflect the attitude of their time, and the fact that a well-established publisher feels the need to underline this obvious fact speaks to the prevailing presumption that readers need to be safeguarded from exposure to the attitudes of people living in the past. Introductions that explain the historical and social background to a classical text can offer a useful guide to readers. Such introductions inform readers why the characters in the novel spoke the way they did and illuminate the cultural attitudes of the times. Introductions that provide context enhance readers' experience of reading. Such an introduction to a literary text is very different to the now perfunctory content warning issues by publishers. The phrase that a novel 'reflects the attitudes of the time' does not illuminate but merely warns the reader. It is factually correct but is used to morally indict the author.

A warning that a book reflects the attitudes of its time implicitly calls on readers to beware when reading the text to spare themselves the hurt caused by its problematic/outdated sentiments. Publishers regularly warn people about content in this way. It is difficult to understand what there is to warn about in Virginia Woolf's 1927 novel *To the Lighthouse*. Yet Vintage, owned by Penguin Random House, has decided to alert readers that this novel 'was published in 1927 and reflects the attitudes of its time'. As literature professor Mark Hussey, who has edited numerous Woolf texts, has observed, this warning treats 'the past as a scary place'.[30] That a content warning can be slapped on even a wonderful novel dealing with the complexities and tensions of family life serves as testimony to the obsessive impulse driving the crusade to place outdated sentiments under a moral quarantine.

Cautionary notes and trigger warnings are now standard. A new edition of Nancy Mitford's 1945 novel *The Pursuit of Love*, published by Penguin, alerts unsuspecting readers that this book contains 'prejudices' that were 'commonplace in British society'. Just in case the reader is not aware of why Penguin felt the need to issue its warning, it states that 'these prejudices were wrong then and are wrong today'. In a tone of faux-liberalism Penguin notes that it is 'printing the novel as it was originally published because to make changes would be the same as pretending these prejudices never existed'.[31]

It appears that for Penguin the publishing of *The Pursuit of Love* served as an opportunity for highlighting the prejudices that were 'commonplace' in British society. P.G. Wodehouse's books also now come with a warning about 'outdated language'. The warning asks readers to be 'aware that this book was published in the 1930s and contains language, themes and characterisations which you may find outdated'.[32] The assumption that a reader may well be troubled by coming across language and themes that are outdated, in books famously about the relationship between a gentleman and his manservant, seems particularly infantilizing and purposeless.

The need to censor and alter the language of old classic books is now seen as routine. Ian Fleming's James Bond books have become the target of sensitivity readers, as have the works of Roald Dahl. The target of these censors is often plain old traditional language usage. In the sanitized version of Dahl's *Charlie and the Chocolate Factory*, Augustus Gloop is no longer 'fat' and Oompa-Loompas are no longer 'titchy' but 'small'. And, of course, gender-neutral nouns have been introduced to replace outdated words. Originally, Oompa Loompas were 'small men'; they are now designated as 'small people'.[33]

Movie and television companies have also been in the forefront of outdating the problematic features of their media. The BBC's iPlayer has introduced warnings about outdated 'social attitudes' to some of their TV shows. Its message warns that these shows 'reflect the broadcast standards, language and attitudes' of the time.[34] In turn, Sky Cinema has warned its viewers that some of its movies – such as *Aladdin*, *Dumbo*, and *Aliens* – contain 'outdated attitudes, languages and cultural depictions which may cause offence today'.[35] Disney+ uses the same language to caution its viewers regarding Disney classics such as *The Jungle Book* and *Peter Pan*. Its disclaimer states, 'This program is presented as originally created. It may contain outdated cultural depictions.'

Libraries have also adopted the practice of protecting their readers from the language and attitudes of the past. In March 2023, it was reported that librarians in Devon decided to hide Enid Blyton books with 'outdated' language and place them in the 'off-limits' section of libraries. Documents issued to library staff state that 'where popular books have language that is increasingly outdated', libraries 'continue to purchase new editions where publishers have updated the language within'.[36] Updating language is a euphemism for censoring and rewriting classic texts such as Blyton's *Famous Five* series.

School libraries in Australia have removed 'outdated and offensive books on colonialism' from their collections. The purge of a school library in Melbourne was guided by Dr Al Fricker, a Dja Wurrung man and expert in Indigenous education with Deakin University. In the course of auditing all 7,000 titles on its library shelves, Fricker justified removing books on the grounds that they were almost 50 years old and were 'simply gathering dust anyway'. He stated that 'we wouldn't accept science books being that old in the library, so why do we accept other non-fiction books to be that old, because nothing is static'.[37]

There is something truly disturbing about the idea that a library ought to rid itself of old non-fiction books. In the discipline of sociology, for example, that would mean ridding themselves of the 19th-century pioneers of the field. In effect, expunging old non-fiction books from libraries is a philistine annihilation of the intellectual legacy of the social sciences and the humanities. Once upon a time, old books were treasured and treated with care by libraries, not treated with suspicion.

In the United States, libraries have taken objection to Laura Ingalls Wilder's depiction of Native Americans in her famous *Little House on the Prairie* novels. The American Library Association removed her name in 2018 from a lifetime achievement award it gives out annually, thereby retrospectively annulling her achievement. When books are cancelled by publishers, they are rendered totally invisible to future generations. In March 2021, Dr Seuss Enterprises announced that six Dr Seuss books, including *And to Think That I Saw It on Mulberry Street* and *If I Ran the Zoo*, would no longer be published because they contained racist and insensitive imagery.[38]

The practice of outdating old books – especially those written for children – is often upheld on the grounds that the outdated stereotypes they contain will have a negative impact on them. Researchers claim that their work 'has revealed' that 'children's books are perpetuating outdated stereotypes of gender roles including boys playing sport, doing physical work and girls as passive onlookers'. One researcher, Helen Adams from Edith Cowan University's School of Education, asserted that research has shown 'that adults will often choose books they loved themselves as children, and this contributes to children being exposed to outdated viewpoints of masculinity and femininity as well as gender roles'.[39] What this statement indicates is that parents buying books that they loved for their children are in effect contaminating them with outdated ideas and words. Yet it is precisely these much-loved books that are shared across generations that help cultivate strong emotional and intellectual bonds between parent and child. This approach towards limiting children's access to outdated books has the effect of distancing young people from the culture of their parents and in effect removing them from the emotional and moral influence of the generations who preceded them.

The practice of outdating books and films is often accompanied by the publishing of guidelines that distinguish between outdated and acceptable language usage. Cultural and educational institutions constantly issue statements offering advice and guidance on how to interpret various objects in their collection. At times, it seems that every project designed to distance society from its past comes with a helpful guideline. 'Supporting Decolonisation in Museums', the guidance which, as noted in our introduction, was issued by the London-based Museums Association, 'aims to empower more people to take action and lead change as museums address the legacy of British colonialism'. In the case of the Museums Association, the guidance offered is explicitly designed 'to take action'. It cites with approval a statement made by Rachael Minott, Chair of its Decolonisation Guidance Working Group, which describes how her experience of 'actively' pursuing 'decolonial practice had been an exciting and rewarding learning experience'.[40]

Most guidelines are not as action-oriented as that of the Museums Association. Instead, they focus on nudging people towards adopting the views of the guidelines' authors. Trigger warnings and content warnings by cultural and educational institutions are often promoted as offering 'individuals a choice of when and how they want to interact with the work'.[41] This, however, overlooks how the very existence of the warning communicates a view that the work in question is something that people should be wary of. Such warnings pre-empt people discovering for themselves how to react to and interpret a particular phenomenon.

Critics of trigger warnings frequently draw attention to their censorious impact on cultural and intellectual life. However, the most important feature of trigger warnings is not their mechanism of censorship but their aspiration to influence people's thoughts. They tell people what to expect and they implicitly instruct people how to react. Often, the instruction they offer is one that proclaims 'Beware of the Past!'

The tendency to attach trigger warnings to objects and texts from the past reveals a deep-seated desire to spoil or damage their reputation. Even a text as foundational as America's Declaration of Independence has been subject to a trigger warning by the National Archives in Washington, DC.[42] This document, mainly written by Thomas Jefferson, is famous for its insistence that 'all men are created equal' and possess 'certain inalienable rights'. The National Archives decided that despite its important affirmation of freedom and equality, the Declaration deserved a trigger warning because of the language used to describe America's Indigenous population. The Declaration of Independence self-consciously defied the British Crown and called into question its rule over the American colonies. In this document, Jefferson stated that King George III 'has excited domestic insurrections amongst us and has endeavoured to bring on the inhabitants of our frontiers, the merciless Indian Savages, whose known rule of warfare, is an undistinguished destruction of all ages, sexes and conditions'.

Next to the declaration, the National Archives placed a content warning noting that the views expressed in this document were 'outdated, biased and offensive'. At first sight, the attachment of a content warning on an 18th-century document on the grounds that it is outdated appears bizarre since, by definition, almost anything produced in the 18th century is likely to be outdated. Yet in its day the Declaration of Independence was way ahead of its time. It is a document that would go on to inspire independence movements for centuries to come. Arguably, far from being outdated, this Declaration retains its relevance to our time, and by treating its content as 'outdated, biased and offensive', the National Archives imply that the very founding of the United States was flawed. And if the founding of this new nation was flawed, then everything that follows bears its negative hallmark.

Trigger warnings are frequently used to draw attention to the outdated and offensive language and behaviour used by some of the most important texts in the Western canon. Student activists at Columbia University who demanded that a trigger warning be attached to the Ovid's classical Latin poem *Metamorphoses* argued that, 'like so many texts in the Western canon, it contains triggering and offensive material that marginalizes student identities in the class room'. Their call for the policing of the reading of this Roman classic was justified on the grounds that such texts 'can be difficult to read and discuss as a survivor, a person of color or a student from a low-income background'.[43] The representation of classical literature as 'triggering and offensive' reflects the aspiration to negate its achievements and render toxic its civilizational accomplishments.

It is not only the Greek and Roman era that faces the presentist Inquisition.

Academics at Oxford University have slapped trigger warnings on many of the most important Old English and medieval texts, such as *Beowulf* and *Sir Gawain and the Green Knight.*[44] These trigger warnings, which inform students that these texts may contain 'racist and misogynist views', implicitly instruct them to interpret this literature through the eyes of the 21st century.

A trigger warning attached to Immanuel Kant's *Critiques* sends out the message that readers should beware the language of this central philosopher of the Englightenment. It notes:

> This book is a product of its time and does not reflect the same values it would if it were written today. Parents might wish to discuss with their children how views on race, gender, sexuality, ethnicity and interpersonal relations have changed since this book was written before allowing them to read.[45]

In this instance, the impulse to vilify the era within which Kant lived is coupled with the arrogant assertion that if this philosopher were alive today his works would express values that are different to the original. Yet despite attempts to attach a health warning to his *Critiques*, Kant's ethical principles and moral standards – his categorical imperative – continue to serve as a point of reference for discussions on this theme. Though more than 200 years have passed since his death, his philosophy, which encourages freedom, moral independence, equality and responsibility, is no less relevant today than during his lifetime. His philosophy made an indispensable contribution to our understanding of why it is essential to take seriously the moral worth of all human beings.

No doubt Kant, like all his peers living in the 18th century, possessed prejudices and biases that contradict the temper of our times. It is unthinkable that their language and sensibilities would have been carbon copies of those of today. The disparagement of the philosophers of the 18th century for lacking the sensibilities of our time indicates an absence of historical sensitivity. When this is combined with the attitude of contempt for the past, trigger warnings become a weapon to be wielded against the philosophical tradition of the Enlightenment.

The re-engineering of language

The struggle to gain control over language plays a central role in the War Against the Past. In many instances, words have become the target of grievance archaeologists merely on the grounds that they are old and are therefore likely to have negative associations with the misdeeds of the past. Often, racial sensitivities are mobilized to prohibit the use of certain words. The terms 'blacklist and 'whitelist' used in computer science and cybersecurity to indicate that something is allowed or not allowed have fallen foul of the language police.[46]

Grievance archaeologists are so devoted to unearthing the racist connotations of words that sometimes the most unlikely candidates have been chosen for public condemnation. *The New York Times* columnist John McWhorter (himself black) wrote of a person who was reprimanded for using the term 'brown bag lunch' on the grounds that the 'phrase evokes the crude color scale that some elite (and elitist) African American organizations are said to have used, once upon a time, to determine eligibility for membership, with only people lighter in complexion than a brown bag admitted'. As Whorter remarked, if we ban 'brown bag lunch', it follows that 'we should no longer refer to whipped cream, since enslaved people were whipped, or shucking corn, because the phrase "shucking and jiving" refers to Black people faking glee to placate white people'.[47] Nevertheless, the Office for Civil Rights in Seattle, Washington, has suggested that government workers refrain from using this common term because it could be offensive to some people.[48]

Grievance archaeologists at Brandeis University found an historical justification for banning the word 'picnic', claiming that the word 'picnic' was 'often associated with lynching of black people in the United States, during which white spectators were said to have watched while eating, referring to them as picnics or other terms involving racial slurs against black people'.[49]

Other unobjectionable terms that are said to have past racist connotations include the dance the cakewalk, which was performed by enslaved Africans in the 19th century. According to the *Conscious Style Guide*, cakewalk and the shortened 'take the cake' should be avoided because of their history. It also advises avoiding the use of the term 'grandfathering' because of its origins in racist Jim Crow-era laws.[50]

It is tempting to adopt a light-hearted tone when discussing the verbal gymnastics displayed by numerous language guides published by both public and private institutions. However, semantic engineering is a serious phenomenon that aims to gain control over the way that people see the world. It seeks to achieve this objective by discrediting traditional language and displacing it with words that weaken society's connection with the vocabulary of the past. One of the most important studies dealing with the movement devoted to displacing the language of the past with a new anti-traditionalist vocabulary is the sociologist Alvin Gouldner's *The Future of Intellectuals and the Rise of the New Class* (1979). The main subject of this book is the way that universities and other institutions of higher education have successfully challenged traditional authority through gaining control over what Gouldner characterized as the culture of critical discourse. The language of critical discourse is abstract and independent of the cultural and social context of society and implicitly challenges the reality projected through conventional language usage.

The Future of Intellectuals and the Rise of the New Class argued that academics and administrators in higher education have delegitimized and discredited traditional language and cultural conventions through successfully promoting their professional authority and expertise.[51] The book offers a compelling sociological explanation for the ascendancy of an anti-moral and anti-traditional language and ideology in American universities. Writing in the late 1970s, Gouldner pointed to the role of what he called the new class of intellectual and knowledge workers in promoting the anti-traditionalist turn in society, and especially inside the university. The exercise of the monopoly that this group had over education and expertise unleashed forces that worked towards the de-authorization of traditional and cultural authority.

Gouldner contended that this development was facilitated by the decline of paternal authority within the family. The twin forces of women's emancipation and the expansion of education in the context of growing prosperity weakened paternal authority, which in turn damaged the capacity of the prevailing system of socialization to communicate the legacy and the values of the past.

At the centre of this argument was a development of tremendous cultural significance, which was the disruption and unravelling of the prevailing process of socialization. Parents, and fathers in particular, found it difficult to impose and reproduce their 'social values and political ideologies in their children'.[52] The most significant dimension of Gouldner's analysis was his insight regarding the relation between disrupted socialization and the intensification of cultural conflict. He argued that schools and chiefly universities assumed a central role in the socialization of young people, claiming the right to educate young people in line with their enlightened opinions and, even in schools, sensing no '*obligation* to reproduce parental values in their children'. Consequently, the expansion of higher education reinforced the insulation of parents' cultural influence from their children. Gouldner wrote:

> The new structurally differentiated educational system is increasingly insulated from the family system, becoming an important source of values among students divergent from those of their families. The socialization of the young by their families is now mediated by a *semi*-autonomous group of teachers.

As a result of this development, 'the public educational system' has become a 'major *cosmopolitanizing* influence on its students, with a corresponding distancing from *localistic* interests and values'.[53] Gouldner asserted that 'parental, particularly paternal, authority is increasingly vulnerable and is thus less able to insist that children respect societal or political authority outside the home'.[54]

One of the most striking developments in higher education since the 1970s has been the emergence of linguistic governance and the development of an alternative speech code. Indeed, in public discussions of semantic engineering, it is the high-profile modifications to everyday vocabulary that have caused most comment. Gouldner pointed out that attacks on the conventional vocabulary are not simply manifestations of what conservative critics often decry as 'political correctness gone mad'; rather, one of the ways in which children become culturally distanced from the values of their parents is through their 'linguistic conversion' to a form of speech that reflect the values of the cultural elites. What Gouldner characterized as the 'culture of critical speech' of the new classes 'de-authorizes all speech grounded in traditional societal authority, while it authorizes itself, the elaborated speech variant of the culture of critical discourse, as the standard of *all* "serious" speech'.[55]

Gouldner's analysis of linguistic conversion anticipated the institutionalization of speech codes and the policing of language in the decades to follow. It also illuminates how changing language usage encourages the cultural distancing of society from its past. In their study *Forbidden Words: Taboo and Censoring Language* (2006), the authors Keith Allen and Kate Burridge stated that unlike normal censoring activities, which are aimed at the maintenance of the status quo, what came to be known as PC (politically correct) language campaigning sought to promote political and social change.[56] This attempt to change language was motivated by the objective of altering how people behaved and how they identified themselves. For this reason, it was also directed at influencing the process of socialization of young people, which is why in 1995 the daycare centre at La Trobe University in Australia banned the use of around 20 words, including the gender-related terms of 'girls' and 'boys', to promote its social engineering mission to alter traditional sex roles. Those who violated this code were 'made to pay a fine into a kind of swear box for using a dirty word'.[57]

In effect, language has become a medium through which supporters of identity politics seek to alter the world and change the reality of others. This approach is stridently advocated by supporters of 'transgender language reform'. As one trans activist, linguistics professor Lal Zimman, explains: 'Because one of the most important ways cissexism is constructed is through language, the identification and dismantling of cissexist language is a central part of trans activism and part of the work that cisgender allies are expected to perform.'[58] From this author's perspective, dismantling language is the prerequisite for the institutionalization of a gender-neutral culture. Zimman explains this as follows:

> Language has played an enormously important role in the sea-change the United States is undergoing in terms of its understanding of and orientation toward transgender issues. One of the milestones in this process is the growing interest in trans-inclusive language within linguistic institutions such as mainstream news organisations, medical providers and schools.[59]

Trans activism is centred on 'language reform', which means erasing conventional identity-related words. As Zimman explains:

> The simplest level of trans-inclusive language reform deals with the use of overtly gendered language in the form of gender identity labels (*woman, man, trans, non-binary*, etc.), kinship terminology (*mother/father/parent, sister/brother/sibling*, etc.), less frequent direct indexes of gender such as professional roles (*waiter/waitress/server, masseuse/masseur/massage therapist*, etc.) and pronouns.[60]

The dismantling of traditional language usage creates a new reality which is sometimes institutionally enforced. Guidance issued by the British Ministry of Defence claims that 'not all women are biologically female' and instructs staff to be careful using the word 'female', in case it 'erases gender non-conforming people and members of the trans community'.[61] MoD personnel are advised to publicize their preferred pronouns on their email signatures, on their social media profiles, and at the start of meetings and presentations. The project of displacing the male/female distinction with gender-neutral language is promoted through some of the most grotesque examples of the re-engineering of language. Organizations representing the medical professions have been at the forefront of censoring the word 'woman' out of existence. When 'woman' is replaced by 'menstruating person', 'mother' gives way to a 'parent who gives birth', 'breastfeeding' becomes 'chestfeeding', or 'pregnant women' are reframed as 'pregnant people', a new reality is being constructed.

Internal guidance issued by the British General Medical Council instructs that all female-specific terms be displaced with gender-neutral ones, to the extent of even removing all references to 'mother' from its maternity documents. So 'surrogate mother' gives way to 'surrogate parent'. Its internal menopause policy document has also been updated and is stripped of references to women.[62] The magnitude of this shift in language usage was shown when the leading medical journal, the *Lancet*, decided to call women '*bodies with vaginas*'.[63] For some institutions, even the word 'vagina' needs to be excised from language use. One cancer charity has decided to rebrand it as a 'bonus hole'.[64] This charity, like *The Lancet* and other publications, is interested not simply in forcing people to change the words they use, but also in altering our thoughts about biological sex and what we think about what a man is and what a woman is.

On occasion, the semantic engineers go too far and are forced to roll back their latest linguistic invention. Johns Hopkins University removed an online glossary of LGBTQ+ terms and identities after its definition of the word 'lesbian' used the term a 'non-man attracted to non-men'.[65] Nevertheless, the use of the term 'non-man' to use as a substitute for lesbian is good enough for Britain's Green Party.[66]

The recently revised edition of the Judicial College's *Equal Treatment Bench Book* provides a striking illustration of how leading members of the British judiciary have become zealous advocates for the adoption of a new gender-neutral language. This publication reminds members of the judiciary to use 'gender-neutral language where possible, e.g., "business person" not "businessman", "postal operative" not "postman", "flight attendant" not "air hostess", "chair" not "chairman".[67]

The *Equal Treatment Bench Book* has thoroughly internalized transgenderist ideology and the language recently invented by activists associated with this movement. It instructs judges 'to use the preferred personal pronouns of transgender people'. It warns:

> Be alert to issues about how someone prefers to be addressed: showing respect for a person's gender identity includes using appropriate titles (Mr/Ms) and personal pronouns (he/him/his; she/her/hers). Some trans people prefer gender neutral terminology (Mx/they/them/theirs), which should be accommodated if that is known.[68]

The *Equal Treatment Bench Book* advocates the cultural attitude towards communication associated with the victim narrative of Critical Race

Theory and gender and identity politics. Its central message is 'watch your words and how you express yourself'. The authors claim that 'a thoughtless comment, throw away remark, unwise joke or even a facial expression may confirm or create an impression of prejudice'.[69] When even one's facial expression requires the policing of the self, it becomes evident that an obsessive vetting of communication and language has acquired a disturbing presence in public life. In effect, freedom of expression is trumped by the necessity of avoiding an impression of prejudice.

The Equal Treatment Bench Book is relatively restrained compared with the American Medical Association's publication *Language for Promoting Health Equity*. The AMA self-consciously contrasts what it characterizes as 'traditional/outdated terms' with newly invented 'equity-focused alternatives'. We learn that the equity-focused alternative to 'fairness' is 'social justice'. 'Ex-con/felon' is designated as 'formerly incarcerated/returning citizen/persons with a history of incarceration'. It wants 'illegal immigrants' to be rebranded as 'undocumented immigrants'. It prefers 'historically marginalized or BIPOC [Black, Indigenous and people of colour]' to the word 'minority' and 'social injustice' to 'social problems'.[70]

Inducing social amnesia

The assault against traditional language usage encourages people to gradually abandon the language with which they grew up; one which was habitually used by their ancestors. So-called 'language reform' in combination with the practice of outdating serves to distort people's capacity to remember the past. When subjected to the process of re-engineering, language which historically served as a medium of communication between generations ceases to play that role. Moreover, language that has become detached from pre-existing tradition has no interest in conducting intergenerational conversation. Its main interest is to draw a self-flattering contrast between itself and its outdated opposite.

The pressure to remove words from everyday language usage means that a language that emerged through the experience of the past loses some of its vitality. As this language alienates society from its past, people begin to find it difficult to recall what life was like in their youth. The new language offers a negative frame for interpreting the experience of the past. Once this language becomes entrenched, it is likely to disrupt our cultural memory of our past. This condition, which was diagnosed by Russell Jacoby as that of social amnesia, leads to a collective forgetting by a group of people of their community's past. Though published in 1975, Jacoby's *Social Amnesia: A Critique of Contemporary Psychology from Adler to Laing* retains its relevance for capturing the dynamic that leads to the construction of an anachronistic and distorted understanding of society's relationship to its past.

In his introduction to the 2018 edition of *Social Amnesia*, Jacoby draws attention to the tendency to depict a leading thinker such as Sigmund Freud as intellectually and scientifically inferior to those who followed him. He criticizes those who believe that those born in the 19th century are likely to be less interesting or significant than those living in our times. In this way, the achievements and genius of previous generations of intellectuals is overlooked. He notes that 'for the revolutionary numerologists to be nineteenth century meant to be hopelessly backward. The criticism implied that those who come later are smarter: the critics and their friends.'[71]

Dwelling on the problem of anachronistic arrogance, Jacoby points out that;

> We are convinced that today we know so much more about sexuality, the family, and the individual than previous generations. Perhaps we do. Yet the wholesale rejection of the past as past bespeaks the marketing mentality: the assumption today is necessarily better than yesterday. Though newer cars, telephones, and x-ray machines are superior to older ones, newer philosophers, psychologists, and literary critics may not be.[72]

Jacoby's warning concerning the 'wholesale rejection of the past as past' on the grounds that it is not up to date serves as an important reminder of the need to treasure the wisdom of older thinkers, philosophers, and scientists, since their insights may well be more relevant to our lives than those of our contemporaries.

For Jacoby, social amnesia is the outcome of a cultural zeitgeist that 'scorns the past as antiquated while touting the present as the best'. Jacoby notes that 'today criticism that shelves the old in the name of the new forms part of the Zeitgeist; it works to justify and defend by forgetting'.

He writes that 'today's banalities apparently gain in profundity if one states that the wisdom of the past, for all its virtues, belongs to the past', and adds that 'the arrogance of those who come later preens itself with the notion that the past is dead and gone'. Jacoby fears that 'society has lost its memory'.[73]

Social amnesia has had a profound influence on the outlook of institutes of higher education and institutions of culture. The social sciences in particular are often indifferent to their historical inheritance and have become addicted to the illusion of originality associated with novelty. 'The humanities and social sciences are rife with narcissism and are obsessed with novelty over substance,' argues Sasa Bozic, associate professor of sociology at the University of Zadar, Croatia. Bozic rightly criticizes the 'constant search for novelty' which has 'overshadowed scholarly substance in research, and devalued work which confirms existing knowledge'.[74] Social amnesia within the academy breeds a sense of indifference bordering on contempt for the achievements of generations of scholars and intellectuals who lived in the past.

Jacoby's identification of the phenomenon of social amnesia in the 1970s indicated that a culture of 'forgetfulness' driven by an 'unshakable belief in progress' expressed through the sentiment that 'what comes later is necessarily better than what came before' was already prevalent over half a century ago.[75] Though there is a strong element of continuity between the world discussed in *Social Amnesia*, there is, however, also a vital point of difference. The celebration of the new and disrespect for the old emanated from a self-satisfied cultural temper that did not feel the need to settle scores with the past. The tendency to forget the achievements of the past was not entwined with the practice of going to war against it. At the time, the practice of outdating language, attitudes, and behaviour was just about to gain traction – first in higher education and gradually throughout other institutions in society.

Nevertheless, the crystallization of the phenomenon of social amnesia indicated that society was struggling to take its past seriously. It was prepared to permit what J.C.D. Clark characterized as the 'distinct enterprise of historical disinheritance'.[76] That it lacked the will and the capacity to defend the legacy of the past became all too clear in the decades to follow. It is difficult to disagree with Jacoby when he stated that, 'today, without romanticizing the past', one can say that 'what is new is worse than what is old'.[77]

There has been a significant shift from the condition of collective forgetting discussed by Jacoby in the 1970s to the current historical moment, where society is constantly under pressure to forget. This pressure to forget has important implications for the way that young people are socialized to acquire a view of the past. In effect, they are educated to forget and regard the past as a vast wasteland where darkness reigns. It is to the subject of the impact of the Culture Wars on socialization that we now turn.

7

Disinheriting the Young from Their Past

Although traces of the past are everywhere, its meaning is shaped by how it is understood, and this understanding relates to how ideas about it are transmitted from one generation to another. Young people become acquainted with the experience of the past and learn about the values that have evolved over the centuries through a generational transaction. This occurs principally through the family and young people's education at school. The humanist political philosopher Hannah Arendt regarded education as a 'realm' governed by the 'relations between grown-ups and children'. She believed this relationship was too important to be 'turned over to the special science of pedagogy'.[1] Rather, the education of the young was the responsibility of society as a whole.

Human knowledge and development have evolved from the insights of previous generations. When the scientist Isaac Newton wrote that he stood on the shoulders of giants, he acknowledged his intellectual debt to the many thinkers who preceded him. The transmission of the experience of the past pertains to more than the sphere of science and knowledge, however. Insights into past generations are needed to help people – especially the young – to find their place in the world. Indeed, as we noted in chapter 5, Arendt went so far as to argue that education must be conservative to create conditions where children can feel secure to innovate and renew their world. It is only in relation to the world as it has been preserved that young people develop their understanding and potential for creating something new. In the relationship between preservation and innovation, the former is logically prior for society.

Even in the 1950s, when Arendt published her thoughts on schooling, her claim that conservation has a key role in education went against mainstream pedagogy. By this time, teaching had come under the influence of progressive pedagogy, most systematically developed by the American philosopher John Dewey, which was (and remains) hostile to the role of conservation in schools. Teacher training institutions tended to embrace educational methods that regarded the role of preservation with disdain. The rejection of conservation in education was widely adopted by prominent intellectuals involved in the socialization of the young. Dewey, like his modern-day followers, attached little value to preserving the past through education. His educational philosophy rejected the idea of the intergenerational transmission of knowledge. Instead, he sought to 'free' education from the influence of the past.

Since the interwar era, there have been debates about how education should strike a balance between orienting towards the past and a changing future world. Mainstream policy-makers and pedagogues have tended to be so fixated on the present that they have enthusiastically supported attempts to distance education from the past. This perspective motivated Dewey and other progressive educators, who argued that instead of teaching children about the world as it is, schools should take a lead in challenging outdated norms and practices. 'Is it a good thing to bring up the young with desires and habits that try to preserve everything just as it is today,' Dewey rhetorically asked, 'or should they be able to meet change, to weigh up values and find good in the new?' He added, 'How much of the background and development of our civilisation do children need to be able to understand what is in the world today?'[2] Dewey did not answer his question directly. Still, many of his followers responded with the sentiment, 'not very much'. In effect, Dewey's downgrading of the role of knowledge about the development of civilization was instrumental in reinforcing the presentist outlook of pedagogy.

The unhelpful contrast between conserving the past and preparing the young for the future usually served as a rhetorical device to discredit the former. This mechanistic counter-position overlooked the creative tension and interaction between the transmission of the legacy of the past and integrating it with the latest insights provided by the disciplinary knowledge of the school curriculum. Education works best when it is directed towards providing a bridge between the present and the past. This enterprise is entirely alien to the current presentist cultural mode.

Many educators believe that their role is not to socialize young people to embrace the values of their parents and communities but to undermine them and replace them with what they take to be more relevant, progressive ones. This approach was outlined as far back as 1922 by Dewey in the following terms:

> It is the business of the school environment to eliminate, so far as possible, the unworthy features of the existing environment. ... As a society becomes more enlightened, it realizes that it is responsible not to transmit and conserve the whole of its existing arrangements, but only such as make for a better future society. The school is its chief agency for the accomplishment of this end.[3]

By 'unworthy features of the existing environment', Dewey meant the system of traditional norms that prevailed in many American communities. He called into question the relevance of values that underpinned the outlook of the community that children inhabited, proposing that schools should teach children the values that he and his colleagues upheld, even if they conflicted with the views of their parents.

During the decades that followed Dewey's elaboration of progressive pedagogy, hostility towards the intergenerational transmission of the values of the past in education became steadily more and more strident. In some cases, this response acquired a dogmatic ideological tone. Post-Second World War international institutions regarded the elimination of traditions, ideas, and values from the curriculum as necessary for diminishing the authority of the legacy of the nation. From their perspective, the intergenerational transmission of traditional norms had to give way to the ideals the anti-conserving curriculum experts upheld. This approach was adopted by the psychiatrist Brock Chisholm, the first director of the World Health Organization, whose views anticipated the outlook of 21st-century culture warriors in education. He complained that

> Old ideas and customs are generally called 'good' or 'sound', and new ideas, or experimental thinking or behavior, are usually labeled 'bad', 'unsound', 'communist', 'heretical', or any of many other words. The power these words have obtained over much of the race is astonishing. They are the symbols of the control that older people and the past have, and cling to, over young people and the future.[4]

Chisholm blamed the outbreak of world wars and conflicts on the imposition of outdated ways on young people. 'We have swallowed all manner of poisonous certainties fed us by our parents, our Sunday and day school-teachers, our politicians, our priests,' he argued.[5]

Chisholm's attack on outdated ways was linked to his romanticized idealization of children. He called for the protection of 'that freedom present in all children', which has been 'destroyed or crippled' in the past through the imposition of adult control. His call for liberating children from the clutches of their elders was conveyed in a radical and provocative tone. But similar sentiments were widely circulated by child professionals, who expressed them far more restrainedly. As director of the World Health Organization and a leading figure in the international mental health establishment, Chisholm enjoyed significant global authority. In a foreword to Chisholm's published lecture on this subject, Abe Fortas, the American Under Secretary of the Interior, praised his call to put aside the 'mistaken old ways of our elders'.[6]

Educationalists who regard the past as outdated are hostile to the notion that schooling should devote itself to the task of conservation. For more than a century, a section of the teaching profession have sought to disrupt the transmission of past values in their classrooms. In recent decades, their standpoint has gained wide influence in education. Unsurprisingly, its supporters are sympathetic to the objective of insulating schools from the influence of the past. Many of them are drawn towards the ideals and objectives of the War Against the Past and actively promote these views in the classroom.

Schools and other institutions devoted to educating young people have become an important site for the War Against the Past. Schools in Anglo-American societies have adopted a form of pedagogy that seeks to distance young people from the ways of their ancestors. Instead of transmitting the values upheld by previous generations, educational institutions are often complicit in dispossessing young people of their cultural inheritance. Consequently, they are responsible for promoting the condition of social amnesia, in which the younger generation knows little about where they come from or of a past that has important significance for their community. Since the outbreak of the current Culture Wars, anti-traditionalist activists have targeted young people, seeking to influence how children and youngsters see the world. This is why so much of the Culture Wars is focused on how young people are educated and socialized.

It is important to situate the current battle over education in an historical context. During the past century, the school was the key site of the War Against the Past. It aimed to 'free' children from their parents' influence and their communities' traditions. From the 1970s, the dominant forms of pedagogy practised in schools were self-consciously anti-traditional. Their goal was to free children from what they understood to be outdated prejudices. Pre-existing forms of schooling were caricatured as old-fashioned Victorian rote learning. Instead, it was argued that the classroom should become child-centred and democratic. Until the turn of the 21st century, the most important feature of this so-called 'child-centred pedagogy' was the introduction of a form of socialization that relied on psychological techniques of validation and the introduction of therapeutic values such as emotional literacy, wellness, and self-esteem in place of traditional values such as courage, duty, patriotism, and solidarity.

At the turn of the 21st century, the 'socialization through validation' project retained its influence over schooling in the West. However, with the outbreak of the War Against the Past, schools have become subject to an unprecedented degree of indoctrination. Pedagogy has become thoroughly politicized, and during the past two decades, many schools have come under the influence of an ideological curriculum. In the early stage of this development, its importance for the schooling of the young was often overlooked. Most of the public's attention was captured by conflicts over the rise of Cancel Culture in universities and institutions of culture such as museums. Controversies surrounding identity-related issues in the private and public sectors, as well as in the sphere of politics, were widely reported and discussed. However, there was relatively little interest in parallel developments in schools.

In effect, until recently, those championing the War Against the Past in schools were overlooked; the politicization of the school curriculum gained momentum and faced virtually no opposition. Gradually, by stealth, the influence of identity politics became deeply entrenched in the classroom. The curriculum and the educational resources that supported it aggressively promoted transgenderist dogma, the racialized representation of a world associated with Critical Race Theory, and the project of the decolonization of the legacy of Western civilization. The teaching of history was strongly influenced by a presentist outlook that taught children to assess events in the past from the standpoint of contemporary sensibilities. Often, the history curriculum was more devoted to disabusing pupils' beliefs in the celebrated accounts of their communities' past than to acquainting them with their history. This curriculum is more likely to motivate children to feel emotionally alienated from their ancestors than to feel a sense of pride about their nation's past. Apologists for an anti-patriotic curriculum continually protest that the past needs to be painted in even darker colours than is the norm. One American apologist for this approach complains:

> History is an essential theme of the education curriculum. This is because learning about a nation's origin is very important. However, in children's history classes, kids are deprived of the parts of history considered murky. The curriculum is more focused on portraying America as a rational and noble Nation'.[7]

Disabusing the young of the belief that their country is a noble nation is one of the drivers of a curriculum designed to deprive pupils of a sense of national pride.

The war fought out in the classroom

It was not until the outbreak of COVID and the subsequent lockdown that sections of the public became aware of the climate of indoctrination that has enveloped the school system. Parents who were listening in on their children's online discussions with their teachers were often taken aback by what they heard. Concern regarding the values promoted in the classroom led some parents to organize and challenge the political direction of their children's curriculum. In 2021, ideological conflict erupted over the school curriculum in the United States. Parental backlash against the regime of indoctrination gained the support of politicians, which, in some cases, led to state legislatures drawing up alternative curricula. Today, the Culture Wars are evident in classrooms on both sides of the Atlantic.

One of the most significant events of 2021 was a revolt of frustrated and angry parents in Virginia which precipitated the shock electoral defeat of the Democratic former governor Terry McCauliffe by the Republican Glenn Youngkin. His defeat indicated that the conflict over the curriculum could have important electoral ramifications. The spread of parental activism against indoctrination in the classroom is frequently dismissed by its opponents as an outcome of the machination of Republican political strategists. Former US President Barack Obama told Virginia voters to ignore what he called 'trumped-up culture wars'. He dismissed parental concerns as 'fake outrage'. His version of events ignores the main driver of the revolt against the regime of indoctrination in the classroom: namely, that for millions of parents, their child's academic and moral education is of the utmost importance. That is why many adults who are normally reluctant to involve themselves in the Culture Wars reacted angrily and chose to fight back when their children were dragged into them by sections of the teaching establishment.

Whereas many people are prepared to stay quiet when confronted with manifestations of the War Against the Past in everyday life, they will react when they realize their child is being brainwashed to adopt values that are antithetical to theirs. Since the summer of 2021, this conflict has also spread to other parts of the world, and the school will likely remain one of the most consequential battlefields on which the War Against the Past is fought. In England and Scotland, even parents who considered themselves progressive reacted angrily when they discovered what went on in the classroom.

In an interview, Sheila, a mother of three from Crouch End in London, told me, 'I used to be a hardcore woke.' However, she totally flipped after being confronted with incessant questions about white privilege by her three children (two boys and a girl). Her 12-year-old son kicked up a fuss in school when he rejected the claim that he was suffering from 'white fragility'. Sheila is now on a personal crusade opposing guilt-tripping educators. Another mother recounted her furious reaction when her 16-year-old daughter relayed her history teacher's explanation that it was the job of students to educate their parents and disabuse them of their 'outdated ideas'. She raised the matter with the history teacher, who first of all became aggressively defensive and then denied that he had used that phrase.

Understandably, in the current debate over the curriculum, most of the attention has been directed at highly charged issues surrounding the question of gender and race. These issues are symptoms of a more important trend, however, which is to dispossess the young from their historical inheritance. One of the main objectives of the politicization of the classroom is to encourage children to believe that their views are more enlightened than the antiquated ideas held by their parents.

Schooling has always been subjected to a succession of pedagogic fads.[8] Most of the time, these fads attempt to find a technical solution to the problem of classroom motivation. The current practice of outdating pre-existing practices, however, has a different aim, which is to discredit the conventions and values still found in schools which bind young people to the generations who preceded them. In effect, the politicization of the curriculum aims to institutionalize a form of socialization that disinherits the younger generations from their past. In the current era, the main medium used is the narrative of decolonization, which represents the conventional curriculum as outdated and pernicious.

Recently published resources and course material for teachers consistently advocate the need to educate children in the language of decolonization. Publishers of textbooks have enthusiastically signed up. In July 2021, Pearson Edexcel – a British multinational education and examination body – boasted of its 'active commitment' to decolonize the subject of drama. The Head of English, Drama, and Languages at Pearson stated, 'We want all learners to see themselves in the literature they study.' For this publisher, the dictates of the politics of decolonization trump the study of 'outdated classics'. That is why it stated that it 'will also be considering adding playwrights that give us greater representation across gender, heritage, LGBTQ+ and disability'.[9]

Religious education is also affected. For example, 'Anti-Racist RE: 20+ Key Ideas for Teachers of RE' encourages religious education teachers to use their subject as a medium for challenging ideas that it deems outdated.[10] It promotes the virtues of a 'decolonized curriculum' and calls on teachers to familiarize their students with the vocabulary that dominates campus politics. Anyone reading this document would struggle to find anything that even remotely has any educational or intellectual connection with religion. What it offers is an account of RE that is devoted to the exploration of concepts such as intersectionality, whiteness, white privilege, unconscious bias, cultural appropriation and microaggression.

In many ways, it is fitting that RE has been reinvented to serve as a medium for the moral re-education of children. The arguments promoting the decolonization of the curriculum often adopt a zealous quasi-religious tone previously associated with old-school fundamentalist preachers demanding atonement and repentance. That children are encouraged to embrace the dogma of white guilt indicates that for some schools the very act of questioning white privilege is interpreted as a contemporary form of sacrilege.

The project of decolonization has enveloped every school subject. In England, the former president of the National Association of Schoolmasters Union of Women Teachers (NASUWT), Michelle Codrington-Rogers, argued at her union's conference that

> All subjects need to ensure that there is inclusivity in their teaching. That there is black visibility in design and technology, modern foreign languages, science and English, music and geography, art and maths, computer science and citizenship, food technology and drama, and all subjects have a responsibility to change the narrative that black people only have a history of enslavement and colonisation.[11]

Her motion was passed by delegates. In the same vein, the Chartered Institute for Archaeologists has demanded that the subjects of archaeology and history must be decolonized.[12] Others have called for the decolonization of science, maths, and geography.[13] Even the food children eat is not exempt from becoming the object of decolonization. Paulette Ennever, a food tech teacher in Ealing, West London, told the NASUWT conference that she 'decolonizes' her lessons so pupils are aware of the origins of the food they eat.[14] Reading between the lines, it is evident that her discussion of the sources of food is not so much about imperialism and race but about altering the way that the past is perceived and understood.

Decolonizing the curriculum is not simply about changing children's reading material or tinkering with the curriculum. It aims to capture the levers of socialization and fundamentally change how people perceive themselves. That is why the campaign to decolonize the curriculum is intensely hostile to Britishness and symbols of British identity. The ambition to re-socialize the young is explicitly promoted by the guidance issued by the Scottish government. The introduction to its teacher guide declares:

> If you are socialised as white, you grew up in a world where you were consistently told/fed by the culture around you that your way of life is the right, sophisticated, enlightened way to be. Of course, it is painful and disappointing to hear that some of these choices cause someone else harm. Fragility is the urge to justify your actions, to have a defensive reaction and to fight off any accusations (to reason and explain your actions and why you made this decision . . . 'I am a good person, I didn't know').[15]

That's another way of signalling that if you want to be seen as a good person, you had better leave behind the values and the way of life into which you were socialized.

Many parents are unaware that their values are systematically denounced and demonized in this way. The imposition of a new curriculum that seeks to indoctrinate pupils with the outlook of the decolonization movement occurs without their knowledge. Some educators also claim to possess the authority to not only discuss intimate questions concerning the sexuality and gender of young children but also to keep parents out of the loop. In Scotland, children as young as four will be allowed to change their name and gender at school without their parents' consent.[16] Sometimes, the parents are the last to know that their child has – with the approval of the school – decided to transition.

The teachers' unions seem to have unhesitatingly decided that ideological indoctrination is more important than education. A document produced by the National Education Union (NEU) in the summer of 2021 asserts that there is an 'urgent' need to 'decolonise' every subject and every stage of the curriculum. It declares that the urgency of taking these dramatic measures is justified because action needs to be taken in response to Black Lives Matter public protests.

In what is, in effect, a call to arms, the NEU document warns that 'from curriculum to routines to classroom layout, our education system has been shaped by colonisation and neo-liberalism'. Its conclusion is that the decolonization of the school can leave nothing untouched.[17] It suggests that everything is pervaded by the toxic influence of British events that occurred two to three centuries ago, from the way children sharpen their pencils to the songs they sing in the classroom. When, as noted in chapter 3, even the layouts of school classrooms are said to be 'shaped by colonization', it is evident that just about anything linked with the past is implicated in the NEU's teleology of evil. This teleology of evil exemplifies how Year Zero ideology provides an interpretative narrative for educators. To demonstrate that colonization constitutes a clear and present danger, the NEU asserts that there is a 'silence around British imperialism and racism' in the education system, and British culture is 'saturated with a longing for return to Empire'. The unsupported and arguably foolish assertion that British culture longs for the return of the Empire legitimates the claim that nothing has changed and that, despite appearances, this country continues to live in the colonial past.

For its part, the General Teaching Council for Scotland (GTCS) has decided that its mission is to indoctrinate rather than educate schoolchildren. Guidance issued by GTCS in 2021 asserted that teachers must commit to promoting 'social justice, diversity and sustainability'. It stated that 'Scotland's teachers help to embed sustainable and socially just practices in order to flourish as a nation'.[18]

Embedding 'socially just practices' in the classroom is a euphemism for indoctrinating pupils with the GTCS's political values. Historically, the attempt to embed a distinct system of political values in the classroom was associated with the practices of totalitarian regimes like the Soviet Union. In Western democracies, it was understood that a teacher's proper role is to educate and serve as a guide, not to play the role of a political commissar instructing students what to think.

The promotion in schools of the narrative of decolonization – which represents a version of Year Zero ideology – aims to achieve its objective through questioning and undermining the conventional values that guide the behaviour of most people. Its supporters have little interest in the academic content of the school subjects they wish to decolonize. Instead, they regard the decolonization of an academic discipline as a means for exacting revenge on the past and putting right what they perceive as its inequities. So, the call to decolonize science is indifferent to the question of method or epistemology. Instead, it aims to criticize the contributors to the field of science for possessing the wrong skin colour and coming from the wrong gender. A monograph on curriculum decolonization advises:

> Perhaps we might help pupils to understand some of the social context of science; to help them to know why, for example, historic privileges have

> meant that many scientific discoveries are credited to men rather than women, and White rather than ethnic minority people. And, importantly, more can be done to strengthen the representation within the curriculum of key scientific knowers from ethnic minority backgrounds. Incorporating this thinking within the curriculum might help more children to see themselves within the curriculum, or at least to understand some of the social factors that have limited the representation of particular groups within science.[19]

Encouraging children to regard a science lesson as an opportunity to explore their identity will do little to help them understand biology, chemistry, or physics. But then the decolonization of the classroom is not about the encouragement of the intellectual development of children. Instead, it wishes to foster a sense of resentment towards a school subject for failing to validate the group identity of sections of the classroom.

The Culture Wars promoted in the school aim to saturate the classroom with the outlook of Year Zero ideology. Designating every dimension of the classroom experience as marked by the residue of colonialism serves to remind the young that their past is bereft of virtuous moments. In this way, supporters of the project of decolonization seek to rupture the links – emotional, moral, intellectual – that bind children to their past. One of the most important spheres where this process is played out is in the field of teaching history.

History rendered contemporary

The influence of the conflict over cultural values in education has important implications for the future of society. The socialization of young people requires acquainting them with their cultural inheritance and the historical experiences that bind them. The common ground on which people live requires a shared understanding of where members of a community come from. Learning about the past helps children to know their place in the world and develop their identity. Erik Erikson, who formulated the concept of an identity crisis, attached great importance to providing young people with a sense of cultural continuity. He noted that 'true identity … depends on the support which the young individual receives from the collective sense of identity characterising the social groups significant to him: his class, his nation, his culture'.[20] For

Erikson, a 'collective sense of identity' is closely linked to the capacity of the adult world to provide the young with a sense of historical continuity.

One of the most important ways that schools can assist young people to gain a sense of cultural continuity is through the teaching of history. Understanding history allows children to cultivate their individual, community, and national identity. How a community views its history influences its members' perceptions of who they are and how they view the wider world. It is for this reason that in the modern era the teaching of history has often been the subject of controversy. Different interpretations of the past have led to disputes about what to emphasize and what kind of meaning to assign to important historical episodes. Controversies over whether to teach a version of the past that instils national pride or one that draws attention to the mistakes committed by ancestors continue to this day. Since the eruption of the War Against the Past, the debate about the teaching of history has deepened so that the very role of this subject is often called into question.

For better or worse, the history curriculum has become politicized and a battlefield where the War Against the Past is fought. As the authors of *The History Wars* explain, the expansion of this conflict into the classroom 'has added a new and vital dimension to the contemporary historical debate: it is through the image of the child, a symbol of the future, that the struggle over the past is increasingly conducted'.[21] It is in these debates that the values and theoretical assumptions that motivate supporters of the War Against the Past are rendered explicit. Often, these debates are not so much about past events but about the legitimacy of protagonists' views about their nation, culture, and identity. From their standpoint, what matters is not the facts of history but whether the past validates their point of view.

For example, there is a heated debate about whether patriotism should be taught in schools. Critics of promoting patriotism dismiss the idea that schools should encourage a sense of loyalty to the nation. They insist that more time should be spent teaching children about the dark side of their past to make pupils aware of the damage caused by colonialism and racism. The response of supporters of a patriotic history curriculum mirrors their opponents: they argue against placing any emphasis on the misdeeds of the past. Regrettably, the need to provide children with a thorough acquaintance of history tends to be subordinated to the political agenda on both sides of the debate.

Supporters of both sides in the History Wars invariably stray into the realm of propaganda. However, in the current era, the intellectual and academic supporters of the War Against the Past are most zealously committed to politizising the study of history. The 1619 Project of *The New York Times*, which we discussed in chapter 3, is a paradigmatic example of political propaganda masquerading as legitimate historical analysis. The 1619 Project is unapologetic about abandoning historical evidence. Some of its academic apologists have openly embraced a contemporary version of Plato's Noble Lie. In her review of the project, the Cornell University historian Sandra Greene explains that the 'publication of *The 1619 Project* is so important despite its flaws', which include 'factual errors' and 'several chapters [that] simplify to the point of distortion'. According to Greene, it is a 'necessary book', and its errors 'should not be used as an excuse to deny the reality that slavery and racism have influenced every aspect of US history'.[22]

When a scholar appears so relaxed about sending out a text containing distortions and factual errors to schoolchildren, it becomes evident that a politicized agenda is trumping academic integrity. There are better ways of sustaining the claim that slavery and racism influenced much of US history than to rely on falsehood and political dogma.

In its devotion to render the events of the past contemporary, the 1619 Project follows a trend that has become deeply entrenched in teaching history in schools for many decades. The history curriculum throughout the West possesses a strong presentist bias. In some cases, the teaching of history has been displaced by social studies. Knowledge about the past is often dismissed as irrelevant to providing children with the skills necessary to engage with contemporary issues. This philistine orientation towards studying the past was memorably articulated by Charles Clarke, a former Labour Party education secretary, in May 2003. While visiting University College, Worcester, he dismissed medieval history as a waste of public money. He stated, 'I don't mind there being some medievalists around for ornamental purposes, but there is no reason for the state to pay for them.'[23]

Thankfully, policy-makers and educationalists do not go as far as Clarke in the contemptuous and instrumental way he regards the past. Nevertheless, they find it difficult to take seriously the necessity of encouraging students to develop a genuine interest in history. Unfortunately, they tend to limit their historical vision to the near past and rarely provide children with the opportunity to learn about the history of more chronologically distant periods. Consequently, history as a school subject has become marginalized, and its content redefined. This point was noted by the historian J.C.D. Clark when he observed:

> In so far as students still study history, they do so in later and later time-frames: in History Departments in US universities, courses on Hitler and the Holocaust attract hundreds of students, while courses on ancient Rome or the Reformation attract mere handfuls. In Britain, medieval history was withdrawn from the GCSE syllabus in 1997, and a controversial attempt made to drop Anglo-Saxon history from the A level syllabus of one examining board in 1999.

Clark drew attention to one significant development, which was that the 'assumption has taken root that events and episodes are more "relevant" to the present the closer they are to it in time'.[24] The teaching profession has become wedded to the curriculum of relevance, which in the discipline of history means using the past as a sounding board for the discussion of contemporary issues.

The failure to appreciate the importance of studying the past as an enterprise that is good in and of itself has encouraged the tendency to instrumentalize the curriculum. The emphasis on relevance has had the unfortunate tendency to ignore the study of the past as a medium through which a common view of the world can be cultivated. On the contrary, the curriculum of relevance asserts that stories that are relevant to white middle-class children cannot be used to motivate those from ethnic minorities. With the expansion of the politicization of identity, there are a growing number of calls to include material of relevance to girls and members of the LGBTQ+ community. The premise for the advocacy of a curriculum of relevance is that a young girl cannot possibly find the story of Julius Caesar compelling and instead needs to be entertained with stories about Florence Nightingale. The idea that children can learn to cultivate their imagination by learning about people and places that are unlike their own is overlooked by identity-addicted curriculum engineers.

The synthesis of the pedagogy of relevance with identity politics leads to the elaboration of a curriculum that assumes that people learn through becoming acquainted with knowledge that is attuned to their subjective experience. This approach is fully endorsed in the Council of Europe's statement *Quality Education in Europe in the 21st Century: Principles and Guidelines*. It states that 'to be relevant, history education should allow for learning experiences that are either directly applicable to the personal aspirations, interests, or cultural experiences of students (personal relevance) or that are connected in some way to real-world issues, problems, and contexts (life relevance)'.[25] Taken at face value, a curriculum of relevance would undermine the very purpose of quality schooling, which is to provide young people with the kind of knowledge that allows them to transcend their experience and learn to think abstractly.

Good teachers will always consider the subjective interests of their pupils. But if they allow the personal and cultural concerns of pupils to determine what is taught, then the curriculum becomes stripped of knowledge that is objectively necessary for the intellectual development of young people. In the case of history, the emphasis on pupils' lived experiences leads to an approach where students learn about a version of the past that mirrors their lives in the present. This 'it's all about me' approach risks turning history from an academic study of the past into an exercise in emotional validation. The focus on relevance invariably contradicts studying the past as such. If what is 'really relevant' is in the here and now, interest in studying history for its own sake is diminished.

Education is not, and should not be, reducible to ideas that are directly relevant to a pupil. Its aim should be to impart the knowledge and insights gained through the experiences of others in faraway places and different historical circumstances. The main significance of formal education is that it provides people with the capacity for generalization and the acquisition of what social scientist Michael Young describes as 'context-independent or theoretical knowledge'.[26] This is knowledge that is distinct from the practical knowledge that people acquire through the experience of their everyday life.

The knowledge acquired through formal education is not always useful or directly relevant. Indeed, one of its characteristics is that it is the kind of knowledge that most people cannot acquire through their everyday existence. Often, the knowledge provided through education is 'detached from the immediate, local world of the learner' and demands a redirection of interests away from their direct experience.[27] Education involves providing answers to questions that the young have not yet asked.

This kind of knowledge is important because it helps students rise above their particular experience and gain insights into the wider world. The premise of this type of formal education is the understanding that there are real limits to what can be learned from direct experience. Indeed, it demonstrates that we rely on knowledge gained through theoretical reflection to make sense of our immediate experience. As the philosopher of education R.S. Peters wrote, reflection on the world often involves the 'postulation of what is unobservable to explain what is observed'.[28] Since the way the world appears is often not the way it is, we rely on abstract theoretical knowledge to interpret it. In putting the case for a knowledge-based curriculum, Young observed that 'because the world is not as we experience it, curriculum knowledge must be discontinuous, not continuous with everyday experience'.[29]

The purpose of education is to help young people develop their capacity for thinking, knowing, reflecting, imagining, observing, judging, and questioning. At its best, such education provides students with an understanding of the past and the knowledge to think about and engage with the present and future issues. Of course, formal education also requires the acquisition of skills that are relevant to their lives – reading, writing, counting – but these are aids that are necessary for acquiring knowledge.

The curriculum of relevance invariably endorses the presentist outlook of reading history backwards. From this perspective, every identity – no matter how recently invented – must be given a place in a reinvented past. An explicit endorsement of this approach is outlined by the Historical Association in its statement titled 'How Diverse Is Your History Curriculum?' The statement begins with the observation that 'the past was full of diverse people and our students are entitled to learn about this diverse past'. This really means that since the contemporary world is obsessed with identity and diversity, it will ensure that the past reflects this contemporary concern. The statement poses several questions that draw attention to its demand for an inclusive curriculum, including 'Are the pasts of all students we teach represented in our curriculum?' and 'Are the pasts of the people of modern Britain represented in our curriculum?' A history curriculum directed towards the representation of all students can only achieve its objective by projecting the identities possessed by students onto the screen of the past. From this perspective, the past is transformed and simplified into an early version of the present.

In spelling out its objectives, the Historical Association's curriculum presents itself as committed to identity representation and validation. It indicates that:

> When students have finished learning our history curriculum will they have learnt that:
> - 50% of people in the past were women?
> - Black people and people of colour have lived in Britain since very ancient times?
> - The story of Black people and people of colour is not just one of people as victims of white oppression?
> - Jewish people and Roma and Traveller people have a long history that is not just one of suspicion and oppression?
> - There have always been less visible groups, such as LGBT+ people and people with disabilities in society?
> - Women were not all white, not all Black people were men, and so on ... that is we are thinking about people having different identities?
> - People were more rounded and complex than the labels people in power/society gave them – they do not just appear in our curriculum to be 'done unto' by people in power?
> - The diverse past helps to understand the diverse present?
> - History can be studied at different levels – from the local to the global?[30]

It is evident that the curriculum is entirely dominated by a commitment to the propagation of the cultural politics of identity. Every identity group gets a mention, but the curriculum is devoid of any attempt to offer an understanding of historical development. It does not offer any guidance that could help students understand the different stages of history or gain a sense of chronology. Instead of dealing with how communities were bound together through the ages, this curriculum represents diversity as the defining feature of the past.

The current vogue for projecting the politics of inclusivity back into the past has the unintended consequence of distorting the significance of the content of what historical figures achieved. At times, it seems that art critics are more interested in whether or not Caravaggio was gay than in his undisputed artistic identity as a great Baroque Italian painter. Far too many school textbooks dwell on the fact that Florence Nightingale was a woman. They are distracted by her female identity to the point that they underestimate her significant contribution to the use of statistical analysis and the improvement of nursing practices.

Rather than a nuanced understanding of the past, 'How Diverse Is Your History Curriculum?' offers a presentist tunnel vision in which contemporary concerns are forcedly projected onto very different past circumstances.

The presentist approach of the history curriculum is most clearly expressed through its insistence on the need for children to empathize with the people they are studying. This approach assumes that it is through the forging of an emotional connection between pupils and their historical subject that deep learning occurs. The Council of Europe's previously mentioned report *Quality History Education in Europe in the 21st Century* asserts the 'importance of emotion in response to historical events'.[31] The importance that curriculum experts attach to empathy is underpinned by the conviction that pupils learn through subjective identification with a subject. Unfortunately, encouraging students to acquire an emotional connection with an historical subject risks losing any understanding of context and historical specificity. Empathy across the temporal divide encourages an ahistorical orientation towards people who lived centuries ago.

Advocates of historical empathy believe that if students are encouraged to put themselves in the position of someone from the past, they will gain important historical insights. They argue that 'historical empathy not only helps students connect with the past but also provides them with the tools to understand better how that past has shaped the present'.[32] From this standpoint, empathy is regarded as a skill that 'refers to the ability to perceive, emotionally experience, and contextualize a historical figure's lived experience'.[33] However, while students can sympathize with the situation and predicament faced by historical figures, the goal of getting them to experience an historical figure's lived experience emotionally is likely to lead to little more than playing an imaginative game.

The representation of empathy as a skill speaks to a technocratic narrative that overlooks the relational dimension of emotional connection. The abstraction of empathy and its transformation into a generic skill can assist the task of impression management but not of deep learning. Moreover, the pedagogic orientation towards cultivating empathy overlooks the importance of subject-based knowledge about historical events. Empathy becomes emptied of relational content when practised by students trying to connect with people whose circumstances and outlooks they cannot understand through emotional identification. As J.C.D. Clark argued in his *Our Shadowed Present*, empathy 'presupposes the possibility of immediate access to the real meaning of the past, without wrestling with the arcane, biased, "constructed", "invented" apparatus of historical writing'.[34] Access to the real meaning of the past can only be approximated through the acquisition of disciplinary knowledge and not through exercising empathy.

The Black Armband view of history

The teaching of history has always been subject to conflicting political pressures. Since the 19th century, discord over history teaching has been a recurrent theme in Western educational discussion. Since the establishment of the European Union, policy-makers have sought to ensure that children are mainly exposed to the history of Europe rather than of their nations. In Australia, Canada, and the United States, the representation of the founding of these nations in the classroom has been a source of controversy. In Britain, the desirability of teaching patriotism has polarized the views of educators.

Recently, the influence of Year Zero ideology in the classroom has significantly impacted children's schooling. As journalist Jenni Russell noted in her column in *The Times*, there is a growing conviction amongst 'today's digital generation that "everyone in the past was wicked"'.[35] Many educators are devoted to the task of disabusing children of any idealism towards their nation's past that they may still possess. One contribution, 'Why Children Ought to be Taught the Bad Side of American History Too', finds it difficult to find traces of the good side of America's past.[36] It cautions against 'inferring America as a moral and honorable nation' because it 'brings about confusion when kids witness the Capitol uprisings'. Ensuring that young people do not regard their nation as moral and honourable is also one of the principal objectives of the 1619 Project. The version of this project sent out to schools informs children to question the claim that '1776 is the year of our nation's birth'. It notes:

> What if, however, we were to tell you that this fact, which is taught in our schools and unanimously celebrated every Fourth of July, is wrong, and that the country's true birth date, the moment that our defining contradictions first came into the world, was in late August of 1619?[37]

It was in 1776 that the Second Continental Congress, held in Philadelphia, voted unanimously to issue the Declaration of Independence of the United States of America. By inciting children to become sceptical about the significance of America's Declaration of Independence, the 1619 Project attempts to influence them to regard their nation's founding negatively.

Calling into question the moral status of the nation is also advocated by sections of the education profession in Britain. According to a report published by researchers Michael Hand and Jo Pearce from the University of London's Institute of Education, patriotism should not be taught in school. Based on a survey of 300 teachers, the report concluded that patriotism should only be taught as a 'controversial issue'. Hand and Pearce claimed that Britain, with its 'morally ambiguous' history, should no longer be made into an object of school pupils' affection.

Hand and Pearce's study is not simply a critique of Britain's past but of loyalty to the tradition it embraces. They rhetorically ask, 'Are countries appropriate or fitting objects of love?' and call for an implicit cultural hostility towards national histories. Their advice is that 'loving certain things may be bad for us', especially when 'loving what is morally vicious, depraved or corrupt'. The report warns that 'to love what is corrupt is itself corrupting, not least because it inclines us to ignore, forget, forgive or excuse the corruption'.[38] The statement infers that loving Britain and its past is corrupting and, therefore, needs to be condemned rather than praised.

The influential Israeli historian Yuval Noah concurs that the teaching of history needs to change to insulate children from all 'the damaging stories' taught to previous generations. He regards the traditional stories about humanity's past as both false and harmful:

> Another thing we cannot shield children from is exposure to false historical narrative. From a very early age, the young are bombarded with myths and disinformation, not just about current events, but also about the basic storyline of humanity itself – who we are, where we come from and how we got here.
>
> In my home country of Israel, for example, even secular schoolchildren typically learn about the Garden of Eden and see colourful images of Noah's Ark long before they hear about Neanderthals.

Harari contends that biblical stories about the Garden of Eden and Noah's Ark are harmful and are actually responsible for the ecological crisis facing humanity. He writes that 'it's possible to trace a direct line from the Genesis decree of "fill the earth and subdue it" to the Industrial Revolution and today's ecological crisis'. His representation of stories from the Old Testament as the source of humanity's environmental irresponsibility taints a text that has inspired people for thousands of years.

Harari joins the chorus of naysayers who insist that 'it's crucial to talk about the dark side of history'. For him, history ought to be an instrument for estranging people from their past and not one for remembering it. He affirmed this thesis with his concluding remark: 'After all, the point of learning history is not to remember the past, but to be liberated from it.'[39] This call captures the attitude that motivates the War Against the Past. The term 'liberation' implies that there is something oppressive or malevolent from which it is necessary to be freed. From this perspective, the past possesses a tyrannical and oppressive power that damages those who have not been able to free themselves from its influence. That is why there is little point in remembering it. Of course, Harari is a professional historian, and it is unlikely that he is really disinterested in the past. What he means by questioning the value of remembering the past is that we should take a safe distance from it.

Despite Harari's warning, the relationship between liberation and the remembrance of the past can be conceptualized in a creative manner.

John Lewis Gaddis, the eminent American historian of the Cold War, noted that historians 'liberate their subjects from the prospect of being forgotten'.[40] Instead of forgetting the past or simply denouncing it, a more productive approach is to engage in a dialogue with our ancestors. Certainly, the most effective way of teaching history in the classroom is through motivating children to enter a dialogue with the past and remembering it.

The darkening of history

The cumulative effect of cultural and educational institutions' negative framing of the past is to alienate children from their nation's history. That is one possible reason for students' decline in interest in their nation's history. The school curriculum fails to provide young people with a sense of the chronology of key events and historical development. The negativity encourages scepticism and contempt for the legacy of the past.

Numerous publications, videos, and podcasts dwell on what they characterize as the dark side of British history. Some of these books and videos present their material as if they are acting as courageous whistle-blowers who are finally exposing the truth about a past that has been intentionally hidden from the public view. A YouTube video titled 'The Dark Side of British History You Weren't Taught in School' presents a story that treats the impact of the British Empire on India as not unlike the Holocaust. Incredibly, it asserts that perhaps as many as 29 million people may have died in India due to famine manufactured by the British from 1876 to 1878 and that inmates in labour camps received the same rations as those in Buchenwald.[41] Black studies professor Kehinde Andrews also claims that the British Empire did more damage than the Nazis.[42] Another historian, Amaresh Misra, actually uses the term 'Holocaust' to refer to the brutal methods used by the British in the mid-19th-century India.[43] Others echo Misra, going a step further and insisting that the British self-consciously introduced what they call 'the Indian Holocaust'.[44]

Aside from distorting and trivializing the Holocaust, the project of demonizing Britain's imperial past seeks to corrode any version of British identity that retains positive qualities. In this way, Britain's past possesses no redeeming features. Inevitably, many schoolchildren have internalized the miserabilist and cynical accounts regarding the historical achievements of British society.

In April 2001, pupils at Pimlico Academy in South London protested against their school's policy of flying the Union Jack. The response of the school authority was to swiftly agree to the children's demand to take down the 'racist' Union flag and applaud the students' behaviour: 'Our students are bright, courageous, intelligent young people, passionate about the things that matter to them and acutely attuned to injustice. I admire them hugely for this though I regret that it came to this,' wrote Daniel Smith, the headteacher.[45]

In effect, the school's response to this incident indicates a preparedness to live in a world where expressions of hatred for the symbol of the nation exist on the same moral plane as that of British identity.

Stripping symbols of Britishness of any trace of moral authority is not confined to the nation's flag. Pride in Britain's important role in defeating Nazi Germany during the Second World War is now countered by the claims that downsize the nation's contribution to the Allies victory. 'Britain has built a national myth on winning the Second World War, but it's distorting our politics,' argues one commentator in *The New Statesman.*[46] There is a veritable industry devoted to dispelling the conviction that Britain played a unique and historically significant role during the Second World War. David Edgerton, in his 'The Nationalisation of British History: Historians, Nationalism and the Myths of 1940', decries the idea that Britain 'stood alone'.[47] He seems to suggest that a version of history that has served as a source of pride in the post-Second World War era is more or less a myth. If these critics are to be believed, just about everything associated with the pre-existing social memory of this war is a myth, and there is very little left in this story that can serve as a source of pride.

The questioning of official versions of historical events is a legitimate scholarly pursuit. There is little doubt that government propaganda played an important role in how events during the Second World War were represented to the British public. Propaganda regarding the management of the Empire played a significant role in promoting a benevolent image of the role of British colonialism.[48] It is the task of historians to call into question apologies for the Empire. But there is a difference between the aspiration for historical accuracy and the impulse to distort it by highlighting only the ignoble deeds of the past.

The single-minded objective of the current project of negating the symbols of Britishness is to corrupt its historical legacy. That is why a positive account of the nation's history is conspicuously rare within the school system. The use of terms like 'Victorian values' or 'Victorian morality' in Britain is now almost entirely derogatory. These terms connote narrow-minded and bigoted attitudes, a rigid social code of conduct, an unhealthy culture of sexual restraint, and the scandal of child labour. Young people today are rarely acquainted with this era's significant scientific, technological, moral, and political achievements. They are more likely to be told about concerns around anthropogenic pollution and fossil fuel reliance stemming from this era than about the positive contribution of the Industrial Revolution to human development.

The reaction of teachers and pupils alike in Pimlico Academy is symptomatic of a distorted historical memory in education. J.C.D. Clark characterized this development as a 'distinct enterprise of historical disinheritance'.[49] In the 20 years that have passed since Clark's comment, the War Against the Past has gone from strength to strength and has successfully inflicted the condition of historical amnesia on society. To be sure, historical amnesia does not mean that society and its people forget everything about their past. It is a selective form of amnesia where social memory is drawn towards remembering some events and overlooking others. Unlike the individual experience of amnesia, which is a psychological phenomenon, the historical amnesia of a society is a cultural accomplishment. Like all cultural accomplishments, it is the result of human cultivation. In the context of our discussion, it refers to the projection of darkness on the past and the remembering of far too little of humanity's inspiring achievements.

It is important to underline the fact that the framing of the past as dark is not simply pursued through history lessons. Virtually every subject in the school curriculum can serve as a vehicle for communicating a script that demeans the past and discredits the values associated with it. Sex education, which has been rebranded as sexuality education, transmits a message of parents' incompetence and of their outdated values. A textbook titled *Evidence-based Approaches to Sexuality Education* (2015) warns that 'generations of parents have had poor experiences with learning about sexuality, which they have passed on to their own children'.[50] UNESCO's *International Technical Guidance on Sexuality Education* explicitly informs teenagers that 'as children grow up, they develop their own values which may differ from their parents/guardians'. One of the learning outcomes of this guidance is to teach students to 'differentiate between values they hold, and that their parents/guardians hold about sexuality'.[51] Students are left in no doubt that their values, the values they are taught in sexuality education, are superior to those of their parents, and certainly to the views held by their ancestors in the past. It is worthy of note that schools have adopted the guidance issued by UNESCO throughout large parts of the Western world.

If it is really the case that parents' values are inferior to those advocated by sexuality education and other curricula, then there is little point in encouraging the transmission of the legacy of the past. On the contrary, these values should be avoided and replaced by the most up-to-date ones. The guidance offered by UNESCO and related educational resources promoting sexuality education is informed by the objective of re-engineering the socialization of the young. The implicit assumption that underpins sexuality education is the necessity for instructing the young to adopt norms of behaviour that are at variance with the conventions of the past.

The re-engineering of socialization requires that previous versions are discredited and that the commitment to transmitting values is displaced by the promotion of new, up-to-date norms. The historian of psychology Kurt Danzinger has characterized the re-engineering of socialization as 'a matter of changing obsolescent individual attitudes'.[52] The practice of changing 'obsolescent' attitudes dominates not only sexuality education but also numerous other school subjects. This is why primary and secondary education has become such an important site for conducting the War Against the Past.

Unlike socialization, which involves the transmission of pre-existing values, its re-engineering is devoted to gaining support for attitudes that lack majority support in society. That is why the indoctrination of the young is conducted in such a manner as to leave parents in the dark. Most parents and adults do not realize that the latest fashionable values of tomorrow are already being taught in schools.

The cumulative outcome of cultivating social amnesia through the re-engineering of the curriculum is to make people forget where they come from and that they are part of a cultural community. As the English author and philosopher G.K. Chesterton explained:

> Education is simply the soul of a society as it passes from one generation to another. What we need is to have a culture before we hand it down. It is a truth, however sad and strange, that we cannot give what we have not got and cannot teach to other people what we do not know ourselves.[53]

When Chesterton wrote this in 1924, we knew far more about ourselves than we do today. Unfortunately, education's refusal to play the role of the soul of society threatens the young with becoming totally disinherited from their past.

Conclusion

Cicero's phrase *historia magistra vitae*, history is life's teacher, may seem a little trite. It has been repeated so frequently that we may dismiss it as a cliché. However, this phrase contains an important truth: humanity's experience of the world provides us with the insight, clarity, and confidence required to make our own way. The failure to assimilate this experience dispossesses humanity of the vision required to confront the challenges of the future.

Paradoxically, those who wish to be liberated from the past invariably become its prisoners. As we noted previously, supporters of the crusade against the past frequently end up living their lives through it. There is little that is liberating about fixating on the misdeeds of the past. Avoiding responsibility for learning from history is, as Cicero implies, to remain forever a child. The self-inflicted condition of historical amnesia deprives its practitioners of the important insights gained over centuries of trial and error.

The refusal to take on board Shakespeare's statement that 'there is a history in all men's lives' leads to a rupture between people and their past. Indeed, one of the most regrettable outcomes of the War Against the Past has been the weakening of the consciousness of history and the emergence of the condition of social amnesia. In effect, the writing-off of the past and the legacy of human achievement calls into question the moral status of humanity itself, which is hardly surprising if people have achieved so little in the past that is worthy of preservation and praise.

Presentism limits society's understanding of historical variability and change and the role of humanity in the making of their world. Often the polemic hurled against the past is specifically directed at the legacy of Western society, but contempt for the achievements of our ancestors is often communicated through a narrative that upholds the moral superiority of the entire contemporary world over what preceded it. However, implicitly, its patronizing assumptions pertain to the achievements of humanity as a whole and not just to those of our forebears.

Western society's pessimistic and cynical outlook towards the past breeds complacency and resignation towards the future. To counter this outlook, it is necessary to elaborate a balanced account of the achievements of the past. Only if people gain clarity about what humanity has achieved so far can they gain insight into what it can attain in the future. A nuanced view of the past shows that people are not just the objects but also the subjects of their destiny.

The ideological orientation driving the War Against the Past represents a dramatic break with the philosophical worldview of virtually every social and political movement of the modern era. That history constituted an important intellectual and cultural resource that provided insights about the conduct of human affairs was rarely questioned. Previous political foes on the Left and Right – despite their differences – all drew something positive from the experience of human history making. Scientific and liberal thought recognized that remaining connected with the achievements of the past was a precondition for moving forward. For conservative thinkers, the past is an important source of enlightenment. They regard tradition as possessing the capacity to confer wisdom and insight on human action in the present. Both liberals and conservatives viewed the accomplishment of human civilization in essentially positive terms and used the word without a sense of embarrassment.

From the 18th century onwards, those drawn towards a conservative outlook went so far as to claim that the traditions of the past could convey transcendental truths relevant to people for all times. Others drew different lessons and regarded history as an inspiration for making significant improvement to the condition of humanity. Today's practitioners of Year Zero Ideology adopt a very different approach. As far as they are concerned, the past is not a source of inspiration and should not be used to provide guidance. Their infantile behaviour towards the past leads them to renounce the achievements of humanity. If little good was achieved in the past, why would humanity improve on its record in the future? Unwilling to offer a balanced account of how history was made in the past, they call into question the contribution that human agency can make to improving the future.

Although, historically, the conservative and liberal views of the past are informed by fundamentally different perspectives, they both affirm the importance of embracing aspects of the human experience. There is a common heritage of enlightened thought that needs to be preserved and taken forward by all those who possess a humanist instinct. The differences on this issue between the two traditions is negligible compared to the chasm that separates them from the contemporary anti-humanist worldview of the authors of the War Against the Past. Their devaluation of the past and its transformation into a horror story encourages a sense of estrangement from a humanist sensibility.

The construction of a past that continually highlights human selfishness and destruction results in a deeply anti-humanist outlook on the world. It has contributed to the widely held view that it is the development of human civilization, particularly the advance of science and technology with the resulting subordination of the natural order to the demands of human society, that is the source of today's problems of environmental destruction and social disintegration.

Civilization is seen to bear responsibility for the perils we face today, and this perspective assigns an undistinguished, if not low, status to the human species. In its most extreme form, this outlook expresses loathing for humanity. People are often portrayed as parasites that threaten the existence of the earth. Human activity is blamed for threatening the survival of the planet. Scare stories that exaggerate the scale of human destruction are regularly broadcast in the media and promoted by advocacy groups and politicians. Telling and retelling a negative story of humanity to date breeds complacency and resignation towards the future. In this way the loss of the authority of the past has led to the emergence of a fatalistic zeitgeist.

In the 21st century, the modernist belief in humanity's potential for subduing the unknown and mastering its fate has given way to the belief that we are powerless to deal with the perils confronting humankind. A loss of faith in humanity's capacity to assume a degree of control over its destiny coexists with a pessimistic vision of the future. The external manifestation of the downsizing of the moral status of humanity is the prevailing influence of fatalism over society. For its part, fatalism is steeped in the presentist zeitgeist discussed in earlier chapters.

In his study *Politics and Fate* (2013), the political theorist Andrew Gamble described the mood of fatalism prevailing in society in the following terms:

> There is now a deep pessimism about the ability of human beings to control anything very much, least of all through politics. This new fatalism about the human condition claims we are living through a major watershed in human affairs. It reflects the disillusion of political hopes in liberal and socialist utopias in the twentieth century and a widespread disenchantment with the grand narratives of the Enlightenment about reason and progress, and with modernity itself. Its most characteristic expression is the endless discourses on endism – the end of history, the end of ideology, the end of the nation-state, the end of authority, the end of the public domain, the end of politics itself – all have been proclaimed in recent years.[1]

If one were to believe all the claims made on this score, it would be difficult to avoid the conclusion that we are doomed to remain in a presentist purgatory.

In our times, fatalism has acquired some unique qualities. Previous debates about human destiny and how much of our fate is predestined occurred within a moral framework which expected people to exercise judgement and responsibility. Today, fatalism has become a cultural orientation; an outlook that diminishes the value of choice and subjectivity. It negates the need for judgement and hollows out the meaning of responsibility.

It wasn't always this way. History has thrown up numerous answers to the question of who decides our individual fate. Time and again, communities struggled with the issue of how much the actions of people influence our future. In ancient times, different gods were endowed with the capacity to thwart our ambition or bless us with good fortune. The Romans, who worshipped the goddess Fortuna, conceded her great power over the outcome of human affairs. Nevertheless, they still believed that her influence could be contained and even overcome by the deeds of men of true virtue. This belief that the power of fortune could be restrained through human effort and will is one of the important legacies of humanism.

Without a close connection with the past, we become prisoners of fate. Why? Because we can only truly understand what humanity has achieved so far and acquire insight into what it can achieve in the future by evaluating the experience of our forebears. The legacy of the past provides the moral and intellectual resources for developing a 21st-century narrative of what solidarity and community looks like. Very importantly, it also provides the foundation for freedom.

The French liberal political philosopher Benjamin Constant's warning about those who attempt to 'liberate individuals from local ties and prejudices' is apposite in this respect. He observed: 'How bizarre that those who called themselves ardent friends of freedom have worked relentlessly to destroy the natural basis of patriotism, to replace it with a false passion for an abstract being.' He claimed that peoples invariably lose their way when they are

> detached from their native soil with no contact with the past, living only in a swift-moving present and thrown like atoms on a monotonous plain, [they]take no interest in a fatherland they nowhere perceive and whose totality becomes indifferent to them, because their affection cannot rest on any of its parts.[2]

In the presentist purgatory, people who are estranged from the past will find it difficult to forge the kind of connections essential for social solidarity. In Constant's view, we have a moral responsibility to protect the achievements of the generations who preceded us from their detractors. We must fight for our history because, without it, the foundation for genuine solidarity is eroded. Historical or social amnesia is just that: a failure of memory. And when we forget what made us who we are and what binds us together, society cannot but become depressingly fragmented and polarized.

Once society becomes de-historicized and uprooted from its past, it will become lost in a timeless wasteland. Those with an impoverished historical imagination are doomed to embark on an eternal quest for meaning because we become connected and situated in time through cultivating an empathetic relationship with the past as members of a community. Without such an attachment, we struggle to intuit where we have come from and are constantly in search of an identity. Navigating our way into the future is harder when we are deprived of a means to assimilate the experience of our ancestors. Put simply, to determine where to go, we need to know where we came from.

Should society become overwhelmed by the ideology of Year Zero, it risks forgetting the valuable lessons gained through thousands of years of hard-earned experience. The loss of historical memory is not a small problem that only afflicts a handful of people interested in the past. Historical memory reminds society of insights and invaluable experience that cannot be simply created from thin air.

Social amnesia dislocates people from the process of history. It limits their capacity to grasp their lives in the here and now. Presentism strips the events of the current era of their historical context. It offers an artificially frozen view of a world indifferent to its origins. The failure to appreciate influences that evolved over decades, if not centuries, and which continue to shape the current times leads to historical illiteracy. Society becomes dislocated from its origins and existentially disconnected from the experiences that humanized our world.

There are countless schools of history and numerous conflicting interpretations of the past. But their differences notwithstanding, they are likely to reach the conclusion that history provides some of the most important moral and intellectual resources that are essential for human flourishing. The past provides important insights about the human condition and can be a source of inspiration. Historical achievements are a precious legacy which must be protected and preserved, and today the adult world must relearn the art of passing it on to the younger generations. Society needs to take control of its history, to learn from it and embrace its achievements with enthusiasm to counter the crusade against the past.

Taking control of history is not a backward-looking desire to hold on to what can never return but the preservation of legacy that provides the foundation for civilized existence. This legacy includes the language we share with the generations who preceded us, along with our moral sensibility about what we judge to be right or wrong. It is through its influence that we develop ideas about who we are and ideals about what we would like to become. Since in effect our very identity is at issue, the stakes are extraordinarily high in the War Against the Past.

It is not nostalgia – a sentimental longing for something from the past to comfort us – but the impulse to understand where we come from that demands the reclaiming the authority of the past so that we can take our rightful place in the world. The past is not simply a temporal phenomenon that we can write off as something that we are done with. It represents the stock of human experience through which different societies developed their knowledge, their codes of behaviour and values. The past is a story of enormous strides and of setbacks and catastrophic errors. Through this experience, humanity was forced to confront the evils for which it bore responsibility as well as to learn the power of doing good. It learned to distinguish between right and wrong and developed a sensibility that was at times directed towards compassion, benevolence, and care. The influence of this civilizational process did not guarantee that individuals and communities would always act in accordance with the norms of civilized behaviour. But the existence of these norms meant that there was a commonly understandable language with which to challenge their violations.

The understanding gained through the experience of the past made it possible for philosophers like Pierre Bayle and John Locke to develop ideas that would eventually be codified through the modern value of tolerance. The precondition for its development was the willingness to learn from the bloody clashes that afflicted Europe over the centuries. Centuries of thinking and reacting to religious conflict and, later, bloody sectarian wars provided the lessons that compelled a small group of thinkers to challenge the prevailing hegemony of unyielding zealotry and dogma and demand the toleration of competing views.

As late as 1691, the French Bishop Jacques-Bénigne Bossuet boasted that Catholicism was the least tolerant of all religions, stating that 'I have the right to persecute you because I am right and you are wrong'.[3] Protestant religious figures more than matched Bossuet's intolerance. Indeed, the Walloon synod of Leyden, mainly composed of Huguenot refugees, condemned religious toleration as a form of heresy.[4] There was nothing natural about tolerance. Without the prevalence of intolerant behaviour and being forced to face up to its destructive consequences, the ideal of tolerance would not have emerged. The idealization of intolerance is not only chronologically but also logically prior to the valuation of tolerance. All the important values of the contemporary world, such as freedom and equality, emerged in response to their opposite. It was the capacity to learn from the experience of the past that has allowed human civilization to develop attitudes that influence attitude and behaviour today. At a certain point, the discomfort and suffering of sections of society provoked the sensibility of repugnance amongst a relatively small number of individuals. However, with the passing of time, their sensibility gained ascendancy and came to influence wider sections of society. If we turn our back on this cultivation of civilized behaviour and write it off as outdated, society will lose touch with the understanding of both what to value and how to value.

The outlook and sensibilities of the contemporary world have evolved through a civilizational dialectic that humanized people's response to the spilling of blood, violent behaviour, slavery, oppression in its different forms, inequality, and unfreedom. In his fascinating study on the 'civilizational process', the sociologist Norbert Elias drew attention to the profound change in human behaviour during the era from AD 800 to the turn of the 20th century. These changes to human behaviour touched on attitudes towards violence, forms of speech, sexual behaviour, table manners, and so on.[5] Following the work of Freud, Elias highlighted the internalization of the mode of 'self-restraint' in the exercise of people's conduct during the course of their interpersonal relations. It should be noted that many of the attitudes that are integral to the outlook that patronizes the past and deems it morally inferior are themselves the accomplishment of the civilizational process discussed by Elias. The moral sensibility that demands atonement for the alleged misdeeds of our ancestors evolved historically through the crystallization of civilized values.

We must fight for our history to ensure that the achievements of our civilization are protected from those who seek to undermine its moral authority. That requires that we must engage in a battle to protect some of the most important civilizational achievements of our ancestors. There are potentially numerous historical achievements to choose from. However, the most inspiring story that transcends the ages is the way in which time and again humanity has rediscovered the idea of liberty and freedom as fundamental principles that bear upon their existence. It was in Europe that these ideals first pushed out their roots. The ideals of toleration and the freedom of individual belief and of individual conscience were crucial in providing societies with a capacity to be open to new ideas and experiences. Such sentiments encouraged our ancestors to become curious about their world. An openness to exploration and risk-taking became integral to the DNA of modern society.

Once freedom gained cultural validation, it was only a matter of time before the freedom to act in accordance with one's conscience gained hold. The conceptualization of a separate sphere of individual conscience and belief created the foundation for the distinction between public and private life. The emergence of these two separate spheres and the valuation of privacy accorded the individual affirmation and respect. One of the important legacies of the European Enlightenment is the ideal of individual moral autonomy and its attendant recognition of the importance of individual choice making. Today's recognition that we exist both as members of a community and as distinct individuals would be unthinkable without the ascendancy of the 16th-century ideal of individual conscience.

Over the centuries, the combined contribution of the ancients – Greeks and Romans – the Renaissance and the Enlightenment helped to consolidate an openness to experimentation leading to the growing influence of reasoning and science. The Judaeo- Christian tradition provided history with a system of moral ideals as well as a tradition that takes ideas seriously. The cumulative outcome of these influences was the development of a cultural tradition that is hospitable to the development of new ideas. Typically, the religious, philosophical, and scientific movements begat by this tradition have transcended cultural and national boundaries. The experience of the Renaissance and the Enlightenment serves as a testimony to the vitality of this tradition. It is a tradition that transcended its historical origins and retains its relevance in our time. It is a tradition that is open to yielding to new experience and can therefore continue to thrive and develop.

That history is a living phenomenon is demonstrated by the continuous discovery and rediscovery of tradition. As Alasdair MacIntyre explained, 'An adequate sense of tradition manifests itself in a grasp of those future possibilities which the past has made available to the present.' These are 'living traditions, just because they continue a not-yet-completed narrative', which 'confront a future whose determinate and determinable character, so far as it possesses any, derives from the past'.[6] Ezra Pound regarded tradition as 'a beauty that we preserve and not a set of fetters to bind us'. He added that 'a return to origins invigorates because it is a return to nature and reason'.[7]

The civilizational process that links the people of the 21st century to their forebears thousands of years ago was frequently disrupted by setbacks and events that threatened to undo the achievements of the past. Nevertheless, despite periodic outbursts of destructive and oppressive behaviour, humanity has been able to move forward and build on its legacy. It is as if a self-correcting mechanism is at work; one that sooner or later reacts to violations of human dignity and of civilizational norms.

As a result, those who despise the past are trapped in a temporal quarantine of their own making. When they ridicule the culture of ancient Greece, they come across as oblivious to anything other than the fact that the ownership of slaves was widespread in these city-states. They decry the significance of the discovery of democracy in ancient Athens and seek to undermine Greece's contribution to the foundation of Western civilization by calling into question its moral standing. Yet our world today is much more influenced by the Athenian spirit of democracy than its instrumental use of slavery. The experience of ancient Athens, with its celebration of the *demos* (the people), the *agora* (the assembly), and its valuation of rhetoric, science, and philosophy, continues to possess a foundational significance for contemporary life. This connection to an ancient civilization must be carefully guarded and its history protected from the naysaying assault on it by grievance archaeologists.

That the legacy of Athenian democracy has triumphed over that of slavery demonstrates that there is much of value in our history. Here what is at issue is not the reinterpretation of history but the mission of exacting a self-serving form of collective punishment on it. The pursuit of collective punishment extends across the temporal divide from the past to the present. Denunciation of the past goes hand in hand with the demand for an act of atonement, contrition, and reparation. In Numbers 14: 89 in the Bible, it is said that the Lord will visit 'the iniquity of the fathers on the children, to the third and the fourth generation'. The current version of ancestral sin advocated by grievance archaeologists is far more unforgiving. It argues that the sins of the father are passed on to generations in perpetuity.

It is paradoxical that the grievance entrepreneurs who are entirely comfortable with the temporal transmission of sins committed centuries ago are totally hostile to the continuing relevance of historical tradition. They forget that the traditions of the past cannot be easily rendered invisible because they are still alive within us, the language we use and the way we reason.

Throughout the previous chapters, we have questioned the attempt to represent the past as morally inferior to the practices and modes of behaviour of society today. Drawing a moral contrast between the present and the past is pointless. The past is not morally superior to the present, but nor should it be interpreted as a temporal era in need of our moral instruction. Historical societies like those of today should be assessed and understood in relation to the specific circumstances and context of their time. Our role is to learn and understand from the experience of the past and not to subject it to a retrospective ideological or political experiment.

The harm done by the vandalization of the past is all too evident in the contemporary world. Young people, growing up with a weak and troubled sense of connection with what preceded them, are the human casualties of the War Against the Past. The imposition of the condition of historical amnesia contributes to the perpetuation of a mood of cultural malaise. Trapped in a presentist quagmire, Western society, which once prided itself in its orientation towards the future, has turned on itself. Winston Churchill was right when he stated that 'a nation that forgets its past has no future'.

To recognize this is also to recognize the existence of an additional virtue, the importance of which is most obvious when it is least present: the virtue of having a clear sense of the traditions to which one belongs. This virtue is not to be confused with any form of backward-looking antiquarianism; I am not recommending an uncritical embrace of tradition or the association of the past with a golden age. Instead, we must recognize that when we appreciate and understand tradition, we see how future possibilities might be grasped. The lessons of the past, learned in the present, enrich the future. Living traditions continue a not-yet-completed narrative and confront a future whose the determinate and determinable character derives from the past.

Notes

Introduction

1 Clark (2004), pp. 27–8.

2 https://www.theguardian.com/books/2021/feb/02/the-new-age-of-empire-by-kehinde-andrews-empireland-by-sathnam-sanghera-review.

3 https://www.museumsassociation.org/campaigns/decolonising-museums/supporting-decolonisation-in-museums/#.

4 https://www.oed.com/search/advanced/Meanings?textTermText0=scrutiny&textTermOpt0=WordPhrase.

5 See Thompson (1963), p. 12.

6 Kant (2005 [1795]), p. 92.

7 https://www.telegraph.co.uk/books/authors/eradicating-bad-stuff-unwelcome-return-book-burning/?WT.mc_id=tmgoff_psc_ppc_performancemax_dynamiclandingpages&gclid=Cj0KCQjwoK2mBhDzARIsADGbjeqeq7WUk3MIRUZ-peWSarxnSOuovw2q2TNnwHhDFZFhkGNQoeHnT1gaAvGLEALw_wcB.

8 https://www.telegraph.co.uk/news/2023/04/08/british-library-emotional-support-trigger-warnings-blm-woke/.

9 https://www.thetimes.co.uk/article/critical-race-theory-uk-schools-scmnfddnm.

10 Furedi (1992).

11 Hoffman (1979), p. 9.

12 Ibid.

13 Nisbet (1980), pp. 332–3.

14 Thatcher (1977), p. 29.

15 Cited in https://www.cultureontheoffensive.com/leftist-critique-of-the-left/.

16 Himmelfarb (2001), p. 118.

17 Hoffman (1979), p. 25.

18 For a 1970s version of this argument, see Keniston (1970). He wrote of 'a rate of social change so rapid that it threatens to make obsolete all institutions, values, methodologies and technologies within the lifetime of each generation' (p. 633).

19 https://www.irishexaminer.com/lifestyle/celebrity/arid-31006230.html.

20 https://unherd.com/2022/07/the-west-needs-to-grow-up/.
21 Eksteins (1989), p. 291.
22 https://www.theguardian.com/us-news/2020/sep/18/first-thing-whitewashing-us-history-with-patriotic-education.
23 https://www.independent.co.uk/voices/trump-speech-1619-project-critical-race-theory-b473614.html.
24 https://trumpwhitehouse.archives.gov/briefings-statements/remarks-president-trump-white-house-conference-american-history/.
25 See Furedi (1989b, 1994a, 1994b, 1998).
26 Táíwò (2022), p. 8.
27 Inglis (2014), p. 113.

Chapter 1 What Is the Past?

1 https://www.theguardian.com/the-scott-trust/ng-interactive/2023/mar/28/the-scott-trust-legacies-of-enslavement-report.
2 https://www.theguardian.com/world/2023/apr/09/archbishop-of-canterbury-justin-welby-100m-fund-c-of-es-past-links-to-slavery-easter?CMP=share_btn_tw.
3 Lowenthal (2015 [1985]), p. 1; Hartley (2015 [1953]), p. 5.
4 https://en.wikipedia.org/wiki/The_Past.
5 https://www.oed.com/search/advanced/Entries?q=past&sortOption=Frequency.
6 Condit (2013), p. 3.
7 Hobsbawm (1998), p. 32.
8 Trilling (1957), p. 189.
9 Hobsbawm (1972), p. 3.
10 Furedi (1992), p. 3.
11 Wright (1985), p. 5.
12 Merriman (2016), p. 3.
13 Plumb (1969), p. 66.
14 Ibid., p. 14.
15 Ibid., p. 51.
16 https://guides.lib.sussex.ac.uk/decolonisation.
17 https://www.change.org/p/the-university-of-missouri-remove-the-statue-of-thomas-jefferson-from-campus.
18 https://uk.style.yahoo.com/oxford-students-want-racist-statue-removed-091520271.html.
19 See the discussion in Furedi (2016).
20 Eyewitness News, 19 March 2015 (link no longer available).

21 https://www.telegraph.co.uk/world-news/2023/10/31/robert-e-lee-statue-melted-down-virginia-inclusive-monument/.
22 https://www.theguardian.com/culture/2020/sep/13/off-with-the-heads-pitt-rivers-museum-removes-human-remains-from-display.
23 https://www.oxfordmail.co.uk/news/18718189.pitt-rivers-museum-oxford-removes-shrunken-heads-exhibit/.
24 https://www.dailymail.co.uk/news/article-7124947/V-accused-infantilising-visitors-putting-warning-signs-history-exhibition.html.
25 https://www.marxists.org/archive/marx/works/1852/18th-brumaire/ch01.htm.
26 https://www.fondazionepirelli.org/en/corporate-culture/blog/the-usefulness-of-the-classics-in-science-and-business-re-reading-and-discussing-gramsci-in-il-sole24ore/.
27 Hobsbawm (1972), p. 13.
28 https://antigonejournal.com/2021/11/oedipus-life-path/.
29 Schiffman (2011), p. 7.
30 Ibid., p. 1.
31 Southern (1973), p. 244.
32 Porter (1988), p. 16.
33 Marius (1985), p. 65.
34 Roberts (1994), p. 98.
35 Ibid., p. 177.
36 This discussion on tradition draws on my study on the history of authority (see Furedi 2013).
37 Arendt (2005), p. 48.
38 Arendt (2006), p. 99.
39 Rawson (1985), p. 322.
40 Cicero (2008), Book 1, 70, p. 68 and Book 2, 2, p. 35.
41 Shotter (2005), p. 10.
42 Flower (2004), p. 9.
43 Cicero (2008), Book 2, 65, p. 56.
44 Arendt (2006), p. 99.
45 See ibid., chapter 5.
46 Wood (1988), p. 60.
47 Flower (2004), p. 9.
48 Lowenthal (2015 [1985]), p. 16.
49 Ibid., p. 4.
50 https://www.marxists.org/reference/archive/machiavelli/works/discourses/ch02.htm#:~:text=Men%20ever%20praise%20the%20olden,have%20seen%20in%20their%20youth.

51 Hobsbawm (1972), p. 3.
52 Koselleck (2004 [1979]), p. 5.
53 Hobsbawm (1972), p. 10.
54 https://founders.archives.gov/documents/Adams/99-02-02-6618.
55 Lowenthal (2015 [1985]), p. 185.
56 Ibid., p. 189.
57 https://oll.libertyfund.org/title/emerson-the-works-of-ralph-waldo-emerson-vol-7-society-and-solitude.
58 Bourne (1913), p. 13.
59 Cited in Kaplan (1956), p. 351.
60 Burt (2007), p. 142.
61 Cited in Wallach (1997), p. 154.
62 https://www.societyforasianart.org/sites/default/files/manifesto_futurista.pdf.
63 Ibid.
64 Keniston (1963), p. 153.
65 Erikson (1968), p. 30.
66 Keniston (1963), pp. 178–9.
67 https://www.econlib.org/book-chapters/chapter-vol-4-miscellaneous-writings-speech-on-the-reform-of-the-representation-of-the-commons-in-parliament/.
68 https://www.earlymoderntexts.com/assets/pdfs/burke1790part1.pdf (pp. 42 and 43).
69 Cited in Kahan (2001), p. 19.
70 https://oll.libertyfund.org/titles/256#lf0223-22_label_1091.
71 Ibid.
72 https://oll.libertyfund.org/titles/256#lf0223-22_label_1110.
73 https://oll.libertyfund.org/titles/256#lf0223-22_label_1221.
74 Cited in Ten (1969), pp. 58–9. Later this passage was altered to give it a wider more liberal tone but the emphasis was essentially the same as before. This essay can be accessed here: https://oll.libertyfund.org/titles/mill-the-collected-works-of-john-stuart-mill-volume-x-essays-on-ethics-religion-and-society.
75 Cited in Ten (1969), p. 60.
76 Condit (2013), p. 3.
77 Lowenthal (2015 [1985]), p. 1.

Chapter 2 The War's Long Gestation

1 Lukacs (2002), p. 5.
2 Rosenberg (1994 [1959]).
3 Burckhardt (1943), p. 6.
4 Ibid., p. 63.

5 Burnham (1960), p. 458.
6 https://www.marxists.org/archive/trotsky/1924/lit_revo/ch08.htm.
7 See the discussion in https://www.britannica.com/topic/fascism/Volksgemeinschaft.
8 See https://www.bbc.co.uk/news/magazine-25943326.
9 Abrams (1972), p. 22.
10 Ibid., p. 32.
11 Ross (1991), p. 253.
12 Inglis (2010), p. 110.
13 Wells (2005 [1911]), p. 35.
14 See Furedi (2014), chapters 1 and 2.
15 This point is developed in Furedi (2014).
16 Muller (2009), p. 224.
17 Bracken (2002), pp. 14 and 207.
18 Ross (1991), p. 16.
19 https://oll.libertyfund.org/titles/spencer-social-statics-1851 (chapter 2, § 4).
20 Ibid. (chapter 32, § 7).
21 Ibid.
22 Cited in Ross (1991), p. 150.
23 Ibid., p. 316.
24 Lynd (1932), p. 198.
25 See Moran (2012), pp. 11 and 26.
26 Frank (1940), p. 19.
27 Chisholm (1947), p. 107.
28 Tönnies (1955 [1887]), p. 263.
29 Friedrich (1972), p. 33.
30 Riesman with Glazer and Denny (1981 [1950]), p. xiv.
31 Hobsbawm (2020 [1994]), pp. 327 and 334.
32 See Coles (1974), p. 23.
33 https://www.orlandosentinel.com/2002/07/21/orlando-group-hoping-to-pique-concern-for-slavery-reparations/.
34 https://www.thetimes.co.uk/article/oxford-is-tying-itself-in-knots-over-racism-85lm7ztq7.
35 https://www.spiked-online.com/2020/06/09/why-did-the-protests-over-george-floyd-turn-into-mass-hysteria/.
36 Ross (1991), p. 475.

Chapter 3 The Ideology of Year Zero

1 Cited in Macintyre & Clark (2013), p. 3.

2 https://www.washingtonpost.com/opinions/2021/06/03/slavery-us-germany-holocaust-reckoning/.
3 https://www.theguardian.com/world/2016/nov/09/western-civilisation-appiah-reith-lecture.
4 Paylor (2017), pp. 374–6.
5 https://artillerymag.com/the-pros-and-cons-of-erasing-history/#:~:text=Translated%20as%20%E2%80%9Ccondemnation%20of%20memory,viewed%20as%20worse%20than%20death.
6 Paylor (2017), p. 374.
7 Ers (2011), p. 157.
8 Cited in Fruchtman (2009), p. 58.
9 https://nationalpost.com/news/canada/book-burning-at-ontario-francophone-schools-as-gesture-of-reconciliation-denounced/wcm/479bc35d-856a-42f3-9df3-44ff7b392a8a/.
10 Ibid.
11 Ibid.
12 https://www.nationalgeographic.com/history/article/150414-why-islamic-state-destroyed-assyrian-palace-nimrud-iraq-video-isis-isil-archaeology. See also https://www.youtube.com/watch?v=hrcvVkAomcc&ab_channel=euronews.
13 Ers (2011), p. 164.
14 Paylor (2017), p. 379.
15 https://www.smh.com.au/entertainment/opera/arts-leading-lights-join-opera-anti-violence-push-20190625-p52134.html.
16 https://theconversation.com/opera-is-stuck-in-a-racist-sexist-past-while-many-in-the-audience-have-moved-on-120073.
17 Tziovas (2014).
18 https://www.washingtonpost.com/news/made-by-history/wp/2018/04/06/aristotle-father-of-scientific-racism/.
19 https://medium.com/@bryanvannorden_14478/i-am-puzzled-by-agnes-callards-article-should-we-cancel-aristotle-92a08a4ec6de.
20 Lefkowitz (1996), pp. 13–14.
21 Ibid., p. 9.
22 Lemos (2023), p. 20.
23 See https://www.commentarymagazine.com/noah-rothman/the-1619-project-when-history-isnt-history/.
24 https://html2-f.scribdassets.com/2bmgmmsurk7ynrz5/images/1-fedcb3b0e8.jpg. (The name 'Nicole Hannah' here is an editorial error.)
25 https://www.wbur.org/hereandnow/2020/07/20/1619-project-nikole-hannah-jones.

26 https://www.theguardian.com/commentisfree/2021/jul/01/this-canada-day-lets-remember-this-country-was-built-on-genocide.
27 https://nationalpost.com/opinion/canadas-not-a-genocidal-state-despite-what-our-self-hating-pm-would-have-you-believe.
28 https://twitter.com/kehinde_andrews/status/1224347295199776773?lang=en.
29 See the discussion in Kühne (2013).
30 https://indica.medium.com/colonialism-was-worse-than-nazism-94d9b0e6fe64.
31 https://unherd.com/2023/05/how-the-history-wars-came-for-garibaldi/.
32 https://www.telegraph.co.uk/news/2022/11/19/teach-britain-founded-racism-say-almost-half-young-people-poll/.
33 https://www.telegraph.co.uk/news/2023/05/14/gender-poll-trans-school-teenagers-civitas-parents/.
34 https://www.theguardian.com/commentisfree/2022/oct/01/slave-traders-names-are-still-stamped-on-native-plants-its-time-to-decolonise-australias-public-gardens. See also https://theconversation.com/hibberts-flowers-and-hitlers-beetle-what-do-we-do-when-species-are-named-after-historys-monsters-172602.
35 https://therevelator.org/decolonizing-species-names/.
36 https://theconversation.com/hibberts-flowers-and-hitlers-beetle-what-do-we-do-when-species-are-named-after-historys-monsters-172602.
37 https://www.theguardian.com/science/2021/mar/18/kew-gardens-director-hits-back-at-claims-it-is-growing-woke.
38 https://frankfuredi.substack.com/p/challenging-the-woke-dictionary.
39 https://entsoc.org/news/press-releases/spongy-moth-approved-new-common-name-lymantria-dispar.
40 https://www.smithsonianmag.com/smart-news/these-moths-will-be-renamed-stop-use-ethnic-slur-180978151/.
41 https://www.reuters.com/article/minneapolis-police-protests-britain-idINKBN23G0XG.
42 https://www.telegraph.co.uk/news/2021/05/11/church-englands-slavery-review-takes-un-christian-starting-point/.
43 https://www.bbc.co.uk/news/uk-64228673.
44 https://www.telegraph.co.uk/news/2022/08/24/anti-slavery-mp-edmund-burke-put-transatlantic-slave-trade-register/.
45 https://www.palatinate.org.uk/durham-university-explores-its-past-as-part-of-race-equality-charter-plans/.
46 Ibid.
47 https://www.telegraph.co.uk/news/2021/07/03/decolonise-desks-demands-teaching-union-sinister-new-escalation/.

48 https://www.architecturaldigest.com/story/interior-race-theory-design-concept.
49 https://www.thetimes.co.uk/article/decolonise-the-english-oppressors-say-welsh-o6b8rppqf.
50 Kendi (2020), p. 19.
51 https://europeanconservative.com/articles/commentary/decolonization-is-not-a-metaphor/.
52 https://www.ids.ac.uk/opinions/contextualising-gaza-colonial-violence-and-occupation/.
53 Deleted. Retweeted at https://twitter.com/MsMelChen/status/1711085203081543894.
54 https://twitter.com/sandeepbak/status/1710619462959841344.
55 Cited in https://nationalpost.com/opinion/canadian-academics-decolonization-israel.
56 Baumeister (1986), p. 45.
57 See the discussion in Furedi (2021).
58 Davis (1940), p. 217.
59 Giles (1997), p. 60.
60 See Furedi (2018), pp. 89–93.
61 Jarausch (1997), p. 16.
62 E.g. Stephenson (1981), pp. 321–7.
63 https://www.theguardian.com/football/2012/feb/22/david-cameron-government-racism-football.
64 Meier (2005), p. 17.
65 Cvijic & Zucca (2004) p.739.
66 https://encountersmissionjournal.files.wordpress.com/2011/08/fountain_2011-03_schumann_and_europe.pdf.
67 http://aej.org.ua/statements_en/1069.html.
68 Ibid.
69 Jarausch (2010), p. 314.

Chapter 4 The Present Eternalized

1 Orwell (1949), p. 118.
2 https://www.oed.com/search/advanced/Meanings?textTermTexto=anachronism&textTermOpto=WordPhrase&dateOfUseFirstUse=false&page=1&sortOption=AZ.
3 https://www.psychologytoday.com/gb/blog/inclusive-insight/201809/has-gender-always-been-binary.
4 https://www.oed.com/search/advanced/Meanings?textTermTexto=gender

&textTermOpto=WordPhrase&dateOfUseFirstUse=false&page=1&sortOption=AZ.

5 Goldie (2014).
6 https://www.lbc.co.uk/news/joan-of-arc-non-binary-shakespeare-globe-theatre-production/.
7 https://www.shakespearesglobe.com/discover/blogs-and-features/2022/08/08/it-was-necessary-taking-joan-of-arc-on-their-own-terms/.
8 https://www.spiked-online.com/2023/02/01/the-dangers-of-trans-washing-the-past/.
9 https://www.advocate.com/arts-entertainment/2016/9/20/15-lgbt-egyptian-gods.
10 https://www.spiked-online.com/2022/11/30/no-jesus-was-not-trans/ and https://www.telegraph.co.uk/news/2022/11/26/jesus-could-have-transgender-claims-cambridge-dean/.
11 https://www.theguardian.com/world/2021/aug/09/1000-year-old-remains-in-finland-may-be-non-binary-viking-researchers-say.
12 https://www.spiked-online.com/2022/08/10/theres-no-such-thing-as-a-nonbinary-skeleton/.
13 https://www.telegraph.co.uk/news/2023/11/20/trans-roman-emperor-hitchin-museum-claim-pronouns-woke/.
14 https://www.bbc.co.uk/news/entertainment-arts-67484645.
15 Ibid.
16 https://unherd.com/thepost/even-the-roman-empire-isnt-safe-from-trans-ideology/.
17 https://www.worldhistory.org/article/1774/ten-ancient-lgbtq-facts-you-need-to-know/.
18 https://www.telegraph.co.uk/news/2023/08/08/mary-rose-museum-lgbt-queering-collection-henry-viii/.
19 https://maryrose.org/blog/collections/the-collections-team/queering-the-mary-rose-s-collection/.
20 https://www.telegraph.co.uk/columnists/2022/12/20/please-spare-us-woke-rewriting-shakespeare/.
21 https://www.shakespearesglobe.com/whats-on/anti-racist-shakespeare-titus-andronicus-2023/.
22 https://www.folger.edu/podcasts/shakespeare-unlimited/critical-race-theory-titus-andronicus/.
23 Stoll (1910), p. 557.
24 Ibid., p. 551.
25 Little (2022), p. 1.

26 https://www.penguinrandomhouse.com/books/691287/the-great-white-bard-by-farah-karim-cooper/.
27 https://www.newstatesman.com/culture/books/2023/05/shakespeare-race-problem.
28 https://www.slj.com/story/to-teach-or-not-to-teach-is-shakespeare-still-relevant-to-todays-students-libraries-classic-literature-canon.
29 https://jacobin.com/2016/12/trump-hitler-germany-fascism-weimar-democracy/.
30 https://tdkehoe.medium.com/thirteen-similarities-between-donald-trump-and-adolf-hitler-3a97a8055dde.
31 https://slate.com/news-and-politics/2016/11/his-election-that-november-came-as-a-surprise.html.
32 https://www.nytimes.com/2021/01/09/magazine/trump-coup.html?referringSource=articleShare.
33 https://www.algemeiner.com/2021/01/14/nazi-comparisons-in-us-politics-are-desecration-of-the-sacred-memory-of-innocent-victims-says-algemeiner-editor-in-chief/.
34 https://www.youtube.com/watch?v=GV8YPcdVVIs&ab_channel=HindustanTimes.
35 https://www.voanews.com/a/is-putin-the-new-hitler-/6476408.html.
36 https://oxfordre.com/literature/display/10.1093/acrefore/9780190201098.001.0001/acrefore-9780190201098-e-1188;jsessionid=0408489FB8135FD2A6A01CEA4BB296CE?rskey=Matqmo&result=1.
37 Himmelfarb (1971), p. 311.
38 Hughes (2014).
39 Hughes (1992).
40 https://www.uc.edu/news/articles/2022/06/ancient-maya-used-sustainable-farming-forestry-for-millennia.html.
41 Febvre (1982 [1942]), p. 5.
42 https://www.telegraph.co.uk/news/2022/12/28/bbc-guilty-rewriting-british-history-promote-woke-agenda-biased/.
43 Hartog (2017), p. 201.
44 Ibid., p. 107
45 Ibid., p. 203.
46 Bauman (2008), p. 54.
47 Hartog & Lenclud (1993), p. 26.
48 https://www.historians.org/research-and-publications/perspectives-on-history/may-2002/against-presentism.
49 Markides (2021), pp. 3–5.

50 Halévy (1948).
51 Hartog (2017), p. xv.
52 Nora (1989), p. 7.
53 Rosa (2013), p. 418.
54 Nietzsche (1967 [1901]), p. 3.
55 Cited in Hartog (2017), pp. 80–1.
56 Adams (2019 [1919]).
57 Inglis (2010).
58 Assmann (2020), p. 197.
59 http://v21collective.org/%20manifesto-of-the-v21-collective-ten-theses/.
60 https://www.iccrom.org/news/thematic-discussion-decolonizing-heritage.
61 https://www.theguardian.com/world/2023/jun/20/fitzwilliam-museum-cambridge-explores-founders-slavery-links.
62 Rousso (2016), p. 13.
63 https://3quarksdaily.com/3quarksdaily/2009/05/moral-anachronism.html.
64 https://public-history-weekly.degruyter.com/8-2020-8/kant-a-racist/.
65 Simon (2019), p. 12.
66 Rousso (2016), p.13.
67 Ibid.
68 Hartog (2017), p. 151.
69 Courtemanche (2019), p. 470.
70 https://www.washingtonpost.com/wp-srv/style/longterm/books/chap1/onhistory.htm.
71 Walsham (2017), p. 213.
72 Rubin (2017), p. 236.
73 Ibid., p. 241.
74 Ibid.
75 Torpey (2004), p. 26.
76 Fernie (2005), p. 169.
77 DiPietro & Grady (2012), p. 44.
78 https://www.historians.org/publications-and-directories/perspectives-on-history/september-2022/is-history-history-identity-politics-and-teleologies-of-the-present.
79 https://thetattooedprof.com/2022/08/19/on-presentism-and-history-or-were-doing-this-again-are-we/.
80 https://twitter.com/DavidVeevers1/status/1560151459601195008.
81 https://www.historians.org/publications-and-directories/perspectives-on-history/september-2022/is-history-history-identity-politics-and-teleologies-of-the-present.

82 Ibid.

83 https://www.telegraph.co.uk/news/2020/06/29/charles-dickens-museum-defaced-graffiti-calling-author-racist/.

84 https://www.kentonline.co.uk/kent/news/my-3-500-graffiti-spree-against-racist-council-was-justifi-251688/.

Chapter 5 Identity and the Past

1 Gergen (2005), p. 117.

2 MacIntyre (2007), p. 223.

3 Gergen (2005), p. 116.

4 Korsgarad (2009), p. xii.

5 Ibid., pp. 7 and 19.

6 Eisenstadt (1998), p. 229.

7 https://newrepublic.com/article/92857/against-identity.

8 See Ruben Navarrette Jr at https://eu.usatoday.com/story/opinion/2019/02/04/identity-politics-trump-julian-castro-stacey-abrams-beto-orourke-column/2733935002/.

9 Izenberg (2016), p. 24.

10 Erikson (1963), p. 256.

11 See Gleason (1983), p. 910.

12 Moran (2015), p. 3.

13 Ibid., p. 11.

14 See White (1844), p. 64.

15 *Tracts of the American Unitarian Association*, nos 71–125 (1827), p. 75.

16 Xiang (2018), p. 21.

17 https://www.vectornator.io/blog/the-queer-history-of-art/.

18 Hobsbawm (1996), p. 39.

19 'A Civil Rights Theme for a Writing Course Campus Life: Texas' (https://www.nytimes.com/1990/06/24/nyregion/a-civil-rights-theme-for-a-writing-course-campus-life-texas.html).

20 Berger, Berger & Kellner (1974), p. 86.

21 Erikson (1963), p. 138.

22 Rieff (2006), p. 4.

23 Arendt (2006), p. 188.

24 Gramsci (1971), p. 103.

25 Oakeshott (1989), p. 68.

26 See http://www.carolhanisch.org/CHwritings/PIP.html.

27 https://www.nybooks.com/articles/1999/04/08/the-joys-and-perils-of-victimhood/.

28 https://unherd.com/2023/06/how-the-identity-cult-captured-america/.
29 See 'Conclusion' to Furedi (2021).
30 https://www.afr.com/politics/woolworths-disowns-rober-corbett-over-antisamesex-marriage-comments-20170919-gyk394.
31 https://www.nationaltrust.org.uk/who-we-are/research/addressing-our-histories-of-colonialism-and-historic-slavery.
32 https://www.reuters.com/article/uk-global-race-britain-slavery-idUSKCN26D1P6.
33 https://www.civilsociety.co.uk/news/a-third-of-national-trust-properties-linked-to-colonial-histories-according-to-review.html.
34 https://www.thetimes.co.uk/article/churchill-rap-wasnt-our-finest-hour-says-imperial-war-museum-splbwsnpq.
35 https://www.express.co.uk/news/uk/1836054/Winston-Churchill-branded-war-criminal-talkTV.
36 https://www.theguardian.com/culture/2023/jun/27/elizabeth-winkler-shakespeare-was-woman-author.
37 Cited in ibid.
38 https://www.telegraph.co.uk/news/2023/06/03/anglo-saxons-arent-real-cambridge-student-fight-nationalism/?li_source=LI&li_medium=liftigniter-rhr.
39 https://www.smithsonianmag.com/history/many-myths-term-anglo-saxon-180978169/.
40 https://www.brown.edu/Departments/Joukowsky_Institute/courses/deadwhiteguys/6561.html.
41 https://www.theguardian.com/commentisfree/2018/oct/22/western-civilisation-is-not-under-threat-even-if-conservatives-want-you-to-think-so.
42 Patterson (1997), p. 91.
43 Ibid., p. 57.
44 Ibid., p. 59.
45 https://edinburghuniversitypress.com/book-toxic-masculinity-in-the-ancient-world.html.
46 https://newbostonpost.com/around-new-england/new-hampshire-is-too-white-to-have-the-first-primary-in-the-country-democratic-national-committee-chairman-says/.
47 https://newrepublic.com/article/161280/criminal-justice-diversity-merrick-garland.
48 https://vtdigger.org/2021/01/21/in-a-survey-minority-business-owners-say-local-chambers-too-white/.
49 https://www.scientificamerican.com/article/disaster-management-is-too-white-official-tells-congress/.

50 https://medium.com/@mdonnell6145/american-tv-is-too-white-6b60b4a5c35e.
51 https://www.thetimes.co.uk/article/lenny-henry-television-is-too-white-after-four-decades-on-screen-i-still-feel-lonely-2zqzkltjz.
52 https://www.thesun.co.uk/news/6578895/monty-python-bbc-not-commissioned-too-white-oxbridge/.
53 https://www.theguardian.com/environment/2021/feb/11/too-white-green-sector-launches-work-scheme-to-be-more-diverse.
54 https://edition.cnn.com/2019/11/24/uk/extinction-rebellion-environment-diversity-gbr-intl/index.html.
55 https://www.forbes.com/sites/drnancydoyle/2020/09/05/our-dyslexia-heroes-are-too-white-addressing-representation-in-business-with-marcia-brisset-bailey/?sh=542a7c16756e.
56 https://www.youtube.com/watch?v=CAMIdHurINo.
57 https://www.telegraph.co.uk/education/2017/01/08/university-students-demand-philosophers-including-plato-kant/.
58 https://www.thetimes.co.uk/article/history-is-too-white-claim-academics-7m3znjqnr.
59 https://www.dailymail.co.uk/news/article-9171987/Leicester-University-denies-dropping-Chaucer-white-proposals.html.
60 https://www.smh.com.au/national/why-the-statues-must-fall-20200612-p5521s.html.
61 https://www.theguardian.com/commentisfree/2016/dec/15/pale-stale-males-blamed-brexit-trump.
62 https://www.telegraph.co.uk/business/2023/05/29/reece-tomlinson-saone-uk-first-trans-led-investment-firm/.
63 https://www.independent.co.uk/travel/inspiration/travel-tv-show-white-male-presenters-b2394859.html.
64 https://gript.ie/the-very-dull-white-pasty-ireland-irish-politicians-talk-white-privilege/.
65 https://sapirjournal.org/social-justice/2021/05/critical-race-theory-and-the-hyper-white-jew/.
66 https://www.nytimes.com/2023/12/01/business/susan-sarandon-apology-pro-palestinian-rally.html.
67 https://www.jpost.com/opinion/article-773642.
68 https://www.i24news.tv/en/news/international/americas/1700326648-canadian-sexual-assault-center-cosigns-denial-of-hamas-rapes#:~:text=A%20rape%20crisis%20center%20at,during%20the%20October%207%20massacre; see also https://www.thetimes.co.uk/article/5cde7d20-7ff4-4e2d-9c34-95584121515I?shareToken=93d7f85bbf181fc644a838cdb74cc017.

69 https://www.arabnews.com/node/2.
70 https://www.washingtonpost.com/arts-entertainment/2023/05/12/queen-cleopatra-looks-netflix-controversy.
71 Haley (1993), p. 29.
72 Ibid.
73 Cited in Lefkowitz (2008), p. 125.
74 Cited in ibid.
75 Ibid., p. 6.
76 Lefkowitz & Rogers (2014), p. 448.
77 https://web.archive.org/web/20230920061544/https:/www.telegraph.co.uk/news/2023/09/18/stonehenge-built-by-black-britons-childrens-history-book/.
78 https://www.youtube.com/watch?v=6M-qsVS8zeU. See also the discussion on this trend in https://www.aporiamagazine.com/p/why-is-the-bbc-promoting-ethnonationalism.
79 https://www.routesnorth.com/language-and-culture/were-there-ever-black-vikings/.
80 Ibid.
81 https://www.newsweek.com/swedish-history-tv-series-faces-backlash-using-black-actors-1841695#:~:text=In%20a%20March%202023%20statement,the%20way%20to%20the%20present.
82 https://www.heritagefund.org.uk/our-work/investing-lgbtq-heritage?page=1.
83 https://www.prm.ox.ac.uk/beyond-the-binary.
84 Ibid.
85 https://www.prm.ox.ac.uk/event/beyond-the-binary.
86 https://www.sdlgbtn.com/the-mysterious-sexuality-of-queen-elizabeth-i/.
87 https://www.telegraph.co.uk/news/2023/06/21/national-portrait-gallery-wall-18th-century-trans-spy/.
88 Habermas (1993), p. 129.
89 Brown (2020), p. 73.

Chapter 6 The Struggle to Control Language

1 https://dailynexus.com/2021-07-24/stop-calling-women-females/.
2 https://www.buzzfeed.com/tracyclayton/stop-calling-women-females.
3 https://www.linkedin.com/pulse/why-should-you-stop-referring-women-females-sacha-de-klerk/.
4 https://golin.com/2021/03/31/stop-using-female-when-you-mean-woman/.
5 https://www.oed.com/search/advanced/Meanings?q=female&sortOption=Frequency.

6 https://www.theguardian.com/commentisfree/2017/apr/24/families-evolved-language-words-relatedness-traditional.
7 https://www.telegraph.co.uk/news/2022/10/06/councils-ordered-ditch-mum-dad-homeless-new-language-guide/.
8 https://www.theguardian.com/world/2023/jul/07/lords-prayer-our-father-opening-may-be-problematic-archbishop-of-york-stephen-cottrell?CMP=Share_iOSApp_Other.
9 https://www.earlymoderntexts.com/assets/pdfs/locke1690book3.pdf (p. 189).
10 Ibid. (p. 191).
11 See Dawson (2005).
12 Coleridge (1976 [1829]), pp. 69, 43.
13 Clark (2004), p. 7.
14 https://www.oed.com/search/dictionary/?scope=Entries&q=outdated.
15 https://www.nytimes.com/2022/09/08/opinion/queen-empire-decolonization.html.
16 See *The Salt Lake Tribune*, 22 May 1996.
17 https://www.independent.co.uk/sport/football/news/greg-clarke-fa-kick-it-out-stereotypes-b1720444.html.
18 https://www.theboltonnews.co.uk/news/18808310.councillor-apologises-using-outdated-language-describe-disabled-people/.
19 https://www.bristol247.com/news-and-features/news/crime-festival-apologises-after-hosts-outdated-and-offensive-comments/.
20 https://www.palatinate.org.uk/cuths-jcr-condemned-after-outdated-and-malicious-facebook-comment/.
21 https://www.ala.org/news/member-news/2021/06/decolonizing-catalog-addressing-problematic-language.
22 https://blogs.cul.columbia.edu/rbml/2021/10/19/on-outdated-and-harmful-language-in-library-of-congress-subject-headings/.
23 https://www.archives.gov/research/reparative-description/harmful-content.
24 https://warontherocks.com/2016/09/six-ways-to-fix-the-armys-culture/.
25 https://www.reddit.com/r/books/comments/vg55p9/can_you_still_love_a_book_despite_its_problematic/.
26 See http://nymag.com/daily/intelligencer/2015/07/everything-is-problematic-university-explains.html.
27 https://www.thepinknews.com/2021/10/03/canada-trans-pronouns-human-rights-british-columbia/.
28 https://www.dailymail.co.uk/news/article-12249661/Michigan-residents-charged-felony-face-five-years-prison-using-wrong-pronouns.html.

29 https://www.telegraph.co.uk/news/2023/06/24/ernest-hemingway-novel-trigger-warning-penguin-offensive/.
30 https://www.telegraph.co.uk/news/2023/07/01/virginia-woolf-to-the-lighthouse-trigger-warning-vintage/.
31 https://www.telegraph.co.uk/world-news/2023/06/12/penguin-adds-prejudices-warning-to-mitford-novel/.
32 https://www.nationalreview.com/news/penguin-removes-unacceptable-words-from-p-g-wodehouse-novels-adds-trigger-warnings-for-outdated-language/.
33 https://www.spiked-online.com/2023/06/19/now-theyre-coming-for-nancy-mitford/.
34 https://www.independent.co.uk/arts-entertainment/tv/news/bbc-iplayer-language-warning-netflix-mighty-boosh-league-of-gentlemen-a9595916.html.
35 https://www.thesun.co.uk/news/11908094/sky-warns-viewers-outdated-language-and-attitudes/.
36 https://www.telegraph.co.uk/news/2023/03/18/enid-blyton-books-hidden-counter-libraries-fret-offensive-language/.
37 https://www.theage.com.au/national/victoria/school-library-discards-outdated-and-offensive-books-on-colonisation-20230216-p5cky4.html.
38 https://apnews.com/article/dr-seuss-books-racist-images-d8ed18335c03319d72f443594c174513.
39 https://www.ecu.edu.au/research/worldclass/kidsbooks#:~:text=Description%3A,and%20girls%20as%20passive%20onlookers.
40 https://www.museumsassociation.org/campaigns/decolonising-museums/supporting-decolonisation-in-museums/#.
41 https://languageplease.org/content-advisory-and-trigger-warnings/#:~:text=A%20content%20warning%20comes%20before,speech%2C%20blood%2C%20and%20death.
42 https://www.thetimes.co.uk/article/trigger-warning-put-on-declaration-of-independence-jxkw7mlfk.
43 http://columbiaspectator.com/opinion/2015/04/30/our-identities-matter-core-classrooms.
44 https://www.telegraph.co.uk/news/2023/02/16/medieval-classics-may-racist-misogynist-say-oxford-scholars/.
45 https://www.openculture.com/2014/03/publisher-places-a-politically-correct-warning-label-on-kants-critiques.html.
46 https://www.vice.com/en/article/v7dd3d/we-need-to-stop-saying-blacklist-and-whitelist.
47 https://www.nytimes.com/2021/10/12/opinion/language-words-woke.html.

48 https://newsfeed.time.com/2013/08/06/dont-call-it-a-brown-bag-lunch-seattle-frowns-on-popular-term/.
49 https://www.dailymail.co.uk/news/article-9721153/Brandeis-University-anti-violence-group-bans-trigger-warning-violent-language.html.
50 https://nbcuacademy.com/harmful-ableist-racist-language/.
51 Gouldner (1979), p. 19.
52 Ibid., p. 2.
53 Ibid., p. 3.
54 Ibid., p. 14.
55 Ibid., p. 29
56 Allen & Burridge (2006), p. 90.
57 Ibid., p. 93.
58 Zimman (2017), p. 86.
59 Ibid., p. 85.
60 Ibid., p. 91.
61 https://www.thetimes.co.uk/article/mod-tells-staff-to-state-name-rank-and-gender-pronoun-rcbwcrw5r.
62 https://www.telegraph.co.uk/news/2023/09/16/general-medical-council-removed-mothers-maternity-policy.
63 https://www.dailymail.co.uk/news/article-10029817/Fury-leading-medical-journal-describes-women-bodies-vaginas.html.
64 https://www.telegraph.co.uk/news/2023/07/09/vagina-named-bonus-hole-cervical-cancer-charity-transgender/.
65 https://www.nbcnews.com/nbc-out/out-news/johns-hopkins-pulls-lesbian-definition-uproar-use-non-men-instead-wome-rcna89307.
66 https://www.telegraph.co.uk/women/life/many-terms-for-woman-identity-wars/.
67 https://www.sentencingcouncil.org.uk/wp-content/uploads/Equal-Treatment-Bench-Book.pdf (p. 194).
68 Ibid. (p. 345).
69 Ibid. (p. 7).
70 https://www.ama-assn.org/system/files/ama-aamc-equity-guide.pdf (pp. 12–13, 15).
71 Jacoby (2018 [1975]), p. 16.
72 Ibid., p. 1.
73 Ibid., p. 51.
74 https://uniavisen.dk/en/humanities-and-social-sciences-are-self-obsessed/.
75 Jacoby (2018 [1975]), p. 48.
76 Clark (2004), p. 28.
77 Jacoby (2018 [1975]), p. 7.

Chapter 7 Disinheriting the Young from Their Past

1 Arendt (2006), pp. 118–89 and 193.
2 http://www.the-philosopher.co.uk/2016/08/individual-psychology-and-education-1934.html.
3 Dewey (1966), p. 20.
4 Chisholm (1947), p. 107.
5 Chisholm (1946), pp. 7 and 9.
6 Ibid., p. 1.
7 https://www.historycentral.com/Educators/DifficultHistory.html.
8 Best (2006).
9 https://www.fenews.co.uk/press-releases/72224-pearson-and-the-black-curriculum-join-forces-to-champion-black-british-history-topics-on-the-national-curriculum.
10 https://www.natre.org.uk/uploads/20%2B%20Key%20terms%20for%20anti-racist%20RE.pdf.
11 https://inews.co.uk/news/education/teachers-school-curriculum-decolonised-black-history-all-subjects-942919.
12 https://www.archaeologists.net/civicrm/event/info?reset=1&id=199.
13 Gandolfi (2021); https://decolonisegeography.com/blog/2021/03/challenging-white-gcse-geography-global-development/.
14 https://inews.co.uk/news/education/teachers-school-curriculum-decolonised-black-history-all-subjects-942919.
15 https://www.thetimes.co.uk/article/take-white-privilege-test-to-help-decolonise-schools-teachers-urged-f67tr55qd.
16 https://www.thetimes.co.uk/article/scottish-teachers-told-to-use-pupils-chosen-gender-s9q05038.
17 https://www.telegraph.co.uk/news/2021/07/03/decolonise-desks-demands-teaching-union-sinister-new-escalation/.
18 https://www.thetimes.co.uk/article/teachers-ordered-to-promote-social-justice-bmqgptqbf.
19 https://cstuk.org.uk/assets/CST-Publications/CST_Bridge_Decolonisation%20Final_Steve%20Rollett_062021_.pdf.
20 Erikson (1964), p. 93.
21 Macintyre & Clark (2013), p. 172.
22 Cited in https://hedgehogreview.com/issues/theological-variations/articles/missed-america.
23 https://www.theguardian.com/uk/2003/may/09/highereducation.politics.
24 Clark (2004), p. 6.
25 https://edoc.coe.int/en/teaching-history/7754-quality-history-education-in-the-21st-century-principles-and-guidelines.html (p. 24).

26 Young (2007), p. 67.
27 Oakeshott (1989), p. 68.
28 Peters (1982), p. 15.
29 Young (2007), p. 82.
30 https://www.history.org.uk/primary/resource/9620/how-diverse-is-your-history-curriculum.
31 https://edoc.coe.int/en/teaching-history/7754-quality-history-education-in-the-21st-century-principles-and-guidelines.html.
32 https://facingtoday.facinghistory.org/use-historical-empathy-to-help-students-process-the-world-today#:~:text=Historical%20empathy%20not%20only%20helps,their%20own%20schools%20and%20communities.
33 https://study.com/academy/lesson/historical-empathy-importance-application.html#:~:text=Historical%20empathy%20refers%20to%20the,internalize%20on%20a%20deeper%20.
34 Clark (2004), p. 6.
35 https://www.thetimes.co.uk/article/ignorance-of-history-feeds-certainty-in-young-6v5krootr.
36 https://www.historycentral.com/Educators/DifficultHistory.html.
37 https://www.wsws.org/en/articles/2020/10/23/1619-o23.html.
38 https://repository.kulib.kyoto-u.ac.jp/dspace/bitstream/2433/142977/1/2008-03_GCOE_Rev_Edu_137.pdf (p. 139).
39 https://www.theguardian.com/commentisfree/2022/oct/18/change-future-teach-history-children.
40 http://archives.news.yale.edu/v30.n13/story5.html.
41 https://www.youtube.com/watch?v=TpsA4zMtB8M&ab_channel=DoubleDownNews.
42 https://metro.co.uk/2020/02/04/professor-says-whiteness-psychosis-british-empire-damage-nazis-12178060/.
43 https://www.theguardian.com/world/2007/aug/24/india.randeepramesh.
44 https://www.sanskritimagazine.com/british-raj-induced-indian-holocaust/.
45 https://metro.co.uk/2021/04/01/pimlico-academy-headteacher-vows-to-change-racist-uniform-rules-14339725/?ito=cbshare.
46 https://www.newstatesman.com/politics/2017/08/britain-has-built-national-myth-winning-second-world-war-it-s-distorting-our.
47 Edgerton (2021).
48 Furedi (1989) and Furedi (1994a).
49 Clark (2004), p. 28.
50 Ponzetti (2015), p. 142.
51 https://unesdoc.unesco.org/ark:/48223/pf0000260770.

52 Danzinger (1976), p. 25

53 Cited in https://c2cjournal.ca/2021/08/content-over-process-albertas-new-k-6-curriculum-is-a-welcome-shift-in-educational-thinking/.

Conclusion

1 Gamble (2013), p. ix.

2 Cited in Garsten (2017), p. 255.

3 Cited in Sabl (2009), p 512.

4 Kamen (1967), p.7.

5 Elias (2000 [1939]).

6 MacIntyre (2007), p. 18.

7 Pound (1914), pp. 137 and 139.

References

Abrams, P. (1972) 'The Sense of the Past and the Origins of Sociology'. *Past & Present*, 55, pp. 18–32.

Adams, H. (2019 [1919]) *The Education of Henry Adams*. New York: Good Press.

Allen, K. & K. Burridge (2006) *Forbidden Words: Taboo and Censoring Language*. Cambridge: Cambridge University Press.

Arendt, H. (2005) *The Promise of Politics*. New York: Schocken Books.

Arendt, H. (2006) *Between Past and Future: Eight Exercises in Political Thought*. London: Penguin.

Assmann, A. (2020) *Is Time out of Joint? On the Rise and Fall of the Modern Time Regime* (trans. S. Clift). Ithaca, NY: Cornell University Press.

Bauman, Z. (2008) *The Art of Life*. Cambridge: Polity.

Baumeister, R.F. (1986) *Identity: Cultural Change and the Struggle for Self*. Oxford: Oxford University Press.

Berger, P., B. Berger & H. Kellner (1974) *The Homeless Mind*. Harmondsworth: Penguin.

Best, J. (2006) *Flavor of the Month: Why Smart People Fall for Fads*. Los Angeles: University of California Press.

Bledsoe, E.M. (2016) 'Make It New' In *The Routledge Encyclopedia of Modernism*. London: Routledge. doi:10.4324/9781135000356-REM1131-1.

Bourne, R.S. (1913) *Youth and Life*. New York: Houghton Mifflin.

Bracken, P. (2002) *Trauma: Culture, Meaning and Philosophy*. London: Whurr Publishers.

Brown, W. (2020) *States of Injury: Power and Freedom in Late Modernity*. Princeton: Princeton University Press.

Burckhardt, J. (1943) *Reflections on History*. London: George Allen & Unwin.

Burnham, J.C. (1960) 'Psychiatry, Psychology and the Progressive Movement'. *American Quarterly*, 12(4), pp. 457–65.

Burt, S. (2007) *The Forms of Youth: Twentieth-Century Poetry and Adolescence*. New York: Columbia University Press.

Chisholm, G.B. (1946) *The William Alanson White Memorial Lectures*. Baltimore: W.A. White Psychiatric Foundation.

Chisholm, G.B. (1947) 'Can Man Survive?' *A Review of General Semantics*, 4(2), pp. 106–11.

Cicero (2008) *The Republic and The Laws* (trans. N. Rudd). Oxford: Oxford University Press.

Clark, J.C.D. (2004) *Our Shadowed Present: Modernism, Postmodernism, and History.* Stanford: Stanford University Press.

Coleridge, S.T. (1976 [1829]) *The Collected Works of Samuel Taylor Coleridge*, Vol. 10: *On the Constitution of Church and State* (ed. J. Colmer). Princeton: Princeton University Press.

Coles, R. (1974) Review of *Dimensions of a New Identity* by Erik H. Erikson. *New Republic*, 8 June, p. 23.

Condit, T. (2013) 'Living in the Past'. *Archaeology Ireland*, 27(3), p. 3.

Courtemanche, E. (2019) 'Beyond Urgency: Shadow Presentisms, Hinge Points, and Victorian Historicisms'. *Criticism*, 61(4), pp. 461–79.

Cvijic, S. & L. Zucca (2004, 'Does the European Constitution Need Christian Values?', *Oxford Journal of Legal Studies*, 24(4), pp. 739–48.

Danzinger, K. (1976) *Socialization.* Harmondsworth: Penguin.

Davis, K. (1940) 'The Child and the Social Structure'. *Journal of Educational Sociology*, 14(4), pp. 217–29.

Dawson, H. (2005) 'Locke on Language in (Civil) Society'. *History of Political Thought*, 26(3), pp. 398–425.

Dewey, J. (1966) *Democracy and Education.* New York: Free Press.

DiPietro, C. & H. Grady (2012) 'Presentism, Anachronism and the Case of *Titus Andronicus*'. *Shakespeare*, 8(1), pp. 44–73.

Edgerton, D. (2021) 'The Nationalisation of British History: Historians, Nationalism and the Myths of 1940'. *The English Historical Review*, 136(581), pp. 950–85.

Eisenstadt, S.N. (1998) 'The Construction of Collective Identities: Some Analytical and Comparative Indications'. *European Journal of Social Theory*, 1(2), pp. 229–54.

Eksteins, M. (1989) *Rites of Spring: The Great War and the Birth of the Modern Age.* Boston: Houghton Mifflin.

Elias, N. (2000 [1939]) *The Civilizing Process*, Vol 1: *The History of Manners* (trans. E. Jephcott). Oxford: Blackwell.

Erikson, E.H. (1963) *Youth: Change and Challenge.* New York: Basic Books.

Erikson, E.H. (1964) 'Identity and Uprootedness in Our Time'. In E.H. Erikson, *Insight and Responsibility: Lectures on the Ethical Implications of Psychoanalytic Insight.* London: Faber & Faber, pp. 83–107.

Erikson, E.H. (1968) *Identity: Youth and Crisis.* New York: W.W. Norton & Company.

Ers, A. (2011) 'Year Zero: The Temporality of Revolution Studied Through the Example of the Khmer Rouge'. In H. Ruin and A. Ers (eds), *Rethinking Time: Essays on History, Memory, and Representation.* Huddinge: Södertörns högskola, pp. 155–65.

Febvre, L. (1982 [1942]) *The Problem of Unbelief in the Sixteenth Century: The Religion of Rabelais* (trans. B. Gottlieb). Cambridge, MA: Harvard University Press.

Fernie, E. (2005) 'Shakespeare and the Prospect of Presentism'. In P. Holland (ed.), *Shakespeare Survey.* Cambridge: Cambridge University Press, pp. 169–84.

Flower, H. (2004) 'Introduction'. In H. Flower (ed.), *The Cambridge Companion to the Roman Republic.* Cambridge: Cambridge University Press, pp. 1–12.

Frank, L. (1940) 'The Family as Cultural Agent'. *Living,* 2(1), pp. 16–19.

Friedrich, C.J. (1972) *Tradition and Authority.* London: The Pall Mall Press.

Fromm, E. (1941) *Escape from Freedom.* New York: Farrar & Rinehart. (Also published as *The Fear of Freedom.* London: Routledge & Kegan Paul, 1942.)

Fruchtman, J. (2009) *The Political Philosophy of Thomas Paine.* Baltimore: Johns Hopkins University Press.

Furedi, F. (1989a) 'Britain's Colonial Emergencies and the Invisible Nationalists'. *Journal of Historical Sociology,* 2(3), pp. 240–64.

Furedi, F. (1989b) *The Mau Mau War in Perspective.* London: James Currey/ Athens: Ohio University Press (Kenya edn, 1990; 2nd edn, 1991).

Furedi, F. (1992) *Mythical Past, Elusive Future: History and Society in an Anxious Age.* London: Pluto Press.

Furedi, F. (1994a) *Colonial Wars and the Politics of Third World Nationalism.* London: I.B. Tauris.

Furedi, F. (1994b) *The New Ideology of Imperialism: Renewing the Moral Imperative.* London: Pluto Press.

Furedi, F. (1998) *The Silent War: Imperialism and the Changing Perception of Race.* Rutgers, NJ: Rutgers University Press.

Furedi, F. (2004) *Therapy Culture: Cultivating Vulnerability in an Anxious Age.* London: Routledge.

Furedi, F. (2013) *Authority: A Sociological History.* Cambridge: Cambridge University Press.

Furedi, F. (2014) *First World War – Still No End in Sight.* London: Bloomsbury.

Furedi, F. (2016) *What Happened to the University? A Sociological Explanation of Its Infantilisation.* London: Routledge.

Furedi, F. (2018) *Populism and the European Culture Wars: The Conflict of Values between Hungary and the EU.* London: Routledge.
Furedi, F. (2020) *Why Borders Matter: Why Humanity Must Relearn the Art of Drawing Boundaries.* London: Routledge.
Furedi, F. (2021) *100 Years of Identity Crisis: Culture War Over Socialization.* Berlin: De Gruyter.
Gamble, A. (2013) *Politics and Fate.* Cambridge: Polity.
Gandolfi, H.E. (2021) 'Decolonising the Curriculum in England: Bringing Decolonial Science and Technology Studies to Secondary Education'. *The Curriculum Journal,* 32(3), pp. 510–32.
Garsten, B. (2017) 'From Popular Sovereignty to Civil war in Post-Revolutionary France'. In R. Bourke & Q. Skinner (eds), *Popular Sovereignty in Historical Perspective.* Cambridge: Cambridge University Press, pp. 236–69.
Gergen, K.J. (2005) 'Narrative, Moral Identity, and Historical Consciousness: A Social Constructionist Account'. In J. Straub (ed.), *Narration, Identity, and Historical Consciousness.* New York: Berghahn Books, pp. 99–119.
Giles, G.J. (ed.) (1997) *Stunde Null: The End and the Beginning Fifty Years Ago.* Occasional Paper No. 20. Washington, DC: German Historical Institute.
Gleason, P. (1983) 'Identifying Identity: A Semantic History'. *Journal of American History,* 69(4), pp. 910–31.
Goffman, E. (2009 [1963]) *Stigma: Notes on the Management of Spoiled Identity.* New York: Simon & Schuster.
Goldie, T. (2014) *The Man Who Invented Gender: Engaging the Ideas of John Money.* Vancouver: UBC Press.
Gouldner, W. (1979) *The Future of Intellectuals and the Rise of the New Class.* London: Macmillan Press.
Gramsci, A. (1971) *Selections from the Prison Notebooks* (ed. and trans. Q. Hoare & G.N. Smith). New York: International Publishers.
Habermas, J. (1993) 'Struggles for Recognition in Constitutional States'. *European Journal of Philosophy,* 1(2), pp. 128–55.
Halévy, D. (1948) *Essai sur l'accélération de l'histoire.* Paris: Les Îsles d'Or.
Haley, S.P. (1993) 'Black Feminist Thought and Classics: Re-membering, Re-claiming, Re-empowering'. In N.S. Rabinowitz & A. Richlin (eds), *Feminist Theory and the Classics,* London: Routledge, pp. 23–43.
Hartley, L.P. (2015 [1953]) *The Go-Between.* Harmondsworth: Penguin.
Hartog, F. (2017) *Regimes of Historicity: Presentism and Experiences of Time.* New York: Columbia University Press.
Hartog, F. & and G. Lenclud (1993) 'Régimes d'historicité'. In A. Dutu & N. Dodille (eds), *L'état des lieux en sciences sociales.* Paris: L'Harmattan, pp. 18–38.

Hewison, R. (1987) *The Heritage Industry: Britain in a Climate of Decline.* London, Methuen.

Himmelfarb, G. (1971) 'Mayhew's Poor: A Problem of Identity'. *Victorian Studies*, 14(3), pp. 307–20.

Himmelfarb, G. (2001) *One Nation, Two Cultures: A Searching Examination of American Society in the Aftermath of Our Cultural Revolution.* New York: Vintage.

Hobsbawm, E. (1972) 'The Social Function of the Past: Some Questions'. *Past & Present*, 55(1), pp. 3–17.

Hobsbawm, E. (1996) 'Identity Politics and the Left'. *New Left Review*, 217, pp. 38–47.

Hobsbawm, E. (1998) *On History*. London: Abacus.

Hobsbawm, E. (2020 [1994]) *The Age of Extremes: 1914–1991.* London: Hachette UK.

Hoffman, S. (1979) 'Fragments Floating in the Here and Now'. *Daedalus*, 108 (1), pp. 1–26.

Hughes, J.D. (1992) 'Sustainable Agriculture in Ancient Egypt'. *Agricultural History*, 66(2), pp. 12–22.

Hughes, J.D. (2014) *Environmental Problems of the Greeks and Romans: Ecology in the Ancient Mediterranean.* Baltimore: Johns Hopkins University Press.

Inglis, D. (2010) 'The Death of History in British Sociology: Presentism, Intellectual Entrepreneurship and the Conundra of Historical Consciousness'. In J. Burnett, S. Jeffers, & G. Thomas (eds), *New Social Connections: Sociology's Subjects and Objects.* Basingstoke: Palgrave, pp. 105–24.

Inglis, D. (2014) 'What is Worth Defending in Sociology Today? Presentism, Historical Vision and the Uses of Sociology'. *Cultural Sociology*, 8(1), pp. 99–118.

Izenberg, G. (2016) *Identity: The Necessity of a Modern Idea.* Philadelphia: University of Pennsylvania Press.

Jacoby, R. (2018 [1975]) *Social Amnesia: A Critique of Contemporary Psychology.* London: Routledge.

Jarausch, K.H. (1997) '1945 and the Continuities of German History: Reflections on Memory, Historiography, and Politics. In G.J. Giles (ed.), *Stunde Null: The End and the Beginning Fifty Years Ago.* Occasional Paper No. 20. Washington, DC: German Historical Institute, pp. 9–24.

Jarausch, K.H. (2010) 'Nightmares or Daydreams? A Postscript on the Europeanisation of Memories'. In M. Pakier & B. Stråth (eds), *A European Memory? Contested Histories and Politics of Remembrance.* New York: Berghahn Books, pp. 309–20.

Kahan, A. (2001) *Aristocratic Liberalism: The Social and Political Thought of Jacob Burckhardt, John Stuart Mill, and Alexis de Tocqueville*. New Brunswick, NJ: Transaction Books.

Kamen, H. (1967) *The Rise of Toleration*. London: Weidenfeld & Nicolson.

Kant, I. (2005 [1795]) 'Toward Perpetual Peace'. In D. Karmis & W. Norman (eds), *Theories of Federalism: A Reader*. New York: Palgrave Macmillan US, pp. 87–99.

Kaplan, S. (1956) 'Social Engineers as Saviors: Effects of World War I on Some American Liberals'. *Journal of the History of Ideas*, 17(3), pp. 347–69.

Karim-Cooper, F. (2023) *The Great White Bard: How to Love Shakespeare While Talking About Race*. New York: Penguin.

Kendi, X.I. (2020) *How to Be an Antiracist*. New York: Penguin.

Keniston, K. (1963) 'Social Change and Youth in America'. In E.H. Erikson (ed.), *Youth: Change and Challenge*. New York: Basic Books, pp. 145–71.

Keniston, K. (1970) 'Youth: A "New" Stage of Life'. *The American Scholar*, 39(4), pp. 631–54.

Keuls, E.C. (1993) *The Reign of the Phallus: Sexual Politics in Ancient Athens*. Berkeley: University of California Press.

Korsgaard, C.M. (2009) *Self-Constitution: Agency and Integrity*. Oxford: Oxford University Press.

Koselleck, R. (2004 [1979]) *Futures Past: On the Semantics of Historical Time* (trans. K. Tribe). New York: Columbia University Press.

Kühne, T. (2013) 'Colonialism and the Holocaust: Continuities, Causations, and Complexities'. *Journal of Genocide Research*, 15(3), pp. 339–62.

Lefkowitz, M. (1996) *Not Out f Africa: How 'Afrocentrism' Became an Excuse to Teach Myth as History*. New York: Basic Books.

Lefkowitz, M. & G.M. Rogers (2014) *Black Athena Revisited*. Chapel Hill: University of North Carolina Press.

Lemos, R. (2023) 'Can We Decolonize the Ancient Past? Bridging Postcolonial and Decolonial Theory in Sudanese and Nubian Archaeology'. *Cambridge Archaeological Journal*, 33(1), pp. 19–37.

Little, A. (2022) *White People in Shakespeare*. London: Bloomsbury.

Lowenthal, D. (2015 [1985]) *The Past Is a Foreign Country – Revisited*. Cambridge: Cambridge University Press.

Lukacs, J. (2002) *At the End of an Age*. New Haven, CT: Yale University Press.

Lynd, H. (1932) 'Parent Education and the Colleges'. *Annals of the American Academy of Political and Social Science*, 160, pp. 197–204.

MacIntyre, A. (2007) *After Virtue: A Study in Moral Theory*. Notre Dame, IN: University of Notre Dame Press : Notre Dame.

Macintyre, S. & A. Clark (2013) *The History Wars*. 2nd edn. Melbourne: Melbourne University Publishing.
Marius, R. (1985) *Thomas More: A Biography.* London: J.M. Dent & Son.
Markides, C. (2021) *Organizing for the New Normal: Preparing Your Company for the Journey of Continuous Disruption.* London: Kogan Page.
Meier, C. (2005) *The Uses of History: From Athens to Auschwitz.* Cambridge, MA: Harvard University Press.
Merriman, N. (2016) *Beyond the Glass Case.* London: Routledge.
Moran, D. (2012) *Husserl's Crisis of the European Sciences and Transcendental Phenomenology: An Introduction.* Cambridge: Cambridge University Press.
Moran, M. (2015) *Identity and Capitalism.* London: SAGE.
Muller, J.W. (2009) 'The Triumph of What (If Anything)? Rethinking Political Ideologies and Political Institutions in Twentieth-Century Europe'. *Journal of Political Ideologies*, 14(2), pp. 211–26.
Murray, D, (2023) *The War on the West.* London: HarperCollins.
Nietzsche, F.(1967 [1901]) *The Will to Power* (trans. W. Kaufmann & R.J. Hollingdale). New York: Random House.
Nisbet, R. (1980) *History of the Idea of Progress.* London: Heinemann.
Nora, P. (1989) 'Between Memory and History: *Les lieux de mémoire*'. *Representations*, 26, pp. 7–24.
Oakeshott, N. (1989) *The Voice of Liberal Learning: Michael Oakeshott on Education.* New Haven, CT: Yale University Press.
Orwell, G. (1949) *1984*. New York: Harcourt, Brace and Company.
Patterson, T. (1997) *Inventing Western Civilization.* New York: Monthly Review Press.
Paylor, A. (2017) 'Year Zero, Social Harmony, and the Elimination of Politics'. *Peace Review*, 29(3), pp. 374–82.
Peters, R.S. (1982) 'What Is an educational process?' In A. Finch & G. Scrimshaw (eds), *Standards, Schooling and Education.* London: Hodder & Stoughton, pp. 1–23.
Plumb, J.H. (1969) *The Death of the Past.* London: Macmillan & Co.
Ponzetti, J. (2015) *Evidence-based Approaches to Sexuality Education.* London: Routledge.
Porter, R. (1988) *Gibbon: Making History.* London: Weidenfeld & Nicolson Ltd.
Pound, E. (1914) 'The Tradition', *Poetry*, 3(4), pp. 137–41.
Pound, E. (1934) *Make It New: Essays.* London: Faber & Faber.
Racette-Campbell, M. & A. McMaster (eds) (2023) *Toxic Masculinity in the Ancient World.* Edinburgh: Edinburgh University Press.
Rawson, E. (1985) *Intellectual Life in the Late Roman Republic.* Baltimore: Johns Hopkins University Press.

Rieff (2006) *The Triumph of the Therapeutic: Uses of Faith After Freud.* Wilmington, DE: ISI Books.

Riesman, D. with N. Glazer & R. Denny (1981 [1950]) *The Lonely Crowd: A Study of the Changing American Character.* New Haven, CT: Yale University Press.

Roberts, J.T. (1994) *Athens on Trial: The Antidemocratic Tradition in Western Thought.* Princeton: Princeton University Press.

Rosa, H. (2013) *Social Acceleration: A New Theory of Modernity* (trans. J. Trejo-Mathys), New York: Columbia University Press.

Rosenberg, H. (1994 [1959]) *The Tradition of the New.* New York: Hachette Books.

Ross, D. (1991) *The Origins of American Social Science.* Cambridge: Cambridge University Press.

Rousso, H. (2016) *The Latest Catastrophe: History, the Present, the Contemporary* (trans. J.M. Todd). Chicago: University of Chicago Press.

Rowbotham, S. (1977) *Hidden From History: 300 Years of Women's Oppression and the Fight Against It.* London: Pluto Press.

Rubin, M. (2017) 'Presentism's Useful Anachronisms'. *Past & Present*, 234(1), pp. 236–44.

Sabl, A. (2009) 'The Last Artificial Virtue: Hume on Toleration and Its Lessons'. *Political Theory*, 37(4), pp. 511–38.

Schiffman, Z.S. (2011) *The Birth of the Past.* Baltimore: Johns Hopkins University Press.

Shotter, D. (2005) *Augustus Caesar.* London: Routledge.

Simon, Z.B. (2019) *History in Times of Unprecedented Change.* London: Bloomsbury.

Southern, R. (1973) 'Presidential Address: Aspects of the European Tradition of Historical Writing: 4. The Sense of the Past'. *Transactions of the Royal Historical Society*, 23, pp. 243–63.

Stephenson, J.R. (1981) 'The Two Governments and the Two Kingdoms in Luther's Thought'. *Scottish Journal of Theology*, 34(4), pp. 321–37.

Stoll, E.E. (1910) 'Anachronism in Shakespeare Criticism'. *Modern Philology*, 7(4), pp. 557–75.

Táíwò, O. (2022) *Against Decolonization.* London: Hurst.

Ten, C.L. (1969) 'Mill and Liberty'. *Journal of the History of Ideas*, 30(1), pp. 47–68.

Thatcher, M. (1977) *Let Our Children Grow: Selected Speeches 1975–1977.* London: Centre for Policy Studies.

Thompson, E.P (1963) *The Making of the English Working Class.* London: Penguin.

Tönnies, F. (1955 [1887]) *Community and Association* (trans. C.P. Loomis). London: Routledge & Kegan Paul.

Torpey, J. (2004) 'Introduction: Politics and the Past'. In J. Torpey (ed.), *Politics and the Past: On Repairing Historical Injustices*. London: Rowman & Littlefield, pp. 1–34.

Trilling, L. (1957) 'The Sense of the Past'. In L. Trilling, *The Liberal Imagination: Essays on Literature and Society*. New York: Doubleday Anchor Books, pp. 176–91.

Tziovas, D. (2014) 'Introduction: Decolonizing Antiquity, Heritage Politics, and Performing the Past'. In D. Tziovas (ed.), *Re-imagining the Past: Antiquity and Modern Greek Culture*. Oxford: Oxford University Press, pp. 1–26.

Wallach, G. (1997) *Obedient Sons: The Discourse of Youth and Generations in American Culture, 1630–1860*. Amherst: University of Massachusetts Press,

Walsham, A. (2017) 'Introduction: Past and . . . Presentism'. *Past & Present*, 234(1), pp. 213–17.

Wells, H.G. (2005 [1911]) *The New Machiavelli*. London: Penguin.

White, W. (1844) *Christ's Covenant the Best Defence of Christ's Crown, etc: Our National Covenant, Scriptural, Catholic, and of Permanent Obligations*. Edinburgh: Kennedy.

Wiener, P.F. (1945) *Martin Luther. Hitler's Spiritual Ancestor.* Cranford, NJ: American Atheist Press.

Winkler, E. (2023) *Shakespeare Was a Woman and Other Heresies: How Doubting the Bard Became the Biggest Taboo in Literature*. New York: Simon & Schuster.

Wood, E.M. & N. Wood (1988) 'Socrates and Democracy: A Reply to Gregory Vlastos'. *Political Theory*, 14(1), pp. 55–82.

Wright, P. (1985) *On Living in an Old Country: The National Past in Contemporary Britain*. London: Verso.

Xiang, Z. (2018) *Queer Ancient Ways: A Decolonial Exploration.* Santa Barbara, CA: Punctum Books.

Young, M. (2007) *Bringing Knowledge Back In: From Social Constructivism to Social Realism in the Sociology of Education*. London: Routledge.

Zimman, L. (2017) 'Transgender Language Reform: Some Challenges and Strategies for Promoting Trans-Affirming, Gender-Inclusive Language'. *Journal of Language and Discrimination*, 1(1), pp. 83–104.

Index

Printed in the USA
CPSIA information can be obtained
at www.ICGtesting.com
JSHW011252271024
72278JS00004B/6/J